MW01170066

The Ever-Present Presence

Selected Writings
of

Albert S. Goldstein

Association for
Progressive Judaism

New York, New York

THE EVER-PRESENT PRESENCE

Selected Writings of Albert S. Goldstein

Typesetting and design by **Rossel Books**

10 9 8 7 6 5 4 3 2 1
First Edition

ISBN: 088125-942-X

Distributed by
KTAV Publishing House, Inc.
930 Newark Avenue
Jersey City, NJ 07306
Email: orders@ktav.com
www.ktav.com
(201) 963-9524
Fax (201) 963-0102

✤ Dedication

In Memory of
Hesse Hoffner Goldstein
Paula Goldstein Bertrand

In Honor of
Micah Goldstein
Tamara Goldstein Prince

✿✿ Acknowledgments

The author and the Association for Progressive Judaism extend thanks to the following individuals: **Rabbi Seymour Rossel**, for his expertise in culling and arranging the material for publication, and in design and typesetting; **Rabbi Louis Stein** for his devotion and meticulous proofreading; **Marsha Levine**, for seeing to the author's every need, which included collating the author's manuscripts; and **Joan Miller** for her careful assembling of all of the material prior to publication.

A.G.

Contents

On the Rabbinate

Aspects of Reform Judaism

❧❀ Foreword

The task of compiling and preparing for publication, the writings of Albert S. Goldstein, has been no less than a labor of love for all of us who have had the good fortune to know him as teacher and mentor, and be inspired by his message. In this volume you will find sermonic essays that bear testimony not only to his erudition and artistry, but to his unflagging commitment to the ideas and ideals rooted in Reform Judaism.

He has served both his people and his faith for more than seventy years. If this publication is our way of saying thank you for nourishing our lives, it also achieves the goal of rendering form and permanence to his rabbinical contribution so that his lessons endure.

I was sixteen when I met him, and deeply disenchanted with the Orthodox-Conservative synagogue that my family attended. One Sabbath morning, as chance, or fate, would have it, I ventured into what I was told was a "Reformed" synagogue, Tremont Temple in the Bronx. The environment was unfamiliar—men and women sitting together, organ music in the background—but it was a dynamic, compelling rabbi, Albert S. Goldstein, who spoke from the pulpit. Later on, he invited me to join his confirmation class. It would prove to be a turning point in my life.

A year after this initial encounter, my father, age forty-nine, died suddenly. At this time of inordinate personal tragedy, the presence of Rabbi Albert S. Goldstein made all the difference. He knew how to distract me from the pain of loss and thus facilitate the process of healing. His understanding of people's needs was instinctive. "Robert," he said, (he has always called me Robert), "why don't you conduct summer services?" And the next thing I knew, I was doing just that. With his guidance and support, I was writing sermons that he would review with me, offering constructive criticism and advice that was immensely helpful. The rest, as they say, is history.

I am only one of many, who, under the influence of Albert S., chose the rabbinate. His ability to inspire was formidable, as if he knew precisely what it took to kindle the light in each of our minds. Under his influence we gained a new appreciation for the words of Isaiah (ch. 60): "The Lord hath anointed me to bring good tidings unto the humble; to bind up the brokenhearted; to proclaim liberty to the captives and the opening of the eyes to them that are bound, and to comfort all that mourn." Because that is what he did. He dealt with the lost and the lonely who carried hurt in their hearts; husbands and wives who felt isolated from each other; the bereaved whose pain needed to be assuaged.

To the task of bringing comfort and healing, he brought his gift for language. He was a great craftsman; and he taught me to respect his craft for the way in which it could be used to invest words with luminous meaning. His homilies sparkled and glowed. He would say, "Craft your sermons carefully, Robert; your rabbinate may depend on your preaching." To him, preaching was like digging an oil well: "If you don't strike oil in twenty minutes, quit boring."

He was, and remains, at age ninety-eight, a force; a man with the capacity to have a profound influence on the lives of others. Albert possesses such a retentive mind;

whatever he reads, he remembers. In earlier days, he would always tell me where he read it, and the page number of the text. Of him it could be said, as it was said of Rabbi Eliezer in the Talmud, *Bor sud, sh'ayno m'ahbayd teepa*—His mind is like a "lime-cemented cistern that never loses a drop" (Avot 2:11). He forgets nothing that he has learned.

His world was, and continues to be, the world of Reform, the brand of Judaism that he taught. He wrote that Reform Judaism "washed clean the ancient heritage that was stifled by a tangled underbrush of ritual." Not that he was ever against ritual as a means of supporting an idea or dramatizing a value; it was ritual as an end in itself that he steadfastly opposed. He explicitly stated that the practice of ritual and the act of ethical living were not of equal magnitude. He took his guideline from the words of the prophets, and he lived by them.

In December of 1950 he wrote: "As we grow older, we ought to be growing bigger, not in height or girth, but in mind and soul. We ought to be outgrowing our pettiness: crying when things don't go our way, feeling sorry for ourselves, complaining about being mistreated, nursing our grievances, treasuring our unhappiness, remembering and counting over all our misfortunes, cluttering up our lives with littleness."

Yes, life is too short to be little. He wasn't wrong. We treasure the words as we treasure the man.

Rabbi Robert S. Widom

❧ Dad as Teacher
A Tribute

Dad is a thoughtful and scholarly man as you will see when you read the essays collected here. He has spent his life reading, writing, studying Scripture, commenting on biblical passages, composing sermons, all of which conjures an image, I suppose, of an erudite, perhaps humorless, individual locked away among and protected by his books. Not so. Never has a thoughtful, scholarly man so loved his audience and been so connected to other people.

For Dad, three people on a bus bench made a class and he was ready to teach. If you were among them, you were in his classroom and lucky to be there. He is and was above all a great teacher. This is not surprising: "rabbi" means teacher and he took the title's meaning very seriously. Here are a few things I learned, and the unusual ways I learned them, from my first, and certainly my most memorable, teacher.

When I was twelve, Dad decided he would study Dante in a summer course at Harvard. Since he was studying Dante, everyone else, he apparently felt, should too. Perhaps he had economy in mind: one tuition, many students. I am certain that I was the only pre-adolescent in Boston that summer who had portions of *The Divine Comedy* read to her every afternoon on the back porch. The neighbors, whose screened porches were just a few feet away, heard Dante being read aloud, too. Every day, after

Dad's course at Harvard, the more or less invisible neighbors and I gathered to attend his informal class. Of course, the meaning was well beyond a child's grasp, but I learned the cadences of great poetry and the beauty of certain phrases. (I learned, too, that there was far worse heat than a Boston summer.) Daddy, aged forty-two, was in school and it was summer and to my amazement he had gone voluntarily! So I learned, by example, that the normal condition of everyone, not just children, is to be a lifelong learner. Teacher is also performer and Dad, gifted with a magnificent, resonant voice and a high sense of the dramatic, made the text live for me, as the best teachers always do. I learned to love the sound of words. I learned that a lot lives in the delivery. And I learned about the importance of connecting to the audience.

As a high school student, I was introduced to the idea of literary style by my Dad who loved deconstructing a text to show me how, from phoneme to phrase to conclusion, it grew to be so powerful. *Silas Marner* and *John Brown's Body*, the English class texts of my high school days, would have been just words on the page without the inventive decoding I learned to do under my Dad's enthusiastic instruction. I learned about the contagion of that enthusiasm and that a good teacher, by his passion for what he teaches, engages and inspires the learner—and, quite possibly, paves the way for the next generation of teachers, for teacher is what I eventually became.

One of my earliest memories of Dad as teacher took place before I could even read and has nothing to do with texts or scholarship but everything to do with people and their care. When we were a very young family growing up post World War II in an apartment in the Bronx, Dad decided that despite our limited means we girls, my sister and I, would have a beautiful room to share. I was five and my sister was an infant. That didn't matter; he seemed to think that even small children should be surrounded by lovely things; even if you couldn't afford lovely things, you did the best you could. Dad got army surplus beds and painted them over in deep burgundy—the only color that would cover army green—and then carefully coordinated floor, walls, and window dressing in pale blue. My Dad, trying his hand at interior decoration for a small child and an infant, paying careful attention to and spending time on a project for his babies, seemed to be saying that grace, color, and beauty enrich life in much the same way that form enhances, and is inseparable from, content. And that even the youngest among us deserves to be in surroundings that express our love for them. The best teachers invest time.

I learned to speak French thanks to Dad, who speaks barely enough to get by. He had taken us to Quebec on a family trip and during our stay in a hotel in that city, I happened to overhear him in conversation with a little French-speaking girl about my age. He was doing his level best to answer her questions: What is your name? Where are you from? Who is that little girl with you? That another little girl could speak to my Dad in a language I could not understand was a defining event in my young life and a matter of grave concern requiring immediate redress.

I set about learning French. It became a lifelong passion. I would never again be left out of the conversation. When I was well along in my study of French, I asked my Dad to explain a difficult passage in a seventeenth-century play by Racine that had been assigned. He proceeded to give me a lively and elaborate description of the strict code of honor that all proper heroes of the classical era adhered to. I remember thinking as he left the room, "How in the world does he know all this?"

Dad and teacher are inseparable in my mind. I learned formally and informally, directly and indirectly, by emulation and out of jealousy of the little French girl, about literary style and technique, poetry and aesthetics, about foreign languages, about how to engage my listeners, how to use my voice and, indeed, about how to teach.

Dad once commented to me that "love" was "joy in giving." Perhaps teaching, too, is a kind of love.

Tamar Goldstein Prince
Chair, Foreign Languages Dept.
Edmund Burke School
Washington, DC

On Some Bible Curiosities

❧❀ The Ladder (Stairway?) Linking Earth to Heaven

Sensitive human beings can see more through a tear, than astronomers can see through a telescope. It was not on a pleasure trip that Jacob had his theophony. He experienced his vision of God and His heaven of angels in the depths of a dream, during his sorrowful and desperate flight from home and the dread vengeance which his brother Esau had sworn against him. It was then, in a dream that he beheld the ladder linking earth to heaven.

It was because of his sin against his blind old father, Isaac, and against his twin brother, Esau, that Jacob had to flee from home and dear ones, even his beloved mother, Rebecca. She had sinned, that he might gain the coveted blessing. She imagined that in his happiness and success she would find her own greatest joy. But it was not to be as she had hoped.

True, Jacob had won his father's blessing as Rebecca wished. But, to both, it brought only suffering and separation. She had expected that he would be gone only a few days, perhaps a few weeks, at most. But neither was destined to see the other again.

It was a painful penalty they had to pay. And perhaps it was more punishing to Rebecca because of her great, unselfish mother love.

We can picture her, sitting at the door of her tent each evening after Jacob's flight, peering out through the dusk in the direction her son had gone, and from which he must, in time, return. Looking out, day after day, with ever-growing hopelessness in her eyes, wondering if he would ever come back, that once more, before she died, she might feel his loving arms about her.

He never came. At last she closed her eyes and was laid to rest, without her cherished son present to receive her last kiss and to shed a tear as the doors of the tomb were closed upon her. She had gained for Jacob a father's blessing. But she lost thereby the opportunity to give him all of a mother's blessing and a mother's love.

But it was hard for Jacob too. He fled from home fearing the wrath of his brother, whom he had cheated of birthright and blessing. He did not know what fate lay in store for him, where he was going, or whether he would ever return home. And he began to realize all that he had lost: a mother's love, a father's affection, and a brother's loyal comradeship—all sacrificed to overweening ambition.

As he wandered on, ever farther from his father's house, he felt more and more alone in the world. It seemed to him as if there was no one to care for him at all any more, to cheer him in his trial, to comfort him in his grief, to help lighten this painful fugitive existence, to lift the burden, for a moment, from his tired shoulders.

He may have thought of his dear old grandfather, Abraham. Years before, the first patriarch had gone over this same road, though in the opposite direction. Yet, how differently Abraham had journeyed. He had with him his beloved wife Sarah, and his nephew Lot, and all his household. Above all, he had journeyed at God's command, strong in the faith that God was with him. And God *had* been with him. With Jacob it was different. He was alone and even God, he felt, must have forsaken him, because of his sin.

He probably thought, too, of Cain, driven out (because of his crime against his brother) from the presence of God and men, and forced to wander on and on, solitary and hopeless, until death, at last, overtook him. Jacob's spiritual kinship at the moment was closer to Cain than to Abraham, feeling that God had forsaken him, too, and left him to his fate.

So he wandered on through that long and bitter day. When darkness came upon him, he was in a wild, desolate, forsaken spot. He looked anxiously about him. Rocks on all sides, as far as eye could see, and no sign of a living being in any direction.

More than ever, he was aware of his loneliness. And of a nameless fear of what might befall him in this awful place, without God (or anyone else) to protect him.

But, at last, fatigue triumphed over fear. And he fell asleep , with his head pillowed on a great stone. But it was no restful sleep. Conscience, fear, his sense of loss, and his longing for home, all troubled him.

But gradually this motley infusion of emotions was transmuted by a disquietingly glorious vision. In his dream he saw a shining stairway leading up to heaven from the very spot on which he lay. Angels went up and down upon it. And God himself stood beside Jacob and spoke: "I am the Lord, the God of Abraham and of Isaac. I am with you, I will guard you wherever you go. I will never leave you until I have done what I have promised you." And with these words a great peace descended upon Jacob. And he rested, tranquil and serene.

When he awoke the dream was still with him. A strong spirit of confidence had replaced his fears and forebodings. God was still with him and would be with him throughout his long and weary journey, and would in time bring him home again.

Desolate as this place seemed, forsaken of all mortal creatures, nonetheless God was here. "The Eternal must be here, though I was unaware of it." So spoke Jacob.

Unconsciously he had uttered a great, eternal truth. For God is in every place. We cannot go where He is not. The whole Universe, which He has created, is filled with His presence.

The Lord is my Shepherd, I lack for nothing.
He makes me lie in meadows green;
He leads me to refreshing streams;
He restores life in me.
He guides me by true paths, as He himself is true.

My road may run through a glen of gloom.
Still, I fear no harm with Thee beside me;
Thy rod and thy staff give me courage.

Thou art my host, spreading a feast before me,
In the face of all my foes.
Thou pourest fragrant oil upon my head,
My cup is brimming over.

And all through my life,
Goodness and Kindness will wait upon me—
The Eternal's guest—within His house evermore.

This was the truth, which Jacob now realized, that in the most unlikely of situations, in a spot which, in the gathering gloom, had seemed like the very valley of the shadow of death, God was still with him, and though he had lain down in fear and trembling, God still watched over him to help him arise, refreshed and renewed with confidence.

Note that the angels are mentioned as ascending and descending. If, in the mind of the author of this story, angels were inhabitants only of heaven, then the story should read angels descending and ascending. But they are here spoken of as though they had (all the while) been accompanying Jacob. But he was so enmeshed by his sense of guilt and self-commiseration that he was utterly unaware of their presence or existence. He may indeed have been without human friends, but unseen, there had been angels by his side to guide, protect, and comfort him.

This is one of the oldest and loveliest of Jewish notions: that God has given every man two angels who accompany him, one at his right shoulder and one at his left, wherever he goes.

Whenever he does a good deed, the angel on the right smiles, and writes it in his book and seals the record for all time.

But when he does an evil deed, the angel on the left grows sad, while he writes it in his book… But he does not seal the record until midnight.

If, during the rest of the day, the man repents, and bows his head and prays: "O Lord, I have sinned, forgive!" the record is erased. But if he does not acknowledge his sin, the evil record, too, is sealed forever.

And both the angel on the right and the angel on the left weep sadly for the evil which had to be recorded.

Another tradition tells us that while Jacob rested, his guardian angels went up the stairs to heaven to tell God and the angels there that Jacob lay asleep after his exhausting flight; that they had been unable to make him aware of their nearness when he needed reassurance most.

So God caused Jacob to see Him in a dream while He brought the angels of heaven down to see this man who was to father an "eternal" people.

The experiences of Jacob's life sum up all of Jewish history. Time and again, Israel has had to leave his home, lest he suffer (and perhaps perish) at the hands of those who should have been his brothers.

How often has Israel wandered forth into the strange world, not knowing whither he was going, nor how long the journey would be, or whether God was with him, or whether he was alone in the world, forsaken of God and men.

But always it was only for a moment. Always the conviction returned, (stronger because of the momentary doubt) that God was still with him, and would ever be with him.

In this quiet trust and undying faith in the God of our fathers, though enemies raged and dangers threatened, and we must wander on and on, Israel has thru the ages repeated the inspiring words of the *Adon Olam*:

> *Byodo afkid ruchi b'eit ishan v'oiro.*
> *V'im ruchi givi-oti, Adonai li v'lo iro.*

> Into His hands I entrust my soul;
> Both when I sleep and when I wake;
> And with my spirit my body too.
> The Lord is with me, I do not fear.

Ever He is our shepherd who leads us and we need not fear, who cares for us and we do not want. Ever He is our guardian who slumbers not and watches over us in love both when we sleep and when we wake. And ever when we forget and turn from Him, still is He with us, and we can return to Him, and be assured of His fatherly forgiveness and His blessing and His love. 🌺

❧ The Wrestling Match at Jabok

Once it was believed that every conspicuous natural object—mountain, canyon, desert, oasis, heath, or bog—had its particular resident spirit. The ancient Romans called such a spirit a *numen*. The medieval Danes had their own word for him: *troll*. The Arabs referred to him as a *jinni*. The Hungarians gave us the word *ogre*. It was some such mythical being who resented Jacob's crossing of *his* river.

In the legend of Jacob's wrestling match with this mysterious being at the River Jabok we have a curious blending of gross and gloomy primitive myth, overlaid and shot through with the light of lofty, spiritual insight. This is not an uncommon combination in the Hebrew Bible.

In this, our ancient ancestors set a literary pattern, to be followed in later centuries by Shakespeare, for example, in *Midsummer Night's Dream* and *The Tempest*; by Ibsen in *Peer Gynt*, by Richard Wagner in his *Niebelungenlied*, and by a thousand painters and sculptors who wrought artistic masterpieces using fairies, nymphs, satyrs, goblins, sprites, leprechauns, gnomes, mermaids, dryads, dragons, and other mythical beings to convey an esthetic message beyond the intent of the original material.

It is the Hebrew ethical genius always to invest, with moral significance, the crude stories they borrowed from pagan sources.

In the original pre-Israelite, primitive legend of this struggle at Jabok Ford, there is a word play between the Hebrew word אבק meaning wrestled, and יבק—the name of the river at which the wrestling match took place. The story originally was intended only to explain how the river got its name.

In that pagan story, some mythical being, who presumably inhabited and dominated the place, wrestled with Jacob all night to prevent him from crossing the stream, which he regarded as his own private preserve.

In all likelihood, the original story related that this mere mortal trespasser, the Hebrew hero Jacob, dislocated his antagonist's thigh. As dawn approached, the mythical wrestler urged Jacob to let him go. Apparently, this was a night demon who must not be abroad in the daytime. And Jacob, possibly realizing for the first time, the supernatural character of his antagonist, refused to comply until the other blessed him.

In the original, pre-Israelite story, it was then recorded that his mysterious foe was forced to bless Jacob at that point. It noted the narrow escape of the demon with the sentence: "The sun rose over him as he passed to Peniel," and concluded with a notice that Jacob named the stream Jabok, that is, "wrestling place."

Now, when the Hebrew borrower of this very ancient, pre-Israelite story gets through with his version of the incident, it no longer merely explains the origin of the name of the river. Instead, it attempts to explain why Jews do not eat a certain part of the hind quarters of cattle, and how the name "Israel" came into being.

But out of all this curiously mixed material, one dominant picture emerges. It is that of a man who, in spite of many faults, had an indomitable desire to have his life rightly related to God, but who must be disciplined and chastened before that desire could be fulfilled.

A very different experience is the one here described from the one at Bethel. There, the vision of the ladder and the angels of God had come to Jacob as a benediction as God does come in some first, wondering spiritual experience to the young.

Jacob might have imagined: Not any human foe, however terrible. Not a river-god. No, but the Almighty God of Righteousness, forcing him to confront his own conscience and make his reckoning.

The Hebrew story teller, making his own use of the material he borrowed from pagan sources, is dramatizing here the consequence that comes to every soul who has tried too long to evade the truth about itself.

Thus far, Jacob's life had seemed successful. By one stratagem and another he had outwitted Esau, then Isaac and finally Laban. Coming home—prosperous, all the outward circumstances might have made him boastful and over-confident; but his conscience saw something else. He saw his world shadowed by his guilt. Old memories awakened; old fears rose up from the past in which he had tried to bury them. He had to face these memories and submit to their bruising recollection..

Now that he was to meet Esau, he knew that he was not the masterful person he liked to imagine he was. He had made his way ahead among people who had not known him. Now he had to encounter people who did know him, and would remember him as a sly, tricky, deceitful youth. It brought him up short, to a reckoning with himself, which was also a reckoning with God. He could ignore the prospect of that in the busy daytime. But now it was night and he was alone. And when a man is alone, then, least of all, can he get away from God.

When the mysterious antagonist touched the hollow of Jacob's thigh, and Jacob's thigh was out of joint, it was a symbol of the fact that Jacob was in the grip of a power which his self-assurance could not match. Jacob knew that henceforth he could never walk in lofty arrogance again.

There is another strange mingling of elements here. The exclamation of the unnamed wrestler, "Let me go for day is breaking," seems to have its origin in the dim old belief that spirits could walk the earth only during the darkness. When the day began to break, they had to go back to the place of shadow from which they had come.

But the timeless meaning is in the words of Jacob, "I will not let you go unless you bless me." In the good and evil that made up Jacob, there were two factors of nobility that saved him.

The first was his awareness that life has a divine meaning above its material fact—the awareness that made him seek the birthright and made possible his vision at Bethel.

The second quality, revealed here in his wrestling, was his determination. He had struggled all night until he was lame and agonized. But when his antagonist wished to separate himself, Jacob desperately held on.

When a man is forced to wrestle with moral reality and its consequences, he may try to get rid of them as quickly as he can. But Jacob's quality was otherwise. Caught in the grip of judgment, his prevailing desire was not for escape. He would hold on until something decisive happened.

In punishment, as in prosperity, he would not let the experience go until he had wrung a blessing from it. The shallow man may ignore his sins. The cowardly man may try to evade their consequences. But Jacob now was neither one. Hurt and humiliated though he was, and needing to repent, he still dared believe that his great desire could prevail.

The original pagan story was told to explain how the River Jabok got its name. The present Hebrew story is told chiefly to explain how Jacob got his new name, Israel.

Jacob's name, when he first appears, makes a poor impression. What the name Jacob first suggests is the self-interest and mean spirit of the supplanter, the heel snatcher. That name was not divested of its first unattractiveness, but in the course of his development as a person, as a man, associations were added to it which made the final balance different.

The one who wrestled with him there by the ford of Jabok said he should be called Israel. Strange as it might seem, it was thus, as Israel, a Prince of God, that succeeding generations have thought of it.

Why? Because he had shown another side of himself to which God could give a different name. At his worst, he had been something better than a sensualist. He was not ruled by the appetite of his body as Esau generally was. His ambitions were on a higher level than the physical. The man whose name in the beginning is synonymous with one contemptuous deed identifies that name at last with a great devotion.

Far better is it, of course, if a man can make his name attractive from the outset. But many a man may need the encouragement which comes from the story of Jacob to believe that a name, which has once been shadowed by discredit, can be lifted to honor.

Jacob wanted to know the name of the being with whom he had wrestled. In the course of an all-night struggle he began to suspect that this was God. And if so, then the blessing would be greatly significant. The name of his opponent was not expressly vouchsafed to Jacob. But when the night was over—he knew. That's why he called the place Peniel, "the face of God," saying he had seen God face-to-face. Though that hadn't actually happened either…. The night had been too dark. But, ineffably, he knew that his soul was not only preserved but purified and expanded because he had encountered the transfiguring spirit of the Lord. 🐾

❧ Your Brother, Joseph

The *sedra* for Shabbat *Va-yigash* (Gen. 44:18-47:27) contains the climax of the story of Joseph's confrontation with his brothers in Egypt. In this episode, Joseph has his servants repeat, with some alteration, the device which he had used earlier to bring the eight brothers back into his presence.

Money had been put secretly into all their sacks before. Now his own divining cup is sent out with them. But this time, it is in the sack of Benjamin.

As the story develops, the suspense keeps mounting. The tension was acute enough when the older brothers were in danger of being accused of being thieves.

But now, Benjamin is involved: Benjamin the beloved of his father, Benjamin, of whom Judah had promised his father, "I will guarantee his return. I will bring him back to you. And if I do not, then let me bear the blame forever." Benjamin, whom, without realizing it, the brothers had specified when they said that "if anyone should be found with the cup, let him die, and we will also be my lord's bondmen."

No wonder they tore their clothes when the cup was found in Benjamin's sack. It seemed that the meshes of old guilt had entangled them in exorable punishment now—even in a matter in which they knew they were innocent.

There are not many prose passages in any literature which compare in beauty and poignancy with Judah's plea

to Joseph to spare Benjamin. For here there is no artifice
of wording. Here, instead, are the fundamental emotions
of human life, expressed with a simplicity so immediate
and spontaneous, that they find their echo in hearts of every generation.

We read how when Judah and the brothers were
brought to Joseph's house, they fell before him to the
ground. Joseph says to them, "What deed is this that you
have done? Do you not know that such a man as I can, indeed, divine?"

And Judah says, "What shall we say to my lord? How
can we clear ourselves? God has found out the guilt of
your servants. Behold, we are my lord's slaves. Both we
and he also in whose hand the cup has been found."

But Joseph says, "Far be it for me that I should do so.
Only the man in whose hand the cup was found shall be
my slave. As for you, go in peace to your father."

Then Judah went up to him and said, "My lord, let
your servant, I pray, speak a word in my lord's ears… For
you are like Pharaoh himself. My lord asked his servants
'Have you a father or brother?' and we said to my lord, 'We
have a father, an old man, and a young brother, the child of
his old age. And his brother is dead. He alone is left of his
mother's children and his father loves him!' Then you said
to your servant, 'Bring him down to me that I may set my
eyes on him.' We said to my lord, 'The lad cannot leave his
father. If he should leave his father, his father will die.'

"Then you said to your servants, 'Unless your youngest brother comes down with you, you shall see my face
no more.' When we went back to your servant, my father,
we told him the words of my lord. And then our father
said, 'Go again, buy us some food.' We said, 'We can't go
down. If our youngest brother goes with us, then we will

go down, but we can't see the man's face unless our youngest brother is with us.'

"Then my father said to us, 'You know that my wife bore me two sons. One left me, and I said, that he has been torn to pieces. I haven't seen him since. If you take this one also from me and harm befalls him, you will bring down my gray hairs in sorrow to the grave.' Now, therefore, when I come to your servant, my father, and the lad is not with us, then, as his life is bound up in the lad's life, when he sees that the lad is not with us, he will die. And your servant will bring down the gray hairs of our father with sorrow to the grave. For your servant became surety for the lad to my father, saying, 'If I do not bring him back to you, then I shall bear the blame in the sight of my father all my life.' Now, therefore, let your servant, I pray you, remain instead of the lad as a slave to my lord and let the lad go back with his brothers, for how can I go back to my father if the lad is not with me? I fear to see the evil that would come upon my father."

Then Joseph could control himself no longer and he cried, "Make everyone leave." So no one stayed with him when Joseph made himself known to his brothers. He wept aloud and he said to his brothers, "I am Joseph. Is my father still alive?"

His brothers could not answer him. They were dismayed at his presence. So he said to his brothers, "Come near." They came near. He said, "I am your brother, Joseph, whom you sold into Egypt. Do not be distressed or angry with yourselves because you did this. God sent me before you to preserve life."

The brothers of Joseph had originally seemed to be a rather sorry lot—narrow-minded, jealous, and vindictive. But it may be that the experience of life, especially the lesson of hard years, had begun to change them.

It is a happy thought to have it suggested that men who had been evil may repent. Whether this was wholly true of all the brothers, Judah, at any rate, appears different, and Judah is the spokesmen for the others. What he says is what they all have, at least, begun to feel. They had begun to understand that one of the worst of human sins is hard-heartedness. They had been cruel, because they did not care.

Sin and the retribution of it echo and re-echo in the pages of the Bible. Nathan stands before King David and tells him the shattering story of the rich man who took the poor man's lamb and he makes David condemn himself with the indignant cry, "As the Lord lives, the man who has done this thing shall surely die because he had no pity." (II Samuel 12:5f)

Amos pronounces judgment and doom upon the ruthless people of his time, summing up their evil in this, that they were "not grieved for the affliction of Joseph." They had no sympathy for Joseph's misery.

Joseph's brothers had begun to learn what the real values of life are. They are reflected in the matchless plea which Judah makes to Joseph. He does not know who Joseph is, but he understands the emotions which every decent man responds to: the sorrow of a man's heart over a lost son, the wistfulness of old age, the memory of a dead mother, the protective love for a youngest child.

In the name of these, Judah pleads, because he feels instinctively that such a plea ought not be in vain. And his feeling is not a matter of words only. He is ready to act in a spirit exactly opposite from the spirit he had once exhibited. Once he had helped to sell a brother into bondage. Now he is asking to be put in prison himself in order that another brother may go free.

A chance for the searching of our own hearts is here. What has life done to us and what do we respond to? Has life made us callous, so that we are ashamed lest somebody should call us "sentimental?" Or have we known, like Judah, even if it is by the hard way as was the case with him, that a man can begin to live with himself only when he knows that the great affections are, beyond all other things, supremely worth preserving?

The man who is hard to others, turns his own soul into stone and the whole ground of his life's best possibility for happiness grows barren.

In the Prophet Micah's formative definition of religion are two beautiful words, "love mercy." They make a summary of what Judah had learned and of what he tried to say.

A great change had occurred not only in the character of Joseph's brothers; Joseph himself had, indeed, changed. He changed from the petted, pampered, foppish, gossipy boy to a man of immense stature, not only of prodigious ability, but of great spiritual breadth. He had a right to be angry with his brothers and he was, at long last, asking them not to be angry with themselves. He wanted them to begin to share his concern, which was a divine concern— the preservation of life.

If he had not had that concern for the fate of a whole people, Joseph would have had neither the foresight nor the long patience to become the agent of salvation for Egypt through the years of famine. In spite of reasons he had for returning hurt for hurt, his affection for his family was such now. What he wanted to know was, "Does my father still live?"

And to the men who had wronged him, he did not say, "1 am the authority who can break you." Instead, he said, "I am Joseph, your brother."

✢ The Holy Cow

Revisiting the Totally Incinerated Holy, Wholly Red Cow, First Introduced to the World in the Pentateuchal Book of Numbers, Chapter 19

Two non-residents are sightseeing in Brookline. George is a denizen of Roxbury's Harlem; but he's familiar with the folkways of the populace in the Coolidge Corner neighborhood. Elvis is a recent arrival from the cotton fields of Dixie. They pass a food shop. Painted on the window is a curious geometric figure, flanked by two nearly-identical three-letter words in a non-Roman alphabet. The design consists of two intertwined equilateral triangles, one pointing up and the other pointing down.

The newcomer from Gingrich-land is intrigued. "What's that sign on that window, George?", he asks.

"That, is the 'scutcheon of the Hebrews: the famous 'Morgan Davis' sign."

"Course. But what's the words say?"

"Why, plain as plain, it says, 'Kosher.'"

"Any fool can tell that. But what's it mean?"

"What's it mean?!, Man, you *are* ignorant! 'Kosher' may mean nothing to you, fellah, but to the Jews, it says 'Duncan Hines!'"

There's this to be said for George. He has a more accurate conception of the meaning of *kosher* than, perhaps, nine out of ten Jews. *Kosher* means, not "clean", but "approved," conforming to recognized, accepted, conventional standards.

I submit that a similar misunderstanding exists with reference to the word טמא, *ta-may*, which is almost invariably mistranslated as "unclean." If this word were translated correctly, I believe it would not only enhance the comprehension of scores of passages where it occurs in Scripture, but it would nullify reams of homilizing and exegesis on the opening passage of the *Sidra Hukat*, the synagogue Pentateuchal lection designated for a Sabbath in July/Tammuz.

This lection deals with the production and use of an organic chemical mixture containing, among other things, the total ashes of a completely red and tenderly reared cow. There is, I think, enough mumbo-jumbo behind the magic potency of such substances as cedar wood, hyssop, red string and water, without adding to the mystification by propounding theories as to how and why this cow lotion renders "clean" the "unclean" on whom it is sprinkled, while it renders "unclean" the "clean" who manufacture it. The latter theorizing is a characteristic pulpit practice in traditional synagogues when the *Sidra Hukat* is read.

I am suggesting that *ta-may* should not here be translated "unclean". Here, and elsewhere in the Bible, it is, I submit, better to translate it by the Polynesian loan-word "taboo". Taboo, as you probably know, signifies "sacred" and also "prohibited". Substitute "taboo" for *ta-may* in *almost* any biblical context and I believe you will find that the sense is quite completely covered. The same, I suggest, may very well hold for rabbinic usage, where, for example, we read that certain sacred objects, like the Torah scroll, מטמא את הידים, *m'ta-may et ha-ya-da-yim*. We certainly do not imply that the holy document "dirties" or "defiles" the "hand," renders it "unclean." The hands become taboo, having come in contact with that which is sacrosanct and, therefore, taboo. The contact may be prohibited, not because the object is abominable, but because (as in this instance) it is sacred. The term "taboo" adequately translates both cases.

In *Hukat*, our text, both the ecclesiastical apothecary and the corpse-handler become taboo by contact with that which is ritually taboo. Not only a corpse, but also holy material (in this instance, red-cow ash and the other red ingredients) are both *tamay*, each for its own reason. Translate *ta-may* as "taboo" and you will have less difficulty with this passage.

By the universal laws of primitive magic, anyone who involves himself in ridding another of his taboo becomes involved himself in the taboo, itself: Just as the man who bathes his dog, usually gets himself soapy and wet; and the surgeon may get his patient's blood, and the criminal lawyer, his client's corruption on himself - so the priest, who prepares the magical antidote for the taboo of corpse handling, becomes taboo when he, himself, handles the sacrosanct ingredients of the formula. The ecclesiastical functionary touches these ingredients which go to make the sacred formula. Ultimately, the formula touches the individual who has touched a corpse. All are in spiritual contact with something taboo: a kind of magical electrical current, flowing backward in time, connects them all.

What is the magical potency of these ingredients? Professor Jacob Z. Lauterbach, in his essay on *tashlich* developed the origins and employment of water as a piacular medium, a solvent and vehicle for carrying away every kind of *tum-ah* (taboo). The water, used on the body and clothes of those who concoct the red-cow-ash suspension, is not intended for hygienic or therapeutic, but only for ritual purification.

The priests might have been concerned with physical contamination if 1) they had personally been in contact with a diseased or rotted corpse or, 2) if there were anything physically contaminating in ashes, water, or the other ingredients, or 3) if, indeed, they had the slightest conception of real physical contamination. What they are concerned with is taboo-riddance, and not decontamination in any hygienic or medical sense.

There is, however, ritual contamination in having contact, however distant geographically or chronologically, with a corpse—the earthly house of a human spirit. The priestly druggists handled the components of the magical aqueous suspension which ultimately touch the clothes and the body of someone who has handled a corpse. To rid themselves of this taboo contact with a corpse, however remote in space or time, the sacerdotal chemists must rid themselves of the taboo. This is accomplished by a process that has two steps. The first step is the immersion of themselves and their clothing in water. Obviously the soaking of the priest's clothing and body does not in itself rid him of his taboo. This is only the first step in the ritual of lustration. It is not until the evening that he becomes rid of the *mana* magical power of taboo. Now, it certainly does not take that long for his body to dry; as for his clothing, he might put on other garments. No, the water is but one part of the process; the second step is a thick insulating layer of time. Thus, there are two layers of insulation between the state of taboo and the state of freedom-from-taboo: ritual purity. One of the layers is ritual dipping in lustral water, and the other, a layer of time. The two, together, are apparently considered a sufficiently thick, separating insulation against taboo.

The word **עַל**, *al,* in the phrase **עַל־פִּרְשָׁהּ**, *al pirshah* (in verse 5 of Chapter 19), is usually translated "with," that is, "the hide, flesh, and blood of the cow is burned with its dung". It seems to make more sense, in this instance, to translate *al* simply as "on", "over", or "above"; thus: "the hide, flesh, and blood are burned over the cow's dung," the latter used as fuel, a common practice throughout the Orient. If so, using an animal's ordure as fuel for its own incineration, is kosher Jewish practice, while boiling a new-born goat in the milk of its own mother is forbidden, pagan custom.

Cedar wood, hyssop (which may be a red-colored herbal plant, either caper or marjoram) plus some scarlet thread or cloth are thrown into the midst of the holocaust (a completely incinerated sacrifice) to enhance the magical properties of the ashes of the holy/wholly red cow.

The magical properties of each of these substances is fairly well known. As for the color of the cow and the thread or cloth: red is everywhere regarded as an antidote to taboo. So are herbs and other aromatic substances, like cedar wood. Red also is the color of blood. "*Ha-dam hu ha-nefesh,*"הדם הוא הנפש—blood is the symbol of life itself (Leviticus 17,1). So are oxen, male or female, bulls, bullocks, cows, heifers, or calves (born or fetuses). All are symbols of vitality. The cedar tree is an evergreen, likewise a symbol of life—the antithesis of death. Each of these, in its own right, is a powerful apotropaic. Add water, a sovereign antidote for taboo, and there you have the perfect prescription.

What do I advise the good teacher to do with this red-cow lotion? I suggest that she or he consider it strictly taboo. Leave it alone. If you are so unfortunate as to have to teach this *sidrah*, play leapfrog with the *parah adumah* ("crimson heifer"). Get on to the edifying account of Moses' encounter with God, and its consequences (which follow the red-cow passage) in Numbers. Speak of the significance of

Moses' dire punishment for having blasted his people and lambasted the rock. Tell your audience the noble truth: That the higher the position a man occupies, the greater his responsibility, especially his obligation to honor his God and obey His commandments, and the graver the penalty for failure to live up to religious expectations. Tell them what lofty positions each of them holds—as a Jew, as an American, as a child of God. Dwell on the corresponding obligations that flow from, and balance, the privileges of high position. No pedagogical good can come of stirring up water already muddied with the ashes of crimson cow and cloth, cedar wood chips and marjoram.

If, however, you simply must deal with the *ash und blotteh* (ash and mud) use it to show מאין באת, *may-eye-yin bata,* "whence we came"—that it was up from such lowly material as this that Judaism grew to become a great prophetic faith. Use it, along with the bronze serpent, that was kept in the holy of holies, and *lex talionis* ("the eye-for-an-eye law") and other examples of gross, primitive origins, to illustrate the almost infinite possibilities for development and perfectibility of a mind fixed on God, especially when the mind is that of a whole God-questing people, a folk who first became conscious of themselves as a nation in the *ash und blotteh*, the spiritual ashes and moral mud of Egypt—a miserable mob of suspicious, neurotic, chronic self-pitiers, who rose to peaks of human spirituality. This is your opportunity to stress the truth that the people God chose were not originally anything very special as to character or conduct, aesthetic taste or intellectual curiosity. Indeed, had they possessed special, spiritual qualifications, there would have been nothing remarkable or challenging in God's selection of them, nor astonishing in their subsequent development.

It was precisely the fact that God did not begin with an elite society of saints, but with a motley rabble, that indicates the almost limitless human potential for spiritual growth, as well as God's infinite power, and His endless patience, perseverance, mercy, and hope.

Such a recital of the rise of Jews and Judaism from the ashes of an incinerated cow, soaring to heights of shining splendor, on which heights stood flaming prophets and martyrs who burned, should make an edifying religious Jewish lesson. Taught with appropriate ardor, it should be warmly received. ✣

Addendum
contributed by Dr. Julian Morgenstern (1881-1977), former President, Hebrew Union College

The Mishnah tells us that the red heifer was sacrificed, whenever the need arose, not in the Temple, as were the regular sacrifices, but upon the Mount of Olives. Now we know that in the folk-lore of Jerusalem the Mount of Olives was thought to cover the place of exit from the netherworld. Once a year, the mountain would split apart, at the time of the *Matzot* Festival at the end of the year, as the year was reckoned by the pentecostal calendar, the earliest calendar employed by Israel, borrowed, of course, from the Canaanites. At this time, *Mot* or *Sheol*, the god of the netherworld, would come forth, seeking to take the lives of the first-born. Accordingly, the Mount of Olives was thought to stand in the realm of the god of the netherworld, and the sanctuary which originally stood upon the top of the Mount was sacred to that god (cf. II Sam. 15.32).

Accordingly, the fact that the red heifer had to be sacrificed upon the top of the Mount of Olives indicates that it was originally sacrificed to the god of the netherworld, and also that the institution was of Canaanite origin. This is confirmed by the added facts (a) that the ashes were used in connection with the touching of a corpse, and (b) by the color of the animal and the importance laid thereon. Red is, among many peoples, the color of death and the netherworld. (Cf. a very interesting and important article by Von Duhn; "*Rot und Tot*", in *Archive fur Religonswissenschaft* IX (1906), 1-24, and bear in mind that the devil is always depicted as red in color or clad in red garments.) 🐾

❧ David's Major Wives
And Their Minor Husbands

Time Period 1016-976 B.C.E.
Bible References: 1 Sam. 16:18-30:31;
2 Sam. 1:1-24:25; 1 K. 1:1-2:10

Almost everyone knows and can complete the quotation which begins: "Power tends to corrupt…". Perhaps nine out of ten members of the literate public can identify the author of that statement. But it is doubtful whether one in ten thousand can quote the very next sentence of Lord Acton's letter, written in 1887 to Mandell Creighton, Roman Catholic Bishop of London.

In that communication Lord Acton is explaining his own philosophy of history to Bishop Creighton, who, in his *History of the Papacy* exculpates the popes for their malefactions—out of regard for their "high office and their lofty claims."

In this now famous epistle, Lord Acton responds: "I cannot accept your canon that we are to judge popes and kings unlike other men, with a favored presumption that they did no evil. If there is any presumption it is the other way, against holders of power, [their guilt] increasing as the power increases."

It is doubtful whether Amos, the great prophet of justice, or Akiba, the Talmudic moral giant, could have said it better. Was not *Mosheh Rabbeynu*, our teacher Moses, most severely punished by being refused entrance into the promised land, for an offense: striking the rock (Numbers 20:12), which, in a lesser person, would have been deemed quite pardonable?

Lord Acton continues with the well-known: "Power tends to corrupt; and absolute power corrupts absolutely," which he immediately follows by the otherwise astonishing, but contextually quite logically sequent and altogether understandable statement: "Great men are almost always bad men."

About sixteen centuries earlier than Lord Acton's letter to the bishop, the great Rabbi Abaye learned from an astute informant that, *Kol ha-gadol may-chaveyro, yitzro gadol heymenu*, "The greater the man, the greater his wickedness" (Suk. 52a).

Almost, but not quite as familiar as the quote of Acton on power is the widespread notion that "behind every great man stands a good woman presumably responsible for his achievement": his wife. If this be so, then King David may very well be the paradigmatic rule-proving exception. For, so far as is known, no good woman had any positive influence on his career.

His credentials for the title "great" are formidable. Eminently successful monarch of that impressively productive nation, and founder of a centuries-lasting dynasty, he became the putative ancestor of the world's savior-messiah.

Still, no good woman, of whom the record speaks, played any notable role in his rise to eminence. It would appear that there was only one good woman with whom he was intimate: his first wife, Saul's younger daughter:

ffiichal

* Getting the Bloody Bride-Price:
  100 Philistine Foreskins
  (1 Sam. 18:17-19, 25:44; 2 Sam. 3:12-16)
* Learning the high cost of candor
  (2 Sam 6:14-23)
* Gross Neglect—Palti(el)

She was a woman of probity, who, initially, loved David dearly, demonstrating her devotion at considerable risk to her life. She died childless, in punishment for flouting the first rule in the unwritten, but easily inferable, and sternly absolute "Torah" of David for acceptable wifely conduct: Her mate, a wife, should appetize, aggrandize, idolize, but never, never criticize.

Bathsheba, who influenced David most, was probably as good at aggrandizing and idolizing as she obviously was at appetizing. This was perhaps true, also, of Abigail. So, doubtless was it with most of David's other numerous wives and concubines. However, there is no evidence that they ever dared risk criticizing him. For the only wife who ever did, there was the dire penalty of childlessness forever: i.e., permanent gross neglect.

David had been flattered at the prospect of becoming a son-in-law of King Saul, whom, from the very beginning, he yearned some day to succeed. David was willing to settle for any daughter of Saul. Saul offered him Merab, his eldest female offspring. This apparently pleased David very much but when Saul married her off to Adriel, and her younger sister Michal, (who told Saul of her love for David) was substituted, David humbly pleaded that he was a poor man, hardly able to pay the bride-price for a royal princess. Saul, who had his own infernal reasons, set the bride-price in a medium of exchange which the young warrior, David, might just possibly be able to pay: one hundred Philistine foreskins. Saul, of course, hoped that David, himself, would be slain in the process of accumulating this rather remarkable *mohar* ("bride-price"). When David did succeed, Saul was so deeply disappointed that he fell into one of his recurrent psychotic depressions.

After this bridal fee had been paid, Saul gave his daughter, Michal, to David as his wife. But Saul remained permanently hostile. Saul had psychotic spells brought on even by such things as Jerusalem bobby-socksers chanting: "Saul slew his thousands, David his tens of thousands [of Philistines]."

For centuries, until very recent times, Scottish armies would carry with them into battle, in a metal container, the heart of their historic hero, Bruce. In critical moments, when the situation was desperate and there was danger either of defeat or having to retreat, a designated soldier, with a powerful pitching arm, would throw the container with Bruce's heart into enemy lines.

That roused the ferocity of the Scot's army, which fought in their short plaid skirts to the point to where they followed Bruce's heart, retrieved it, to tear victory out of the arms of the enemy.

The sacred object, which the army of ancient Israel carried into battle, was the Ark of Yahweh, which contained the broken tablets of the Decalogue.

In one of Israel's numerous battles with the Philistines, the Holy Ark fell into enemy hands. Later, it was recaptured, but was not returned to the Hebrew Tabernacle immediately. It spent some time in a "safe, house" before it was finally brought back to the City of David, to the sound of song and music in the midst of jubilant dancing. So infectious was the spirit of the occasion that David, the king, joined the dancing dervishes as he approached his home to greet his household. His wife, Saul's daughter, Michal, was watching from the window and saw King David as he whirled with all his might before the Ark, amidst the rejoicing parade bringing home from exile, as it were, the sacred Ark of Yahweh.

David was wearing only a loose linen gown. Michal, daughter of Saul, watching King David leaping and whirling before the Ark, despised him for behavior she deemed unbecoming for a monarch. When David came home to greet his household, this is the greeting he got from Michal, daughter of Saul: "Didn't the King of Israel do himself proud today, exposing himself in the sight of slave girls of his subjects as one of the riff-raff might?"

This is how David responded: "It was before Yahweh, I danced, the God of Israel, who chose me to replace your father to be ruler over Yahweh's people, Israel." As the sequel to this brief, but brutally cruel, interchange, to her dying day, Michal, daughter of Saul, first wife of David, had no children. She suffered permanent gross neglect, because she had violated the primary law in the unwritten Torah of David, specifically for wives: The rule cited above.

After David fled for his life from Saul's house (1 Sam. 25:44), Saul gave Michal, his daughter, to Palti(el). When David became king, he sent Ishbosheth to take her back (2 Sam. 3:15). Palti(el) followed them weeping until Abner ordered him away. He went away, still weeping. He loved her.

Abigail

❊ Protecting her husband from his protector
(1 Sam. 25: 3-35)
❊ Making herself first a Widow, then a Wife
(1 Sam. 25:36-44, 27:3, 30:5; 2 Sam. 2:2, 3:3)

Hardly the paradigm of an ideal wife (*eyshet cha-yil*) David's next mate, Abigail, wife of Nabal, was a brazenly disloyal spouse to her first husband, a crudely calculating syco-phantic coquette, manipulating the local brigand, David, into accepting her husband's property, taken by her without Nabal's knowledge, and presented as a bribe for spar-ing her life, then marrying the fugitive outlaw, when her husband dies of a stroke ten days after hearing of his wife's treachery. Dear, dear Abigail….

We meet her when David sends word to her husband, Nabal, the sheep-herding magnate of Carmel, asking him for a contribution to David's commissary. On what basis is the request made? On the grounds that David's freeboot-ers were the local "protective" agency: So long as they were around, none of Nabal's flocks was missing and no harm had come to any of his employees. Nabal scoffed at the idea that he owed David and his outlaw band anything. Had he contracted for their alleged services—this so-called "protection"? "Who is David?" Nabal asks. "What makes this son of Jesse someone I must pay tribute to? The country is full of runaway slaves. Am I to take the bread, wine, and meat intended for my workmen and give it to him?!" (1 Sam. 25: 2-12). This account is obviously written, long after the events it recites, from the perspec-tive of a royal chronicler, employed by King David him-self, or by a successor in the Davidic Dynasty. So Nabal is presented as if he were guilty of *lese majesty* in denying Da-vid any claim to tribute or to royal pretensions. But, at the time when Nabal refuses him, David is not a monarch, but only a mobster who maintains himself by practicing extortion against fellow Israelites and massacre amongst the native Canaanite inhabitants of Gesher, Gezer, and Amalek, from Telam to Shur (1 Sam. 27: 8-12). Of these Canaanite natives, David "left neither man nor woman alive. He seized sheep, oxen, asses, camels, and clothing" and made his way back to Achish, to the Philistines, who asked "Where have you been raiding today?" David would answer, "Against the southern part of Judah, or against the Jerahmeelites…." Of the Canaanite natives, David "never left a man or woman alive to be brought to Gath to report."

Was Nabal's description of David and his band inaccurate? Not if we are to believe the chronicler himself, who tells us that escaping, first from the wrath of Saul and later from his Philistine refuge in Gath, David comes to Adullam, where, in addition to his brothers and his father's clan, "Everyone who was in difficulties, everyone who was in debt, everyone who had grievances gathered around him. He was their leader" (1 Sam. 22:1 f.).

The royal archivist amuses himself by deriding the rich sheep rancher, Nabal, for presuming to imbibe excessively "like a monarch" (1 Sam. 25-36; See Esth. 1:5-7, *passim*) when he is, after all, only a magnate. In doing so, the palace scribe chooses to overlook what is, or should have been, obvious, namely, that sheep-shearing time was traditionally an occasion *par excellence* for festal celebration (1 Sam. 35 ff., 2 Sam. 13-23 ff.) and that it was his own wine Nabal was drinking, And he could well afford it, for he had it in such ample supply that he was unaware of the missing quantity his wife had furtively taken to David, until she, herself, informed her husband of the loss when he sobered up the morning after.

One wonders, too, about that name, Nabal. Was it the name his mother gave him at birth or was it a derisive nickname with which he was smeared by his detractors when he was out of ear-shot or after he was dead? And is his Cabelite origin also an aspersive allusion? [*Kelev*="dog"] When David receives word of Nabal's refusal, he says, "To arms, men! By dawn tomorrow there will not be a man alive in Nabal's camp!" Now, even on the crudest eye-for-an-eye basis, where is the equity in this proposed pogrom? Nabal's servants were certainly not responsible for his refusing David's demands.

When Ahab, who *was* a King, demanded Naboth's property, he, at least, went through the motions of having Naboth found guilty by a court of a capital offense and it was Naboth alone who was executed for refusing to relinquish his property to the king (I Kings 21). And, in due course, the Prophet Elijah denounced this as crime. None of his contemporaries, indeed, no one but Nabal himself, faults David for taking Nabal's goods and ultimately causing his death. In Nabal's case, Abigail had to bribe and flatter the extortionist, David, to prevent the massacre of innocent people.

What kind of wife is it who permits, and thus encourages, his employees to speak disparagingly of her husband? "He is such a nasty creature. No one can say a word to him" (1 Sam. 25:17). Undoubtedly, they took their cue from their master's wife, who does not hesitate to deride him. She goes to David with Nabal's property, not in order to save her husband's life, but her own, as she says, "When Yahweh has prospered my Lord [David], please remember your humble servant, Abigail" (25:30-31).

She relieves David of the guilt of murdering Jews, takes care of his immediate needs for food and drink, lavishes praise on him for his prowess, predicts that, for fighting His battles, Yahweh will reward him with the throne and a great long-lived dynasty. She even goes to the fatuous length of saying "No evil is to be found in you all your life"(25:28). That's for David. For her husband, this: "Ignore the rascal, his name, Nabal (="Churl"), bespeaks his character.... May your enemies fare like Nabal" (25:25) (i.e., experience the fate I confidently predict for him? How can she be so sure of what that fate is to be unless she has planned it?).

David promises that, come what may, he will take care of her. With that assurance, she goes home to find Nabal carousing with the men of his household (25:36). She postpones telling him what she has done until morning, when he is sober—or, perhaps, only hung over. The news literally stuns him. "His heart dies in him." He becomes catatonic, motionless as stone. About ten days later "Yahweh smote Nabal so that he died," says David's admiring chronicler.

At the news of which, David blesses Yahweh for relieving him of the necessity of avenging the insult to his dignity—this brigand with, as yet, only pretensions to kingship. Then, remembering their deal, David pays off: He sends for Abigail to become one of his wives. Before his messenger's bringing her the invitation to her wedding, she prostrates herself a "slave, willing to wash my Lord's servants feet." Obsequious lickspittle to the very end.

Then she goes off to become David's wife. Not his only one, for, at about the same time, he took to wife Ahinoam of Jezreel. Thereafter, Abigail is consistently mentioned after Ahinoam as the two accompany David in his pre-monarchial career, as brigand, marauder, and leader of a band of mercenary troops offering their services to the Philistines. Abigail is always identified as "the wife of Nabal, the Carmelite," and as second to Ahinoam (1 Sam. 27:3; 30:5 and Ch. 1:3).

Abigail manages to a) save her life by surreptitious theft of her husband's property, b) become a widow by telling him about it later, and c) become a member of David's numerous harem by fawning self-abasement and fulsome flattery. To accomplish this, she had to ride her ass to meet him, get off her ass and fall on her face before him, prophesy that all his ambitions would be realized, and beg him to remember her when it all came to pass.

Bathsheba

❋ Taking the lethal little ewe lamb
   (2 Sam. 11:1-12:25)
❋ Saying who shall reign and who shall die
   (1 Kg. 1:1-2)

Bethsheba—Uriah, the Hittite's wife—was somewhat more subtle and certainly more successful than Abigail. Doubtless, she had more going for her: her exquisitely voluptuous body. All she had to do was expose it at the right time and place so that the king could get a clear view from the roof of his palace where he strolled when he rose from his afternoon siesta. It was in the springtime of the year, the customary season "when kings go off to war" that King David dispatched his army to devastate Ammon and to besiege its capitol, Rabbah; but David, himself, remained at home (2 Sam. 11:1-12).

Spring… in balmy Jerusalem… nothing to do after a restful mid-day nap but take the air on the palace roof to enjoy the sights…. The fact that what he saw was another man's nude, ravishing wife…. Her husband was one of David's officers, currently away from home, fighting at the front for his king, while the commander-in-chief lolled at ease in Jerusalem. This seemed to bother David not at all.

From start to finish David's affair with Uriah's wife lacks all sophistication and circumspection. The king's lust for this woman is so whelming, it overcomes all semblance of discretion. He sends some person(s) to inquire about her.... Of the people asked, someone or other says she is Uriah's wife. He sends one or more servants to fetch her. She copulates with him. She becomes pregnant and sends some individual to inform David. With all these messengers, go-betweens, inquirers, and respondents—all of them human beings, i.e., *m'dabrim*, "talkers"—how could the scandalous behavior of these two have been kept secret? It simply was not possible.

David's effort at cover up—summoning Uriah from the battle front, unsuccessfully urging him to "go home and enjoy"—it is all so messily managed that the affair would have been ludicrous, had it not turned out to be so obscenely clumsy and ruthless. Uriah's refusal to accept paternity for David's baby, begotten with Uriah's wife, is in no way an indication of the Hittite solder's naiveté. Uriah is no simple-minded ignoramus, no *goyishe kop*. Nor is his speech to David a piece of gung-ho patriotism. He is no military prig, citing Judaean army regulations to his commander-in-chief, quoting the rule that a soldier, during a campaign, may not engage in coitus (2 Sam. 11:11). No, it is a stinging rebuke to his king which Uriah obliquely utters. "While the Ark and Israel and Judah abide in booths [but the king stays snugly in Jerusalem in bed with my wife] and your Field Marshal, Joab, and your majesty's men have nothing at all to cover them but the sky, shall I go to my house, dine and drink and lie with my wife? As Yahweh lives and as you live, I will not do this thing."

Deluded by his overweening pride in his skill at manipulation, in getting his way with men as with women, David does not at all feel the full import of Uriah's speech. Instead, he persists in his frenzied but futile effort to get Uriah to bed with Bathsheba. He spends a whole day getting the man drunk. But even in his intoxicated stupor, Uriah is not stupid. He refuses to cover up the crime of a king who commits adultery with the wife of a heroic soldier at the front, fighting the king's battles and then, when he has got the woman pregnant, expects the husband to accept paternity for a child he has not fathered.

With all David's emissaries and Bathsheba's neighbors involved in the inquiries, etc., was it possible that Uriah did not know what had gone on between these two? The saying may be true that "the husband is the last to find out," but, late or early, he does get to know, and nothing but that knowledge explains Uriah's steadfast refusal to make love to so lush a beauty as Bathsheba, especially given the permission, and persuasion, and even a present of food, from the king, his commander-in-chief.

In all this, the beauteous Bathsheba is passive—always available, the willing acquiescor in anything David requires of her: He sends for her, she comes to him. She does not hesitate, or object. When he tries to coerce her husband into going home to have sex with her—again she makes no protest. One wonders: What if Uriah had been willing to be a cuckold, rather than a corpse? What would have happened to the David/Bathsheba "romance"? How changed would Israel's history have been? Had he been *literally* a bastard, would Solomon have ruled?

Nathan denounces David for his double crime of adultery/murder. The prophet does not fault the adulteress, Bathsheba. Why? In Nathan's oft-cited parable, is Bathsheba accurately portrayed as the "poor man's" innocent one-and-only "little ewe lamb" expropriated by the big bad "rich man"? Was she blameless? Did she demur: that she was a chaste married woman; that this was adultery? It all happened in a big Jewish city, perhaps the biggest; did she cry for help (Dt. 22:23f.) that she was being raped? Didn't she know that what she did—or just let happen to her—was a crime? Does anyone believe that she was that ingenuous? If not, then why is there no condemnation—at least for her being an accessory to sin and crime?

In denouncing the expropriation and murder of Naboth, the prophet Elijah spares neither accomplice: Ahab nor Jezebel. Why, in condemning David, is there no word of blame for Bathsheba? Was the prophet Nathan perhaps smitten by her (literally) fatal charm? Was he more afraid of *her* than of David himself? Did he agree with the sentiment that "The female of the species is more deadly than the male"? Was Nathan being prudent, feeling that she had even fewer moral scruples than her second husband; that she would probably outlive him and had her own terminal way of settling scores; that she would probably have the last word as to what that hired hand, the royal archivist, wrote about her in the official court chronicles?

Apparently David is emotionally devastated by the prophet's denunciation and even more by the curious "punishment" for their sins: the *death of their little son.* David prays, fasts, lies on the ground by the child all night. There is no record of Bathsheba's reaction to the child's plight. When the boy dies, David goes to her, lays with her; she bears him a son.

Thereafter, the record is silent about Bathsheba and Solomon—from the time of his birth (2 Sam. 12:24) to the day when, we are told, at Nathan's insistence, she intercedes with David in behalf of Solomon's candidacy for the throne (1 Kg. 1:15 ff.)

At the latter time, David is so aged and infirm that his courtiers decide he needs a young female as bed-warmer. Abishag, the Shunamite, fulfills this office; but, the condition of the king being what it was, she remains a virgin: "He knew her not" (1 Kg. l:1-4).

Nor did he know much else that was going on. Notably, he does not know when his eldest son, Adonijah, has himself crowned king. Then it is, the court chronicler reports, that Nathan speaks to Bathsheba saying, "Have you heard Adonijah now reigns and David does not know it... If I may advise you on how to save your own and your son, Solomon's, life, go to David and tell him this: 'Did you not swear to me that Solomon, your son, would reign after you? Why then does Adonijah reign?'" (1 K. 1:11-30).

If the king had, in fact, ever made such a promise to Bathsheba, she was certainly not one to need to be reminded of it. But knowing the king's feeble condition in all respects, and especially with Nathan's offer of corroborative testimony, she is willing to risk this royal *aide de memoir*, which strikes this Bible reader as a complete invention, put together either by Nathan with Bathsheba's assistance, or vice versa.

In today's theater parlance, Bathsheba is "a quick study." She goes to the bed chamber where Abishag is ministering to the decrepit old man. She repeats Nathan's words verbatim adding, as her own small contribution, only the phrase "and the king does not know it." Evidently, there is little that the king does know. He is senile and one could tell him just about anything.

To make assurance doubly sure, Nathan assures Bathsheba that, while she is still telling David of his alleged promise, the prophet will come in and corroborate her testimony, which, of course, he does. But, if the king ever did make such a promise and could remember it at all, why would it be necessary for *two* people to remind him of it— one after the other, but as if by mere chance? As a midrashic adage has it, "If one says you are an ass, you may ignore it; but if two say the same thing, get yourself a bridle." Especially if you are dealing with an aged individual, so debilitated that he "does not know" what is going on about him; then two people saying the same thing should be able to persuade him of almost anything at all, including the conviction that he had actually once made such a promise. In any case, for Nathan and Bathsheba, the plan succeeded.

David's subsequent "fatherly advice to his son," his final words to Solomon, his successor, in no way affects this judgment of the doddering king's decrepitude: David says to Solomon, his son and successor, about his great general, Joab: "Joab... do not let his gray head go to the grave in peace" ... About Shimei, a caustic loud mouth critic of David: "bring down his gray head to death with blood" (1 Kg. 2:5,9). In sum, settle my scores with my old enemies... is altogether in keeping with this assessment of the mentality of a spiteful old man, who, to the very end, nurses ancient grudges, hates, and insults to keep them warm; but, no longer having the power to wreak vengeance himself, bequeaths this legacy to his more-than-willing offspring and heir, Solomon.

That Solomon was Nathan's choice as David's successor is quite clear. That Solomon was a stronger king than Adonijah might have been is probable. That Bathsheba would rather have her own son succeed David is evident. But it is not evident, probable (or entirely clear from the record which we have) that David ever made any such promise to Nathan, Bathsheba, Solomon, or to anyone else.

Aided and abetted by Nathan, Bathsheba is able to obtain the throne for Solomon by *informing* the superannuated king that he actually had promised the crown to her son. But to *secure* the throne for Solomon, she felt that she had also to get rid of his closest and only likely rival. Thus, there is the sequel to her final tête-à-tête with her husband, David. It is her tête-à-tête with their son, Solomon. She goes to him with this astounding story: Adonijah, she says, came to her (to Solomon's own mother, mind you) complaining that the kingdom really belonged to him, but, since he cannot have that, then, as a sort of consolation prize, he asks her to request Solomon's permission to take David's last bed mate, Abishag, the Shunamite, to be his— Adonijah's—wife.

As anyone with an ounce of sense (let alone of knowledge about ancient marital practice, especially among royalty) could have anticipated, Solomon goes into a towering rage, saying—what is too obvious even to need saying— that Adonijah is asking for the throne, itself, and, what he is really asking for is his own execution.

In most primitive cultures, it is a rather well-known article of faith that to take for one's own the bed mate of a potentate is to acquire some of the Great Man's *mana* ("mysterious power"), with which his intimacy with her had imbued her. To do this with impunity is a manifestation of a *fait accompli*, a sign that one already has acquired the Great One's power. Unsuccessfully to make the attempt, or to admit wanting the Mighty Man's consort, gives evidence that one aspires to his power: a capital offense if the woman's husband happens to be a king. Thus, when Reuben offends by laying with his father's concubines (Gen. 35:22) Jacob is so incensed that he curses this

first-born son of his with his dying breath (Gen. 49:4).
When Absalom wants to show that he has, indeed, succeeded David as king, he lays with his father's concubines
(2 Sam. 16:21 f.). This might have earned him execution,
had he not died in battle. Still, his intimacy with the royal
concubines rendered them unfit for the king's further use.
And, because they had been used previously by the king,
no ordinary mortal might aspire to wed them. Their miserable fate was sealed: permanent celibacy behind locked
doors (2 Sam. 20:3).

Adonijah certainly knew all this. He could not have
been guilty of the incredible stupidity of which Bathsheba
brazenly accuses him to Solomon. In the nature of the
case, there could have been no witnesses to the alleged dia-
logue between Adonijah and Bathsheba, so that even were
he given a chance to state his case, it would have been his
pathetic denial against Bathsheba's barefaced false asseveration.

When Naboth was framed and judicially murdered, at
least Jezebel and Ahab went through the motions of giving
him a public trial—with suborned witnesses, of course—
but, still there was the ostensible show of legality. Bathsheba sees to it that there is no slip, no hiatus between her
statement to Solomon and Adonijah's execution. "That
very day... he [Solomon] sent Benaiah to kill him [Ado-
nijah]."

It is utterly improbable that any offspring of David
could be so witless as to make such a preposterous request,
in the first place, and, in the second place, to channel it
through Bathsheba, the reigning monarch's mother, who
had gone to such lengths to get her son the crown.

David left his son, Solomon, with the legacy of getting
rid of his father's enemies. Bathsheba saw to it that her
son's chief rival was disposed of, if need be by perjuring

herself, framing Adonijah with treason, with a story as utterly absurd as this one (1 Kg. 2:13-25).

Apparently, it holds true of women, too, that "Power tends to corrupt; and absolute power corrupts absolutely."

"Great men are almost always *bad* men." And usually the only kind of women who can live congenially with them are not "good" women, but *their kind* of women.

Not that David was *all* bad. He was a singularly loyal, concerned, and protective servant to Saul, a memorably devoted friend to Saul's son, Jonathan, a generous, remembering patron to Mephiboshet, a sentimentally doting father to his rebel son, Absalom, and measurably very much less of a ruthless oriental despot than his son and successor, Solomon.

In response to Nathan's parable (2 Sam. 12:3) of the lone little ewe lamb, followed by the shattering accusation "Thou art the man!" David does have the humility to confess, "I have sinned…." In all of Solomon's lengthy career, there was no Nathan or Michal or Joab or wise woman of Tekoah to criticize him for any of his multifarious misfeasance and malfeasance. No one, male or female, would have dared. It is unlikely, even if any had the temerity, that they would have survived to boast of the foolhardy act.

Anent the David/Solomon combination one may apply the punch line of the old *hevra kadisha maisseh* ("burial society tale"): This holy burial society was in a dither about the prospect of having to eulogize a decedent whose cadaver they were preparing for interment. He had lived a very naughty life. To allay their concern, a tardy member of the association arrived with this reassuring announcement:

איך קען דיזעם תכשיט! אפער איך קען
זייין זוהן אויך! אלזאָ האב קיין דאגות ניט
ברודער. אנדגעגען איהם איז ער א מלאך!

"This one I *know*! But, not to worry, fellows. I also know his son!! And compared with *that* character, *this* customer was an angel." Compared with Solomon, David was a model of probity. 🐾

Author's note: This essay was submitted in 1987 to the editor of an American Jewish magazine, who rejected it because he thought its irreverent treatment of the great king, putative ancestor of the Messiah, would lose the magazine great numbers of pious subscribers. It later turned out that this editor was an ignoramus and had probably never read the Bible. An editor of an English magazine, published in Israel, offered to print the essay provided I would agree to have him preface it with a disclaimer. I offered to permit it, provided I was able to see the disclaimer and respond to it, and have my response printed next to the disclaimer itself. That editor refused to permit it. He offered, instead, to print my letter of response to the disclaimer in the next issue of his quarterly. This I turned down. That was the end of it back in 1987. Perhaps, I should have permitted the disclaimer and not insisted on a response to it next to the disclaimer, itself.

✺ The Meaning of Psalm 24:6b

In Psalm 24:6 we read:

זה דור דרשו מבקשי פניך יעקב סלה:

Zeh dor doreshav, m'vak'shei fanecha, Ya-akov, Sela.

Who are the seekers (*m'vak'shim*) in verse 6b? Whose *panim* do they seek?

The proposed answer to the first query is: the *ger* who was a *yerei Yahweh*. The proselyte, converted to the religion of Israel, was assured—by prophet, lawgiver and psalmist—of his favorable acceptance by Yahweh, Israel's God. He felt nowhere near so sure of his benign reception by Jacob/Israel, God's people.

The proposed answer to the second query is: that of Jacob/ Israel. For reasons of personal emotional security, *gerim* needed acceptance and warm welcome among the people whom they had to join when they sought the God of Israel. We shall see that they had good reason to wonder whether this people would accord them the cordial reception (*panim*) they looked for.

Our Psalm verse is variously rendered in Jewish translations:

> Such is the generation that seek after Him, That seek Thy face, even Jacob. Selah (*The Holy Scriptures*, J.P.S., 1917).

> Such is the generation that seek Thee; That seek Thy presence, O God of Jacob (*Newly Revised Union Prayer Book*, CCAR, 1940).

> Such are the people who turn to Him, Jacob, who seek Your presence *(The Book of Psalms*, JPS, 1972).

> Such are the people who turn to Him, Who seek Your presence, O God of Jacob (*The New Union Prayer Book, Gates of Prayer*, CCAR, 1975).

The verse is rendered in still other ways by Christian translators. But, whether Jewish or Christian, all versions of this verse seem to be influenced by the Septuagint, which interpolates *theou* ('God') between *ton* and *Iakob*. However, there is no reason to believe that the Hebrew text ever read *mevakeshei panecha, elohei Ya-akov*. The structure of the psalm as a whole would indicate that *elohei* was never a part of this verse.

Each verse in the psalm consists of two halves, with about the same number of syllables in each half. Verse 6a has four syllables, verse 6b has six. To interpolate *elohei* in 6b would make the second half of the verse more than twice as long as the first half. There is nothing like this imbalance anywhere else in the psalm. Moreover, assuming we are correct in our understanding of who the seekers (*mevakeshim*) in vs. 6b are, the *peshat* translation of *mevakeshei fanecha Ya-akov* makes excellent sense: "They are seekers of your favor, Jacob."

Panim in the sense of favor, approval, approbation, acceptance, being countenanced, or welcomed, is not uncommon in biblical, particularly in hagiographic, literature. Thus:

Prov. 19:6: רבים יחלו פני־נדיב, *Rabim yechalu penei nadiv*—"Many will seek the favor of a bounteous man."

Ps. 45:13: ובת־צר במנחה פניך יחלו, *Uvat-Tsor bemincha panayich yechalu*—"The daughter of Tyre shall sue your favor with a gift."

Ps. 119:58: חליתי פניך בכל־לב, *Chiliti fanecha vechol lev*—"I have sought your favor with all my heart."

In addition, our very phrase, *mevakesh panim*, occurs in Prov. 29:26, רבים מבקשים פני־מושל, *Rabim m'vak'shim penei mosheil*—"Many seek (entreat, bespeak, court) the favor of the ruler." Still, translators of Ps. 24:6b, no matter how they render *panim*—whether as face, presence, or whatever—inveterately assume that it is God's.

The present translator believes that *panim* is that of *Yaakov*, not of Yahweh, and that it refers to Jacob/Israel's favor (acceptance, approval, etc.); that it is this approval which the seekers (*m'vak'shim*) are looking for. They know they have God's; they wish to be countenanced by God's chosen folk.

They have already been accepted by God, as the Psalmist tells us. They are the *dor* ("generation/people") of vs. 6, who have sought to ascend Yahweh's holy hill, to stand in His sacred place (vs. 3). They possess the requisite ethical qualifications: clean hands, pure hearts, etc. (vs. 4). In their encounter with their Redeemer, Yahweh, in His capitol shrine, they have taken away the reward of His benediction, His *berachah* and *tzedakah*.

Not only the psalmist, but the prophets (from Moses to Deutero-Isaiah), all the ecclesiastical officialdom of Israel, have told *gerim* that God welcomes them to His home. What these proselytes still hunger for is the same kind of welcome from His people, i.e., from Jacob/Israel. From biblical times to our own, this has been a major concern of the proselyte: he knows he is approved by God and all His official representatives. But what he needs most is kind reception by the average Israelite with whom he wants to share communal life: residence, work, play, worship—all the simple details of daily existence.

Not infrequently, the proselyte, who seeks to join the congregation of Israel, was (and still is) made to feel not like a *ger*, a dweller among God's people, but like a *nochri*, a *zar*, an *acher*—an alien, a total stranger, an utter outsider.

These *doreshim/m'vak'shim* of our psalm are evidently not *zera Avraham*. Cradle Jews, native Israelites—from the Psalmist's time to our own—would need no other credentials to enjoy an *aliyah* and stand in God's holy place. But these *mevakeshim* are people without inherited rights in the community of Israel. They have turned to Yahweh, seeking to enjoy the privilege of membership in the congregation of Israel, having earned it by their ethical conduct and character.

Already accepted by Yahweh, they were troubled about the reception they might get from born Jews. The *ger* had ample cause for anxiety on this score. He was anything but reassured by the fact that the rule "You must not injure or abuse a *ger*" occurs six times in Scriptures. If this directive were noted for its regular, positive observance, why would it have been necessary to reissue it so often?

Similarly, the commandment "You must have the same law for the native and the *ger*" is repeated six times. There is no need to repeat orders that are regularly observed. Moreover, when the *ger* is mentioned in Holy Writ, it is almost always in the company of pathetic souls: widows, orphans, strangers, etc.

The *ger* was certainly the object of God's grace and mercy and of the prophets' compassionate concern. But evidently he is not invariably the object of the people's pity. The prophet Ezekiel castigates his kinsmen for their maltreatment of *gerim*, thus: "I leave you to the scorn of nations and the mockery of the world ... *Gerim* are oppressed, widows and orphans abused ... You scorn what is sacred to Me. Natives . . . wrong the weak and wretched and inflict injustice upon *gerim*" (Ezek. 24:4, 7-8, 29). We may then understand Psalm 24:1-6 in the following way:

The earth—the planet and all its inhabitants—belongs to the Creator, Yahweh ... Who may ascend to His holy hill, stand in His sacred shrine? Any person of probity who makes the ascent will come away with Yahweh's blessing and the just reward for his good character. This is the sort of person who turns to Yahweh, Israel's God, who seeks acceptance by Israel, Yahweh's people.

Now how shall we account for the Septuagint interpolation? Were those Jewish translators of the classical Greek version of Scriptures unaware that such psalms as Pss. 15, 24, 25 and 34 were written for, about, and perhaps even by proselytes? (See my "Conversion to Judaism in Bible Times" in *Conversion to Judaism*, ed. D.M. Eichhorn, New York: Ktav, 1965 pp. 23ff.) Or, were those ancient Alexandrian scholars themselves antipathetic towards *gerim* and did they, therefore, tilt the meaning of 24:6b in the attempt to deflect the reader from calling *gerim* to mind when reciting this psalm? It is interesting that none interpolated *elohei* before *Ya-akov* in reading the Hebrew text itself.

In any case, neither the formal literary structure of the psalm nor its substantive sense require any such Greek interpolation. The Hebrew makes perfectly good sense as it now stands and doubtless has always stood. At least to one psalm-reader the favor (*panim*) which the questors (*doresh-im*/*m'vak'shim*) were courting clearly seems to be not God's but Jacob's. 🔹

First published in *Journal of Reform Judaism*, Summer, 1981

❧❀ Megillath Esther
The Original Purim Shpiel Stage Script

High on anyone's list of reasons for rejoicing on the jolly feast of Purim should be the certainty that the characters in the Esther story are not real people and the events it records never happened in Ahasuerus' Persia nor in any other place or time.

If the story's protagonists were not caricatures but true portraits of actual persons, we should have to blush for one who would seriously heroize Esther or Mordecai. Their conduct provides no warrant whatever for exhorting worshippers to emulate "the fidelity of Mordecai and the devotion of Esther," and their example of "duty and loyalty to our heritage" (*New Union Prayer Book*, p. 403). Mordecai is faithful exclusively to his own ambition; Esther is devoted only to Mordecai. To the extent that our heritage includes, *inter alia*, pride in one's Jewish identity, avoidance of intermarriage with pagans, and condemnation of vengeance and violence, then neither Esther nor Mordecai evince any loyalty to this heritage. They both connive in keeping Esther's Jewish origin secret, so that she may marry a spineless, mindless, pagan sot, to the end that Mordecai may rise to the utmost peak of power in the mightiest empire on the planet in his time, climbing to this eminence on a heap of 75,811 pagan corpses in a two-day slaughter (Jewish body count not given).

As a piece of escapist reading intended to lift up our people's spirits, if only with fantasy and fun, *Esther* must have been appreciated and warmly welcomed, when first published—probably in the early Hasmonean period. Still today we may enjoy the action in this ancient Jewish version of a possibly even older pagan blood-and-guts All-Fools-Day farce, and can, without apology or embarrassment, laugh at the artificially contrived plot, the predictable behavior of each of the one-dimensional *dramatis personae* in this fast-paced yarn saturated with the gore of slaughtered victims and the wassail of jubilant victors—so long as we know that none of this has any resemblance or relationship to factual history.

However pretentious its pseudo-historiographic verbiage, beginning "It happened in the days of Ahasuerus" (*Esther* 1:1) and concluding, "The full account ... of his deeds ... are they not recorded in the royal annals of Media and Persia" (*ibid.* 10:2), our *megillah* is patently comedy, whose central motif is the triumph over adverse circumstance, resulting in a happy conclusion. More specifically, it is farce, whose plot depends on a skillfully exploited situation rather than on the development of character.

The book's lasting worth lay in its author's (a) insight into the sty of the judophobic mind: a warren of tangled emotions: power-lust, vanity, suspicion, hatred, fear of the unlike, frustration exploding in murderous rage, naked greed; and (b) his apperception of the survival value of humor, his profound grasp of the truth that he who laughs, lasts.

R. Simeon b. Lakish is recorded (J. Meg. 1.5) as having declared that in some distant future, when the rest of Scripture would no longer be esteemed, Torah and *Esther* alone would still be treasured. Why? Because, like the poor, "judophobia" we have always with us? Or because he endorsed the book's prescription of mirth, the gaiety of

feasting, the pleasure of gift-giving and receiving, as ano-
dynes to those who suffer the effects of the acting-out behavior of the carriers of Jew-hatred, the age-old social disease? Resh Lakish might have been knowledgeable about
the therapeutic value of entertainment as a psychological
technique for relieving tensions. He had been a circus performer before becoming ben Zakkai's brother-in-law and
Sanhedrin colleague (B. M. 84).

Torah and *Esther* do have one thing in common. Both
are repositories of Jewishly "inconvenient traditions." The
Torah contains them. The Book of Esther constitutes one
in toto.

There are numerous embarrassing episodes in the Torah: e.g., Abraham and Isaac passing off their wives as their
sisters, in order to save their own skins; Jacob taking advantage of his brother's hunger to acquire the birth-right
and of their father's blindness to obtain the blessing; etc.
These inconvenient traditions, however, comprise but a
fraction of the complete Torah document, and their reten-
tion in the Pentateuch lends the ring of truthfulness and
reliability to the whole record (considering that these unflattering incidents might have been expunged from the
text, and were not).

The situation is far otherwise with the Book of Esther. It is wholly an inconvenient tradition, all embarrassment—were it history. And on both external and internal
evidence it lacks the excuse that it just had to be told because it actually "happened in the days of Ahasuerus"
(1:1). Summarily we may list as external indications that
Esther is not history the following points:

> (1) No corroborating record exists in Persian an-
> nals of a queen Esther, or a vizier Mordecai, or
> any other queen or vizier who were Jews.

(2) In Babylonian-Assyrian myth, however, Marduk was the victorious chief of the celestial pantheon and his beauteous cousin Ishtar was queen of heaven and goddess of love and war, while Humman and Mashti were their counterparts among Elamite deities.

(3) The plausible theory is that the Esther story is a demythologized Hebraic version of some ancient struggle between Assyro-Babylonian and Elamite gods.

(4) Hence, the likelihood that our *megillah* is a stage script for the original Purim carnival *shpiel*, a variety of All-Fools'-Day farce, featuring the typical role-reversal theme, complete with the condemned man playing king-for-a-day prior to his scheduled execution (6:4-11), a figure familiar to folklore through the ages.

Leaving aside these external indications, the reader who scrutinizes the *megillah* text itself can find internal evidence which should impel him to exclaim: "Aren't you glad you know *Esther* is fiction? Don't you wish everyone did?"

Mordecai the Manipulator

To advance his own fortunes, Mordecai exploits Esther's female charms, Ahasuerus' countless weaknesses, even Haman's overweening pride and recklessly blind hatred.

Had Mordecai wished to prevent Esther's marriage to a pagan, he had only to marry her himself (as Meg. 13a. says he did!). But obviously there is more in it for him as Ahasuerus' foster-father-in-law than as Esther's husband. To become vizier he is willing to risk Esther's life, their

people's life, his own life. Esther is Mordecai's instrument
by which he rises to supreme power in Persia. For Ahasuerus, the king, only reigns; his vizier rules. And Persia is
the mightiest empire in the world at the time. Esther
achieves for Mordecai his desire that she becomes Ahasuerus' queen so that he may become the world's most
powerful man.

To Mordecai, the fact that the bridegroom is a king
apparently justifies Esther's marriage to a *goy*. Is such conduct not sufficient precedent and *hechsher* for parents and
guardians of every nubile Jewish female to marry her off to
any gentile, provided only that he be extremely rich or
powerful, and regardless of his character? Why not? So sit-
uated, who knows whether these, too, may not in some cri-
sis be "saviors of their people?"

Once he achieves the first step up the ladder to supreme power, by using Esther, Mordecai seems to have no
occupation at all other then standing or sitting in the king's
gate. Is he a palace doorman or just a loiterer? In any case,
this is the vantage point from which he picks up useful intelligence, like the regicide plot (6:2) which can advance his
ambition. It is the conspicuous spot in which he can be
seen deliberately ignoring the king's order to bow low in
salute to Haman. This refusal has nothing to do with idola-
try. From the time of Jacob-Israel (Gen. 33:3) who bowed
to the ground seven times before Esau, to that of Anna
and the King of Siam, prostrating oneself before a great
personage has been a common oriental form of salute.
What Jew in history ever refused to obey the law of the
land, or just local custom, in a matter of this kind?

Mordecai perpetrates a deliberate, calculated (if risky)
affront to the most powerful man in Persia, whose job the
author of *Esther* intends for Mordecai to get in this way.
Daily the courtiers, who know Mordecai's ancestry, ask

him why he commits this offence; he ignores their question. They repeat all this (as Mordecai knows they must) to Haman, who disdains punishing this one defiant Jew (Esther 3:3-5). Generalizing from the behavior of one Jew Mordecai, Haman accuses all Jews of disobeying the king's laws because they live only by their own peculiar rules (3:8).

When Mordecai's slight to Haman results in the pogrom plan, as he knew it would, he tears his clothes, dons sackcloth, pours on ashes, goes into the public square, and before the king's gate, shrieks and cries bitterly (4:1f). He rejects the fresh garments that the embarrassed Esther sends him (4:4) and, in response to her request that he explain his conduct, he tells her messenger, Hatach, "all [?] that had happened to him" (4:7). But while he includes the detail of the exact sum Haman had agreed to pay for the Jews' destruction (even though Ahasuerus refused the money), Mordecai gives Esther no hint that it was his own flagrant affront to Haman that provoked the edict of extermination in the first place. Instead, Mordecai loads the entire burden of getting him and Jewry out of their predicament on Esther's slender shoulders. He sends her a copy of the edict and demands that she go to the king and petition for its annulment (4:8).

In response to Esther's demurral, Mordecai tells her that she will not escape the general holocaust. Who would tell her secret? Doting Hegai (2:8f.,15)? Faithful Hatach (4:5f.,9f.)? As the go-between in her communication with Mordecai, he must have known the relationship for some time and evidently had not betrayed her. All the courtiers knew Mordecai's ancestry, for he had told them he was a Jew (3:4), and all the harem inmates knew of his relationship to Esther for "daily Mordecai walked in front of the harem to ask how Esther fared" (2:11). And yet, for five years the secret truth was somehow kept from the king and

Haman! No, if her Jewish origin were made known now, it could only be by the machinations of the man who had first ordered her to conceal it, and now demanded that she reveal it—or else her "family" would perish! (4:14). He was the only family the orphan girl had (2:7), and he had her trapped! He would not have to expose her Jewish origin any more than he had already done (a) by going daily to the harem to ask about her (2:11); (b) by telling the courtiers in the king's gate that he was a Jew (3:4); and (c) by communicating with her about the edict of extermination through Hatach (4:5-9). How bright would one have to be to follow the trail left by these clues? How was it possible that in all the citadel of Susa two people—Ahasuerus and Haman—were still ignorant of Esther's origin?

To get her to go to the king, Mordecai threatens her with extermination. She has the choice of risking death if her husband fails to hold out his scepter to welcome her, or courting death by defying Mordecai. With only these alternatives before her, she gambles on the compassion of Ahasuerus! Her choice was not dictated by courage, but by prudence—and fear.

Once he gets Esther to do his bidding, as she always had before (2:20), all is upward mobility on the glory road for Mordecai, and downhill for Haman. Mordecai, the manipulator, had managed all this. *A sheyner Yid, a fayner mentsh!*

Esther: Mordecai's Trilby

Esther does her master's bidding (2:20). Whether in his house, as adopted daughter, or as his agent in the king's palace, she is solely and utterly devoted to Mordecai. But to her heritage? One wonders how she could perform such quintessential pieties as *kashrut*, *hallah*, or *mikveh* without exposing her Jewish origin.

Loyalty, fidelity to our heritage? Pretending one is not a Jew, so that one can marry a bibulous goy (but rich!)? What esteem would a self-respecting man have for a wife who considers him a bigot? If that were an incorrect assumption, why the secrecy about her origin? If Persian law forbade its monarch's marriage to a Jew, then the alliance was illegal as well as being unJewish. What honorable woman would want to marry a bigot who wouldn't have her if he knew her ancestry? What decent person would want his adopted daughter who adored him to marry such a royal clown as Ahasuerus?

Esther submits to the beauty contest and accepts the instruction to keep her ancestry secret. When she does depart from the script Mordecai provides, it is to say—appealing for her life to Ahasuerus—that she would offer no objection to being sold as a slave (7:4). Is this loyalty to the Jewish heritage?! Our sages say that the ear of the voluntary Jewish slave is pierced (Ex. 21:5f) because it is a useless appendage on the head of one who has heard the words at Sinai, "I am the Lord who brought you out of bondage," and is still willing to say, "I love my master" and reject freedom.

Esther does briefly resist Mordecai's order that she speak to Ahasuerus, saying that no one may do so without being summoned. What overcomes her reluctance? Mordecai's lethal threat. Whether or not she goes, her Jewish origin will be discovered and she will die in any event. It is this threat that convinces her, not self-sacrificial dedication to her heritage or people. Her act is basically self-serving: to save her own life and that of the only person she is utterly devoted to.

Why does Esther invite Haman to "two" wassails, letting the ax fall only at the conclusion of the second? Is it because she feels Ahasuerus needs a double dose of drinking bouts to soften him up into fulfilling her petition and to warm his wrath sufficiently against Haman? Or does she derive more vengeful pleasure in building up Haman's impression that he is specially favored by both his sovereigns, as indeed he boasts to Zeresh, his wife, and their gathered friends? (5.12). Is this being true to our heritage? ["Vengeance is mine, saith the Lord" (Nah. 1:2; Dt. 32:35; Ps. 94:1); "Thou shalt not take vengeance" (Lev. 19:18).] No, it is obviously the suspense-building technique of the spinner of this yarn.

In the closing scene of the second *mishteh*, how had Esther managed to position herself on the banqueting couch so as to convey to the angry, wine-fuddled Ahasuerus the impression that Haman, terrified and trembling, prostrate and pleading with her for his life, was a wanton lecher bent on raping the queen? And stupid, too, with her husband just outside the apartment, cooling off in the garden (7 :7f.).

When Ahasuerus gives Esther the body count of the Susans KIA while dutifully obeying their monarch's orders to kill Jews, and asks her what she wants done next, she requests that the slaughter be continued for one more day and that Haman's sons be hanged on the gallows with him (9:12f.). Nice lady, Esther! *A zise Yidine!*

Not only is there no evidence that the laws of the Persians could not be changed (8:8), but the notion is absurd and refuted by the very promulgation of the edict of extermination itself. For this edict obviously changed the laws under which Persia's Jews had been a protected minority. But of course without this touch there would be no story of Esther, the Jewish [?] girl who married ....

Ahasuerus—The Royal Clown

The king is incapable of making up his mind. To those who make decisions for him, Ahasuerus is so grateful that he does anything they ask. He fairly fawns upon them for the favor they confer on him by asking a favor of their king.

Haman has only to say, "If it please the king, let an edict be issued for their destruction and I will pay, etc." (3:9), and Ahasuerus draws off his signet ring and gives it to him, saying, "Keep your money, do what you like with this people." He never bothers to ask: "What people?" He seems so delighted at being asked for his consent—so long as nothing more is expected of him.

Ahasuerus doesn't mind having blood shed (not his own of course); he just doesn't want money as a serendipity. In this respect his Jews are like their monarch. "They laid not a finger on the plunder" (9:15-19).

After presenting Esther with the first body count of Persians slain in the capital and wondering: "What must the Jews have done in the provinces" (as if delighted with the Jews' high score in the open season he has declared on his loyal pagan vassals), he asks her, bubbling with enthusiasm: "Now what is your petition, what is your request? It shall be done for you ..." (9:12). He is so pleased to be able to please.

Ahasuerus' favorite form of entertainment is the *mishteh*, literally, a drinking, a wassail. The word occurs twenty-four times in the narrative, sometime specifically as *mishteh yayin*, a wine drinking. Though the word is traditionally translated "banquet," there is no mention of food at any of these parties. Eating is mentioned only once in the book, and then negatively: "Eat no food" (4:16).

With the chiefs of his 127 provinces, to whom he shows off his treasures and finery, Ahasuerus wassails for six months (1:4). He follows this drinking by an additional week of wassail with all the men of Susa during which he wants to show off Vashti, "wearing [only?] the royal crown" (1:4,11). When she refuses this summons, he consults his wizards and astrologers, takes the advice of Memucan, and deposes Vashti (1:16-21). When he sobers up and misses her, he takes the advice of Harbonah to stage a beauty contest to select Vashti's successor (2:1-4). He celebrates his marriage to Esther with a wassail (2:14).

After listening to Haman's proposal of genocide, Ahasuerus and Haman sit down to drink, though the city of Susa is *nevuchah*—bewildered (perplexed? troubled? appalled?) (3:15).

At Esther's request, he imbibes at two wassails with her and Haman. At the second of these he becomes so apoplectic with rage, between the news of Haman's audacity and the effect of the drinking, that he must leave the *mishteh ha-yayin* to cool off and calm down in the palace garden (7:7). This recess proves insufficiently sobering, for, on returning, he mistakes the tearful, quaking Haman, on his knees pleading with Esther to spare his life, for a concupiscent male bent on violating the queen's chastity (7:8).

On the night between the first and second *mishteh* "the king could not sleep" (6:1) (too much wine?). This insomnia is fortuitous for Mordecai's success. Had it not been for his wakefulness, how would the royal lush have discovered he owed his life to Mordecai? Is it odd that the king did not resort to the usual, tried, tested and true connubial slumber-inducer? That the conventional male cure for sleeplessness never occurred to him is hardly surprising. We have proof that he could dispense with Esther's wifely ministrations for at least a month at a time. Esther herself provides evidence when she admits that she hasn't been summoned to the king's presence for 30 days (4:11f.).

Having first bedded and then wedded the very most beautiful damsel in all his vast realm, stretching from the snowy Himalayan peaks to the source-springs of the Blue Nile, Ahasuerus offers Esther the gravest of marital insults: gross neglect. Lest we summarily condemn him for his lapse, without giving due consideration to all the pertinent circumstances, we might reflect that ....

The burden of responsibility for this failure was not all his, but that of our Common Parents—Father Time and Mother Nature—whose imperious mandates no child of theirs can flout. What Herculean labors Ahasuerus had performed in his brave nightly encounters with battalions of eager young virgins: prodigious feats of prowess among all those multifarious contours and textures, tactics and techniques; a fresh, fragrant bundle of femininity each night! Four wearying years of this grueling exertion.

How four? The bridal beauty contest began immediately after Vashti's unpardonable crime, the Great Refusal (1:12), and her sentence to the supreme penalty: Royal Deposal (1:19). That was in the third year of Ahasuerus' reign (1:3). It was "in the seventh year of his reign" (2:16) that he married Esther. Four years, then, from the dethronement of Vashti to the coronation of Esther, with tryouts for approximately 1460 aspirants between. The figure 1460 is arrived at by assuming that no competitor in the lists of love was ever summoned by the king for a repeat command performance (a possibility, under the contest rules: 2:14) until Ahasuerus discovered Esther. The text's silence on this moot point permits the assumption that there were no repeaters. Three years of 365 nights each, plus one of 366 totals 1461. Subtract Esther. Grand total: 1460 girls between Vashti and Esther.

After all that, Ahasuerus—valorous knight in the service of Ishtar, queen of heaven and goddess of love and war—was a very tired soldier. The call to arms, however perfumed, had somewhat lost its stirring power to rouse his spirits, or much of anything else. *Hors de combat*, Ahasuerus was temporarily out of ardor after so long, arduous and exhausting a tour of duty.

The thirty-day connubial hiatus (4:11f.) occurs in the twelfth year of Ahasuerus' reign (3:13) and, thus, in the fifth year of marriage to Esther. Time enough to recuperate, perhaps. Also sufficient time to accumulate some appetite for repeat performances he had missed among the 1460 new girls he had acquired for his harem (it is unlikely that any could have departed alive voluntarily), aside from the presumably adequate supply of older females who doubtless had staffed the harem in Vashti's time. Remember, Ahasuerus was a very rich man (1:4).

The nature of the male animal being what it is, four years of experiencing a fresh female each night provided opportunity for Pavlovian conditioning to produce a taste for variety, even assuming—what is improbable—that this taste was previously nonexistent ....

Aside from his general fickleness, his concupiscence, and his inability to decide for himself or act on his own, Ahasuerus was given to towering rages (1:12; 2:1; 7:7,10). All in all, a most unsavory character, yet Mordecai unhesitatingly thrusts his gorgeous virgin cousin and adopted daughter Esther into the hands and bed of this psychopathic personality.

Esther' s Jews

When Persia's Jews receive permission "to destroy, slay and massacre ... to kill ... children and women and plun-

der their property … the Jews had light and joy and gladness and honor, banqueting and holiday making" (8:11,
16,17,19,22). Thus *Esther*'s Jews go forth with glee to their
killing spree and, when the slaughter is completed, they
celebrate, "rejoicing, and feasting and holiday making and
exchanging delicacies" (9:19). They are made especially
happy because "many pagans converted to Judaism for
fear of the Jews" (8:17). Their cause prospered, since all
the Persian empire's provincial officials helped them, "for
the fear of Mordecai was upon them; the man grew ever
more powerful" (9:3f.).

Thus, *Esther*'s Jews seemed thoroughly to enjoy "smit-
ing with the sword … slaughtering, destroying, working
their will on their adversaries." But, though they may kill
with pleasure, it is stressed that they disdained doing it for
profit. Like their king, they do not stoop to loot (9:15-19).
After each of three massacres there is the refrain: "They
laid not a finger on the plunder" (9:10,15,16). Are they
morally superior to pagan Persians because their gory or-
gies are untainted by lucre? *Esther*'s Jews are exemplary
subjects of their monarch, who also refused to accept
money related to killing (3:11).

After publishing their edict to exterminate all Jews
and plunder their property, "the king and Haman sit down
to drink, though the city of Susa was troubled" (3:15).
Bothered by what? Their unconscionably callous conduct?
After slaughtering 75,800 Persians, the Jews celebrate "with
feasting and rejoicing" and many pagans became Jews out
of fear (9:17).

What makes *Esther*'s Jews morally superior? Is it because the dead are pagans? (They were also dutiful citizens
obeying their king's orders.) Or is the conduct of the king
and his vizier reprehensible and that of *Esther*'s Jews justi-
fied under the rule "Let not one who is arming [for the

fray] celebrate like one who is unarming" (IK. 20:11) after a successful slaughter?

The Absurdly Symmetrical Plot Line

The structure of *Esther*'s plot line betrays the story's farcicality. No writer, even of fiction (let alone of history) with the slightest pretense of realism, would dare subject his readers to so mathematically balanced a "measure-for-measure" plot as we find in Esther. No author, who wanted his story to be taken seriously and believed, would risk it. Not a Thomas Hardy, or an Ambrose Bierce, or even an O. Henry. But a writer of comedy, and particularly of farce, would not hesitate to enhance the humor of his yarn by just such incredible, ludicrous artificiality.

The *middah k' neged middah* character of this utterly unreal tale is typified and epitomized in Esther 9:1: "The very day when their enemies hoped to lord it over the Jews, the very reverse occurred; the Jews got to lord it over their enemies." But there is ever so much more to Esther's quid-pro-quo, tit-for-tat design:

The Male Antagonists

Haman	Mordecai
Ahasuerus gives him his ring, saying, "Do as you like with this people" (3:11).	Ahasuerus gives him the ring, saying, "Do as you like with the Jews" (8:8).
Envisions himself royally mounted, with an equerry-herald proclaiming: "This is what is done to the man whom the king delights to honor" (6:7ff.).	*Is* royally mounted and led around town by Haman, crying: "This is what is done to the man whom the king delights to honor" (6:11).

Because Mordecai refuses to bow low to Haman, Haman resolves all Jews must die (3:5f.).

Because of Mordecai's provocation, Haman dies and Jews destroy Persians. (9:6, 16f.)

Erects gallows to hang Mordecai on (5:14).

Haman and his sons, instead, are hanged on it (7:10; 9:14).

Keeps secret from Ahasuerus the identity of the people to be destroyed ... (3:8) until the edict of extermination is published (3:13).

On his orders, Esther keeps from Ahasuerus the secret of her own identity ... (2:10,20) until she is coerced into making the revelation (7:4).

Before his rise to power, Ahasuerus consults numerous councilors (1:13ff.,21;2:1f.).

After Haman's demise, Ahasuerus consults only Mordechai and Esther (8:7f.,9:2;10:2f.).

Hopes to wear royal mantle and crown but it never happens to him (6:7).

Enjoys the privilege twice, once before Haman's demise (6:11) and again after it (8:15).

When he becomes vizier, Ahasuerus orders courtiers to bow low to him (3:2).

When he takes over, the whole population of Susa spontaneously shouts for joy (8:15).

Despite his lofty position, he complains bitterly that Mordecai is still alive and not bowing (5:15).

Though still alive, he wails bitterly over the fate decreed for him by Haman (4:1).

The Massacre

As planned by Haman, it is to last one day and include plundering of Jewish victims (3:13).

As executed by Jews, it lasts two days, but no plundering of Persian victims (9).

The enemies of the Jews expected to get the upper hand over them (9:1a.).	The Jews got the upper hand over their adversaries (9:1 b.).

The Victims

75,800 attacking enemies killed by the Jews (9:6, 15, 16).	No Jews reported KIA "defending their lives."

The Beautiful Wives

Vashti	Esther
	Her virtue is obedience; she does not intrude when not invited (4:10). She is also obedient to Mordecai's orders (2:20; 4:16).
Her sin is disobedience. She doesn't come when she is called (1:10ff.).	
The penalty is divorce, deposal, and banishment (1:19f.).	The reward is marriage to the king (2:17) and the inheritance of Haman's estate (8:11).

The Marital Publicity

Vashti's reprehensible conduct and condign punishment are published as a warning to disobedient wives (1:22).	Obedient Esther's nuptials are extensively celebrated as an example to nubile girls of the reward for obedience (2:18).

The Celebration

After the edict of extermination is published "the king and Haman sat down to drink and the city of Susa was troubled" (3:15).	After 75,800 pagans are destroyed, Jews feast, rejoice, exchange delicacies, and establish annual festival (9:18f.,22f.,26-31).
Haman's hatred of Jews results in decree that pagans should destroy Jews (3.13).	Fear of Jews impels pagans to convert and become Jews (8:17).

The Falstaffian Farceur

(*The Author*: Sole Creator of Mordecai, Esther, Ahasuerus, et al.)

The author of *Esther* found the seed for his *maisseh* in Daniel 6.2;8.2;9:1; Ezra 2:2;4:6; and Nehemiah 1:1; 7:71. All these together provide him only with the names Mordecai, Ahasuerus, Susa, and the number of Persian provinces as 120. This last may be an error for 20, Herodotus' figure, or a plain piece of exaggeration on which the author of our story improves. The largest number of provinces that even the most boastful Persian emperor ever claimed owning is 29. Daniel says 120—A nice, round, familiar biblical number. *Esther*'s author gives his story the ring of mock authenticity by boldly using the odd, large, primary 127 (1:1).

Exaggeration is one of the most common comic ploys. Our author uses it early in his yarn: "The rule about drinking was this: No one was compelled to drink, the king's orders being that the servers were to allow the guests to please themselves" (1:18). The narrator is poking fun at the ludicrous character Ahasuerus, who seems eager to let his guest know that, far from having to fear that the liquor might be rationed, so much had been provided that it might be supposed that each man was expected to imbibe a tun. This tall tale is stretched taller and the humor heightened by the author's suggestion that this kind of drinking goes on for six months, followed by a week of wassail with just the people of Susa in attendance (1:5).

Like exaggeration, repetition also is a well-known comic device. To repeat a gag line is one of the oldest tricks in the comedian's bag. We have three instances of exaggeration and repetition in Ahasuerus' formula of invitation to Esther: "What is your wish, Queen Esther, what is your request? You shall have it, were it half my kingdom" (5:3,6; 7:2). Three times, too, there is the proclamation: "Thus shall be done to the man whom the king delights to honor" (6:6, 9, 11).

Thrice also is the litany, after each body count of Persians slain by Jews: "But they laid not a finger on the plunder" (9:10,15,16).

The author enjoys triads. Thrice he favors half-a-year as the optimal period for conditioning people. He has the king lubricate his satraps internally with alcohol for six months (1:4), and he has Hegai, the harem master, lubricate each fresh batch of inventory externally with myrrh for six months and with other aromatic ointments for six months (2:12).

If the average reader fails to chuckle or grin while reading *Esther*, it is probably due to his self-consciousness in perusing Holy Writ, Sacred Scripture, Divine Revelation, God's Word—no less! And, of course, the Hebrew Bible does contain works to which such grandiose titles truly apply. Esther is not one of them.

Remarkable and oft-mentioned is the absence of the words "God" or "prayer" in the story. Not even when the situation seems to demand their use, notably in Mordecai's speech to Esther: "If you do not speak out at this time, help will come from some other place" (4:4). If he means from God, why doesn't the author say so? Why does he deliberately avoid such terms?

On his own, and by Esther's request, Mordecai and the Jews "loudly mourn ... weep, wail, lie in sackcloth and ashes" (4:1ff.,16). Nowhere is it stated that they prayed. To assume that such consistent, invariable omissions are accidental, an oversight on the author's part, would be harder to credit than to take for granted that this competent writer deliberately avoided these holy words.

Why? Because, while Mordecai and Esther are the author's examples of nominal, or—at best—"catastrophe" Jews, the writer himself was a normally reverent Jew. As such, he could hardly bring himself to commit the sacrilege of introducing holy words into so profane a piece as this secular farce of his. He knew the nature and intent of his opus. When, in our time, we sanctify his story as the central scripture in a "Worship Service," some of us tend to forget his purpose in composing this *megillah*. He would be astonished at the regard some of us pay his composition.

However pleased he may have been, he would not be astonished to know that his *oeuvre* was destined to be selected for inclusion in "The Anthology of Representative Hebrew National Literature" we call *TaNaKh*, among such unsanctimonious opera as *Koheleth* (Ecclesiastes) and *Shir Ha-Shirim* (Song of Songs).

Pseudepigrapha were common enough in the age when this *megillah* was written. So were parabolic stories composed by pamphleteers on the theme of xenophobia, e.g., the story of Ruth which, like Esther, also opens with the stock formula: "It happened in the days of ..." When the author of Esther concludes his tale with the formula "and the rest of the deeds of ... are they not written in the chronicles of ...," he is employing literary license common in all ages among fiction writers. And like these writers, the author of Esther flatters his readers with the imputation that *hamaskil yavin* that he is reading comedy, not history. Our author isn't being pretentious, but only indulging in playful whimsy.

Esther is a tale told by a lusty farceur with a talent for colorful, zesty, action-crammed scenes, full of sound and fury signifying that its author is enjoying himself falstaffianly and hoping that his readers will do the same. Were realism, history, or verisimilitude the author's intention, we should have to blush with shame for his chief characters. Only one bit player, Vashti, gives any evidence at all that she is capable of blushing.

Conclusion

Nevertheless, there are a few fine gold needles of insight in the compost heap of ruthless ambition, cruelty, naked greed, vanity, fear, hate, gleeful vengeance and violent death—all the multifarious materials involved in this ancient yarn.

The author exhibits a shrewd understanding of some factors in judophobia. Hatred is, indeed, often sparked by injured pride (Honor me, praise me, or I hate you!) (3:5). This can grow into hostility toward the whole people with whom the offender is associated, however tenuously (3:6). Also, xenophobia can be profitable (3:9,1 3f.).

Then, too, there is the lesson of the "catastrophe Jew." He conceals his identity in the hope of self-aggrandizement and comes out of hiding only when calamity impends. Still, when Jews do unite, however belatedly or ulterior the motivation, they can achieve the most important triumph—survival. In the midrashic paraphrase of Jacob's farewell charge to his sons (Gen. 49:1): "*If* you do gather yourselves together, then I can tell you that you *will* have a future."

As every comedy does, *Esther* has a happy ending: victory and celebration. It initiates Purim, an occasion for feasting and joy. Gladness and the accompanying smiles and laughter are essential to endurance in life. It takes a healthy dose of faith to be able to laugh in the face of present wretchedness and imminent disaster. Yet evidently Jews did manage this in ancient Persia, and Babylon, and Egypt, and ever since down to our own day.

Esther and all the Purim *shpieln* it has spawned down the centuries have shown that he who is able to relieve the tensions of his fear by a sense of humor may be able to surmount that fear and survive the threat to his existence which induced it. Yes, he who laughs, lasts. This is the saving power of humor. Purim proves the worth of mirth. 🌸

First published in *Journal of Reform Judaism*, Spring, 1979

Sermons for Special Occasions

❀❀ The Ever-Present Presence

There is this twice-told tale of the town's outstanding ne'er-do-well who presents the congregation's *tzadik* with a preposterous proposition:

"Rebbe," he pleads, "if I were a rich man I would support this whole Jewish community instead of always begging them to support me. And you, Rebbe, could make me a rich man. All you've got to do is ask the All Merciful One, *HaRahaman.* to see to it that I get the big prize in the state lottery."

With no faith whatever in the plan, the soft-hearted, empathetic rabbi promises that he'll try. To his astonishment the *Ribbono Shel Olam*, "the Master of the Universe," agrees to arrange matters so that the *shnorer* will win First Prize.

A month goes by. Again, the ne'er-do-well is at the *tzadik*'s door. "Rebbe, you promised… and nothing's happened!"

The Rebbe questions The-Holy-One-Blessed-be-He, Who expostulates, "Yes, I know I promised I'd do what he asked. And I would if that man made it at all *possible* for me to do it. But wouldn't you think he'd help Me just a little, say, by getting himself a lottery *ticket?*"

You see, quite evidently, even the power of God has its limits. Our ancient sages observed that without the application of some quintessential human effort, situations abound in which the Almighty is powerless to help us; where the Omnipotent One is, in effect, impotent.

In the realm of things material, for example, the Creator abundantly provisioned this planet with an impressive array of physical energy sources: fossil fuels in every form: solid coal, liquid oil, natural gas; solar, nuclear, electrical, wind, and water power—to mention only some of those sources of energy which Earthlings have so far discovered.

However, none of these serves mankind effectively without some human input. It is necessary for men to drill for oil and gas, to dig for coal and uranium, to construct water wheels, windmills, dams and generators, and storage facilities in which to accumulate. electrical, solar, and nuclear energy.

God has supplied all the requisite ingredients, including the human brain and physical dexterity wherewith to organize all this effectively. But even where a human settlement has an adequate, functioning power plant, there may be no evidence of the plant's existence; no light or power source in any individual residence, shop or factory, unless that specific building is properly connected, wired, and supplied with appropriate fixtures. Even then, there is no light or power evident until someone flips the right switch to turn it on.

All this by way of analogy: to intimate that God's presence and power in our world are made manifest by our contribution to His creative work here.

And, as the immensely powerful generators of electricity set up in the inner city are quite real and continue to exist, with all their potential power, whether we tap and use any of that power or not, so God is there whether we make the needful connection with Him or not.

Now, this post-Auschwitz generation is hardly the first or only one ever to question the presence and power of God, or to doubt the reality of His very existence. Skeptics, cynics, agnostics, and atheists have abounded on planet Earth for millennia.

Not only are there a number of chapters in the Book of Psalms which mention the "wicked," the "arrogant," and the "foolish," who say, "There is no God," but we have evidence that, in the centuries since Bible times, there was frequent urgent need for contrary reassurance to be given to people who were not wicked or arrogant fools, but pious souls, who, for some of the very same reasons which make *us* sometimes doubt and wonder, were occasionally given to pondering, "Is there? or isn't there? Does God, or doesn't He, exist?"

Some two hundred years ago, the famous *tzadik*, Rabbi Levi Yitzhak of Berdichev, ordered his *shamash*, his private secretary, to go to every store in the marketplace and tell the busy Jewish businessmen there to shut their shops and assemble on the town common to hear a momentous announcement which the rabbi most urgently needed to make to them and, of course, which they most desperately needed to hear and respond to.

"But Rabbi," the *shamash* protested, "today is a market day. Everyone is busy with selling and buying. And this is the very busiest time of the day. Could you not wait for Shabbat, when they will be in *shul*, anyway? Or, if it must be today, then for some other time, say, on their way home from work?"

"No!" said the *tzadik*, "Go and tell them what I have said: that Levi Yitzhak son of Sarah of Berdichev, has an urgent message for them, which cannot wait a day or even an hour. And they must stop their trading, and close their stores, and come to the town center and hear what I have to tell them."

Sadly, fearful of the anger of the Jewish store-owners of Berdichev, but dutifully obedient to his universally revered employer, the *shamash* went to every shopkeeper on that busy day, in that busy hour, and told them that the holy *tzadik*, Levi Yitzhak, commanded them to leave their trafficking with money and commodities and come to the town commons to hear a most urgent proclamation which he wished to make to them.

Grumbling and unhappy, yet wondering what could be of such enormous urgency, the Jewish merchants of Berdichev complied. They locked their stores and gathered on the common. When all had assembled, the *tzadik* mounted a box in their midst and began to speak. "I have asked you to close your shops and come here, even at this busy season, on this busy day, in this busy hour, because I have news of tremendous importance for all of you, tidings which could not be postponed for another day or for another hour. And this is my proclamation: I, *Levi Yitzhak ben Sarah miBerditchev, machriz umodia lachem*, 'announce and proclaim to you': There is a God in the world!"

There is a God in the world! But, most times, we seem unconscious of it, unaware, oblivious. And even if we know it with our mind, we may not want to admit it in our heart. Or, maybe, the reverse. And sometimes, God help us, we may even want to forget it altogether. It is sometimes inconvenient, perhaps painful, to remember it. But God is here nonetheless. Whether we know it or not, whether we admit it or not, whether we do like it or don't.

How easy it is to forget God during business hours when we are steeped in the welter of buying and selling, getting and spending. How easy it is to imagine that all we have, all our goods and machinery and our money belong to us and us alone. As if we created the wood and the metal and the stone and the fabric and the fuel, the animals, plants, and chemicals which, put together, produce the gadgets and merchandise we deal in, consume, and profit from. As if they, or at least the substances they are made of, were not here long before we came into the world, and will be here long after we are gone.

We shall not continue to possess all our shops, factories, and offices and cars, and homes and wardrobes, and jewels and cash, and stocks and bonds forever and ever to all eternity....

Is there any Levi Yitzhak today who could make us close our shops and offices and studies for an hour to proclaim the awesome, overwhelming news that there is a God in the world? That God and not we, created all that is; that all we have is but lent to us during part or all of our lifetime—to be used for God's purposes, God's ends; that we are but stewards of whatever we possess; that we hold our wealth as a trust for which ultimately we must render account to Him.

There is indeed a God in the world—not only in the heaving bosom of the ocean deeps and the glistening snow fields on mountain tops and the unimaginably vast spaces of the firmament, dotted with uncountable suns and planets—but in our businesses, our stores and offices, and streets and homes. There, it is we who manifest His presence. There, we are the instruments with which He operates. What we do, and say, and are, there testify to His existence, His reality—or witness against it.

As, at daybreak or sunset, there are light waves, but no glorious vision of splendor in the skies, unless there are eyes to see it. And, as in a forest, when a tree falls, or a nightingale sings, there are airwaves but no sound, unless there is an ear to hear it, a brain to translate it—so, in our busy workaday world, there is no voice of God, unless our tongue gives utterance to it; no power of God, unless our hand expresses it; no truth, or beauty, or glory of God, unless our labor and loving concern manifest it as we speak to another human being, whether it be client or colleague or child or parent or patron or patient or spouse or sibling; each time we use a hand, whether to sign a check or set a table or caress a loved one or comfort a suffering fellow mortal.

It may be strange, but it is nonetheless true, that it is through us frail, finite, transient mortals that the almighty eternal, and infinite God makes known His presence and does His work in the world. In the words of the prophet Isaiah:

> *Atem eydai*, "you are My witnesses," *n'um Adonai*, "says the Eternal," *v'ani el*, "and I am God."

which our sages interpret to mean:

> *Im atem eydai*, "if, when, and where you are My witnesses" [doing My will, effectuating My *mitzvot* of help and healing], *az ani el*, "then [and there] I am God.." *V'im eyn atem eydai*, "but where you are not My witnesses" [My living instruments; My fingers, hands, and arms of justice, mercy, and love in the world], *ki-v'yachol, eyn ani el*, "then, it is as if there were no God."

This is what is meant by being created in the image of God. We are placed here to manifest God's image, to transform the world into His kingdom, and in the process to become transfigured ourselves.

Does God truly exist? Is He real? As real as your kindness and concern, as true as your justice and love, as actual as your compassion and solicitude, as present as your faith in goodness. For He created not only the distant specks of light that shine in the sable heavens at night. He also created those warm and lovely sparks which glow in your heart and could, if you let them, light up the world we share.

In response to some statement that is curious, startling, peculiar, astonishing, remarkable, or doubtful, have you ever heard someone (perhaps yourself) say, "You can't prove it by me"? Well, there is a God in the world and, if you let Him (more especially if you help Him), He could prove it by you.

Dear friends, my prayer and blessing for each of you on this Holy Shabbat is that you will be quickened by a renewed realization. There is a God in the world, and He could prove His existence, His reality, His living presence among us, by you, by your life, your labors, and benefactions, by what you do in, to, and for your family, your congregation, your community, your people, your world; by whatever you accomplish that says, "Thank you, God, for your most precious gift to me: one more week of life." 🕮

January 23, 1999

❧ Three Hebrew Words

Down the long centuries since the *Akeda,* "the binding of Isaac," three Hebrew words have become a classic text for more Jewish sermons perhaps than any other sentence in the Tanach: וילכו שניהם יחדו, *Va-yayl-chu shney-hem yakhdav,* "[Abraham and Isaac] went on together" (Gen. 22:6).

Quite aside from their intrinsic meaning, this sentence fascinated the pious preacher in ages past because it occurred not once but twice in one paragraph of our Rosh Hashanah Torah lection.

To people who were convinced of the divine authorship of Scriptures, and believed absolutely that the whole Torah was dictated verbatim by God and that it contains not a single unnecessary word, a whole sentence occurring twice in one paragraph was a mystery calling for profound analysis. It cried aloud for interpretation and understanding.

But it was not merely the repetition of the sentence in our Rosh Hashanah Torah reading which captured the imagination of the old-time *darshan.* He was fully as much mystified at the use of three words in the sentence *va-yayl-chu shney-hem yakhdav* when just one might have sufficed to say that Abraham and Isaac went up to Moriah, if that was all that Scripture meant to convey.

Va-yaylchu means "they went." What was the need for *shney-hem*—"the two of them," and, again, *yakhdav*—"together?" This seeming repetition was the golden opportunity the old *maggid* seized to prove that there were no superfluous words in Scripture. The old preacher would begin by explaining that *va-yaylchu* meant action, "they went."

Father Abraham had been commanded by God to take his son to Mt. Moriah. When God commands His faithful servants to do something, they do not sit down to take the suggestion under advisement. They get up and go! The old-fashioned preacher would remind his congregation that Judaism is not a speculative philosophy, something you just sit and think about. It's a code of conduct, a pattern of behavior, an active way of living, a matter of doing. God said, Get thee up to Mt. Moriah, *va-yaylchu*—"and they went!"

What about *shney-hem*—"both of them"? Well, lest you imagine that Abraham, prototype of the Jewish parent, thought he had done his tour of duty in the service of the Lord and therefore, felt free to send his son to be offered to God by some representative, an agent—let's say the boy's Hebrew school teacher, for example—Scripture specifies *shney-hem*—"both of them," Abraham and Isaac, father and son, parent and child, the two of them went.

Yakhdav—"together." Both Abraham and Isaac might have gone to Moriah but each at his own pace, in his own time, his own fashion, Abraham taking the high road as it were and Isaac the by-road. Why should they have to suffer the painfully sad experience of the long journey together, each knowing what would happen at the journey's end, wondering what was in the mind of the other? No, they went, both of them went. And both of them went together, companionably, side by side, each lightening for the other the distress of that anguishful trip by his very presence.

Having enlightened his patient congregation as to the real necessity for all three words, the old-time preacher usually said a lengthy word or two about the meaning of *Moriah*, the name of the mountain which was the goal of the father and his son, the parent and his child.

It was a hill that offered a challenge to any climber, of course. But it was not a Mt. Everest, no towering Himalayan peak, no unreachable goal. It was an attainable height, not an effortless ascent but accessible, if reasonable effort were exerted. It was the symbol of Jewish ideals. They are not superhumanly unattainable, basically impossible formulas like turning the other cheek, loving your enemy, or giving away every last cent until you are skinny enough to slide through the eye of a needle and get into heaven. Jewish standards are sound, realistic, reasonable, realizable by normal mortals. Such ideals as justice, kindness, honesty, equity, freedom, peace, service to man, obedience to God.

And how does one reach Moriah? The word *Moriah* is derived from the same Hebrew word as *moreh*—"teacher." One climbs to Moriah by study, by learning. By devotion to Torah, God's word, we come to know His will; and in the process we are trained for the most important part of our religion, namely to do His will.

And then the *darshan* of a former age would make his peroration. He would appeal to the youth to honor their father and their mother by walking with them the well-tried Jewish paths that lead to Moriah. The way of the parents was the good way of spiritual peace, of religious pleasure, and the youths would do well to walk those paths together with their fathers.

Those congregations had an easy time of it, comparatively, because that would be the end of the old time preacher's sermon. Whereas it would only be the beginning, the introduction to mine.

The old time preacher had an easy time of it, too. He could concentrate on the wayward youth. Today, he would have his hands full with wayward parents, as well.

It was simplicity itself to illustrate to the youth of former generations what the rich fullness of Jewish life was. Every Jewish child had an excellent example of Jewish living— at home. There he could experience every day what the preacher was talking about in *shul*.

Would that this were true so today. The old time rabbi could confidently plead with the youth of his congregation to follow in the footsteps of their elders. In our day the preacher would do well to think twice before making any such suggestion.

We do not have to tell modern youth to do what their parents do. They are usually doing it. They are usually going the same way—both of them together. But the direction they are taking is not invariably toward any Moriah.

Too often it is something else and something less which beckons them. No matter what his parents' preachment the modern child sees his parents practice and is quite willing to pursue that practice himself. The Philistine standards for the most part, the shallows of American civilization which Arthur Miller so startlingly revealed in his grim play, *The Death of a Salesman*.

The whole structure of modern Jewish education is feeble and tottering largely because it rests on the fallacious assumption that Judaism is something exclusively for children.

The ceremonies of the synagogue we think are beautiful—*for the children*. The *Kiddush*, if recited, is recited for the children. *Shabbos* and festival candles, if they are lighted, are lighted for the children. The *Seder* is conducted, if it is, for whom? for the children—*nebich, die kinder*.

When our fathers emphasized the training of a child they assumed this education was preparing him for adult Jewish living. They never regarded the ceremonies of his people's faith as baubles wherewith to amuse a Jewish child until he grew up and outgrew them. If the instruction of Jewish children is not a preparation for their life as adult Jews then it is a pitifully useless consumption of their time and that of their teachers and a cynical mockery of their religion. It is kid-stuff, than which nothing is more contemptible in the eyes of sophisticated adolescence. Judaism is not *kinderspiel* but a way of life for the mature.

What, for example, can the prophet Hosea's concept of love, human and divine, mean to a child; or Job's struggle with the problem of pain and evil? What message can the radical prophet Amos or the gentle cynic Kohelet or the author of the Book of Jonah bring to an immature mind? How superficial are the lessons that a half-grown youth can learn from Jewish history with its passion and its glory or from the vistas which spread before the mind from the lofty peaks of our wisdom literature?

For centuries these wonders have engrossed the best adult minds among our people and among Christian scholars in the academic world. And we would presume to package it all in neat little homogenized capsules taken once or twice or, by reason of superhuman strength, three times a week by youngsters until they have reached the advanced age of thirteen or even, by reason of superhuman parental effort, sixteen years.

Certainly, it is important that our children are introduced to our inheritance. But only if it become for them a useful heritage, not a mere heirloom. What is the difference between the two? It is vast. An heirloom is pointed to with pride because it is an antique, but it is never used. An inheritance is useful, usable, and used. Why introduce our children to an old friend of the family if his friendship is no longer valued by the parents who indeed snub him consistently every year from one Yom Kippur to the next Rosh Hashana?

Judaism is not a beginner's course in history or customs or elementary Hebrew or even theology. It isn't a school of archaeology for children. Rather is it what the rabbis say it is: *aron hanosey nosav*—"an ark which carries those who carry it," which exalts those who exalt it. Judaism is not classroom attendance or exams or report cards or curriculum or a Bar Mitzvah diploma or a Confirmation certificate framed and pointed out to the neighbors and friends. Judaism is something to use, to live by. It will survive only if we put it to use. And, if we as adults put it to use, our children may. If we do not, they are not likely to. And if they do not, it won't survive and neither will they. At least, they will not survive as Jews.

10 September 1979.

✿✿ Where Ḩappiness Lies

> This command which I enjoin upon you today is
> not beyond your power or reach—not in heaven
> or overseas—that someone must get it to you
> that you may do it. No, it's very near—in your
> mind and your hand so you can do it [Deuteron-
> omy 30:11-14, *adapted*].

Seventy years ago (when I was a rather new rabbi) the
National Federation of Temple Brotherhoods sent to each
of its thousands of members a questionnaire investigating
the religious beliefs, practices, and preferences of adult Reform Jewish males. One of the questions on that survey I
still remember, as well as several of the answers to it.

The question was, "What do you want your rabbi to
talk about?" A few riotously funny comedians wrote, "I
want him to talk about ten minutes. Preferably less." Some
respondents wrote, "I want him to talk about topics of the
day. As for Bible, Talmud, and Jewish history—what was,
was! None of it grabs me." To offset and cancel that preference, others wrote, "I want him to talk about sacred Hebrew texts and eternal verities. I can read newspapers and
magazines and listen to radio and TV broadcasts about
current events myself. I don't need to hear them, or book
reviews, from the pulpit." But I found one response unforgettable and have remembered it all these years: "I want
my rabbi to talk about *me*."

Whether his parishioners always recognized it or not, from the pulpit *this* rabbi always tried to talk about them. Certainly on this occasion none of you will have the slightest difficulty recognizing the target of my talk. This time you won't be able to *escape* knowing that I am talking to you *about* you, each of you where you *live*, by which, of course, I mean not a certain house on some particular street, but in your mind. As John Milton said, "The mind is its own world."

I want to talk to you about happiness—your personal happiness. How you attain it. The *only way anyone ever* achieves a happy day, or year, or life. You may have noticed I omitted mention of "happy hour"? For that, saloons have the formula; you come there at five o'clock in the afternoon, before the bar gets too crowded, and you can booze up on your favorite flavor of alcohol at bargain prices.

Be that as it may—to get into our subject: Early each September I receive in the mail, from a *secular* Jewish organization, a box of *Shanah Tovah* cards. These are sent, of course, in the hope that recipients will respond with a donation to the source of this mailing.

I stress the fact that this is a *secular* agency. The *Shanah Tovah* cards themselves make that abundantly evident. Because the wish expressed on each of them is for a *happy* new year. And of course there is nothing Jewish or religious about that wish. It is the chant you hear from the throats of drunken revelers when the clock strikes midnight between December 31st and the 1st of January.

"Happy New Year" is a familiar old pagan series of syllables. The Rosh HaShanah prayer is that you be inscribed in the Book of Life for a *good* year—a year of goodness—during which, it is hoped, that the good person receiving the card or greeting will do good things for himself, his family, and friends, his congregation and community, his world. That, whether or not life is good to him or her, this Jew will be good to life.

As for happiness, that is not achieved for anyone merely by words of well-wishing acquaintances, neighbors, and friends expressing the hope that happiness will *happen* to the recipient of those wishes.

For each of us, here and everywhere, happiness depends not upon any external circumstance, event, statement, thing, or any combination of these; but solely upon the decisions each of us makes with reference to all that we have and everything that happens to us. Happiness is always a matter of choice.

Each of us decides for himself whether to be content with his lot or unhappy about it. Addressing themselves to our theme, our sages ask, *Ayzeh hu ashir?* "Who is happy?" (or "rich") and they answer, *"Hasameyah b'helko,"* "The one who decides to be happy with his or her lot"—no matter what that lot may be. Because, whatever it is, there are legions of folk who would gladly swap places and circumstances and rejoice to exchange their situation for yours.

An oft-quoted statement from the Torah reading for these holy days is the commandment *u'vaharta baha-yim,* "choose life!" Now, I ask you: Is that an intelligent, sensible, or necessary commandment? Does anyone ever choose death? You can bet on it! They do! Not only is suicide a popular choice, particularly among our youth today. But countless thousands of others identify happiness with thrills of excitement, which they find in flirting with the *Malach HaMavet,* "the Angel of Death": sky diving, racing cars, climbing mountains, ingesting addictive toxic drugs, or sailing around the world alone in a fifteen-foot boat.

And what about professional assassins, "hit men," terrorists, and self-proclaimed patriots who throng the streets to protest against peace and violently obstruct peace efforts in Somalia, Bosnia, Gaza, the West Bank, and other misery spots on the planet?

As there are multitudes who *choose death* for themselves or others, there are myriads who *choose to be unhappy*. Call them "neurots," if you like. But unhappiness is something that doesn't just happen to them. It is a fate they choose for themselves.

This is hardly a novel, unique, or peculiar view of the source of unhappiness. It is the *consensus* of the best minds who have studied the subject seriously, in depth, and at great length.

Years ago, the brilliant philosopher of history, James Harvey Robinson, opened his classic literary gem, *The Mind in the Making*, with the statement, "It is not the external circumstances of our lives which make or mar our happiness; it is our *attitude* toward those circumstances."

And it is each of us who decides, chooses, fixes, determines that attitude. Characteristically, the wise and witty Will Rogers said it succinctly: "Every one is about as happy as he decides he is going to be."

Consider the alternative. If happiness is not something we choose, but depends on what others say or do, then we have little or no control over our peace of mind—we are manipulated marionettes.

But if happiness *is* a choice we make for ourselves, why would anyone choose *un*happiness. Why would one *prefer* to be depressed; *decide* to be miserable. Well, for all kinds of reasons—most of them unconscious, perhaps.

Possibly to punish themselves for some real or imagined guilt. For example, large numbers of holocaust survivors flagellate themselves because they (who feel they are so unworthy) survived, while their relatives (all of *them* admirable, of course) perished.

Others choose unhappiness in the wistful hope that this will make their spouse, parents, siblings and/or offspring miserable—and also perhaps to get their attention and evoke their sympathy. "She's so depressed, *nebich*"… "What can we do to cheer him up?"

The fact is, of course, that there are both happy and unhappy: princes and paupers, professors and peasants, geniuses and morons, brides and widows, invalids and athletes….

Consider the way that two of our distinguished ancestors related to their life together. When King Saul heard the women of Israel extolling David (his harpist, therapist, and field marshal) in the popular street chant, "Saul has slain his thousands, but David his tens of thousands," the thought that those "military experts" (the housewives and bobby-soxers of Bethlehem and Beersheba) valued David's battle prowess more than his, made Saul so desperately unhappy that his mental health deteriorated precipitously, to a point where finally his mind was shattered and lay in shambles.

What other choice did Saul have? Well, he could have applauded himself for his astuteness in having discovered and appointed to lead Israel's armed forces the ablest military strategist and tactician in the Mideast of that era.

Saul *might* have rejoiced in his good fortune in being able to sit safely and comfortably on his throne, while David was risking his life constantly on the battlefield in mortal combat with the Philistines. Saul might have gladly admitted that David was a fiercer fighter than he, but that he was a wiser ruler.

Instead, Saul chose to keep a jealous eye on David, suspecting that the young five-star general was hankering for his throne.

Saul's unhappiness was so acute, constant, and unbearable, that he tried desperately to eliminate its perceived cause; he sought to murder David. But David eluded the spear Saul flung at him, and fled into hiding.

While Saul was fuming toward insanity, what choices did David make? Did he decide to wallow in self-commiseration? Did he seek to elicit sympathy? pester his colleagues and supporters with the querulous plaint, "What did I ever do to the King to earn his murderous hate?" Did David plot revenge? Did he take advantage of any of the opportunities he had to do Saul in? He could have; but he made other, saner choices.

Saul pursued David into the wilderness of Ein Gedi. When Saul entered a cave to rest, he didn't know that David and his men were hiding in its recesses. His men wanted David to seize the opportunity to dispatch Saul and thus end their plight as fugitives.

Surreptitiously, David did indeed cut off part of the king's cloak as proof that he could have killed him. Proof which he later exhibited (at a safe distance) to Saul. But David's conscience smote him. He said, "How could I have done such a thing to my king, the anointed of God?"

On another occasion, David and his nephew and right-hand man, Abishai, crept into Saul's camp in the dead of night. David said to Abishai, "Do not slay him. Who can lay a hand on God's anointed and be guiltless?"

You see, Saul let the words of the David-adoring women determine how he would feel and, therefore, how he would act. David decided that his choice alone would determine how he *felt* and what he would *do*.

We turn now from the love-hate relationship between Saul and David (two men of immense political power who made news in Israel three thousand years ago) to the hate-love relationship of Yitzhak Rabin and Yasir Arafat, who made news in Israel (and just about everywhere else) by signing a peace accord.

What hope or expectation did you have for peace in Israel when that happened? How did you decide to respond to the events which led to the scene on the south lawn of the Clinton White House?

You had a number of choices—all the way from the dourest pessimism to the most ebullient optimism, and almost anything at all in between. You might justify pessimism on the basis of all the long list of broken promises and broken hopes which have been made and experienced by contending nations in the Mideast. At the other extreme, with no necessary factual justification at all, you could imagine yourself now hearing the footsteps of the *mashiah* coming to reign over a blessed world to the end of time.

For myself, I choose a rather ordinary, moderate, simple, practical, healthy optimism. With reference to Israel, I live in *hope* that all I have supported, stood, worked, and prayed for during most of my long life may yet be realized, and that what happened that day was a step forward on that very long road. Perhaps, before I die, my people (in a very much diminished territory from the area designated for close Jewish settlement by the League of Nations seventy-odd years ago) may, at last, be able to devote the best of its enormous talent, energy, and means to positive, productive discovery, invention, and enterprise: in science, education, literature, medicine, music, philosophy, art, and government, instead of sadly wasting so much of its best brains and other resources on military defense and mere physical survival.

I do not say I am counting on all this to happen. As a practical person with a healthy respect for history and reality, do not take it for granted that wondrously beautiful things are about to happen—for Israelis and Palestinians. I do not *expect* this to happen. Only because I have patiently, painstakingly taught myself to live *without expectation*. I have learned *never* to *expect* anything, good or bad. But I do *hope*. I patiently, passionately, prayerfully hope for what I consider good: for me, my people, and the world's people.

I have lived too long to expect or assume that what I want, hope, and pray for, will necessarily or inevitably be actualized. But what have I lost by hoping and praying for its realization? Absolutely nothing. For, what if my hope is disappointed? *Until* that happens, hope itself keeps me happy. To be hopeful is to be happy. And hope, too, is a *choice* we make. If my hope is disappointed, all I have lost is the sadness and sourness that pessimism would have bought me.

If someone's pessimistic prediction comes true and the Apocalypse (total global disaster) occurs: is the pessimist happy because he guessed right?

No disappointment can convert me permanently to pessimism. Because disappointment seldom is permanent. It is hope which "springs eternal" in the healthy human heart. And, despite countless disappointments in my own life, my heart still seems to be human and healthy.

Pessimism is only a shorter word for hopelessness, and I see no way of reconciling hopelessness, with happiness. As long as I have a choice I choose a quiet, sober, non-jubilant optimism: a happy choice.

I recommend it.

Now, I hope—I really seriously, deeply, and fervently hope—that no one—not one single, solitary individual—is saying to herself or to his neighbor, "What this preacher is saying is easier said than done." (I mention this because that has been a response to my insistence that happiness and unhappiness are choices we make: "Easier said than done.")

If, by any chance that hackneyed, worthless series of syllables occurs to you, don't utter them. Please! They are quite impertinent. "Easier said than done," constitute an absurd cliché, an inane banality, sound without sense, a meaningless utterance, an O. O. ("Obvious Observation").

That, dear friends, is simply because everything, but every thing in this world, is easier *said* than done. Of course, it is easier to *talk* about *anything* than to do it. That is too obvious to need uttering.

I have not *said*, nor do I *believe*, that the choices one *must* make to be happy are easy to make. So, what if they are *hard?* They are necessary, and they are possible, and they are worth the effort. No big, important decision in life is easy to make. But the decision to be happy seems to me a wise and healthy one, a choice worth *whatever* it costs.

You know the story of the hobo who comes knocking at the farmhouse door asking for something to eat. You remember the farmer's response. "Stranger," he says, "ever since Adam was expelled from the Garden of Eden when he got into trouble because he didn't have enough to do to keep him occupied, every man has had to *work* if he got hungry and wanted to *eat*. You want breakfast, fella? Earn it. Split those logs out there for my stove and fireplace."

In an hour the log-splitter knocked on the kitchen door to tell the farmer the job was finished. The farmer was astonished, but checked to see whether this was *true*. It was. He invited the man in for a lavish and leisurely breakfast, at the conclusion of which, the farmer said, "You're the best worker I've ever had, and I want to keep you— alive! I don't want you to kill yourself working. For the rest of the day I'm going to give you an easy job."

The farmer took him out to the barn where there was a heap of apples, and gave him these instructions: "All you've got to do is separate this fruit into two piles. The small apples to the left, and the big apples to the right. Easy does it."

The farmer came back in an hour to get a progress report, only to discover the man stretched out flat on his back on the barn floor, not just asleep, but unconscious, in coma! It took the splash of a full pail of cold water in the man's face to bring him around.

"What happened?" asked the farmer. "You did so well this morning with the woodpile. Why did this easy job knock you out?"

"Easy job!" the hobo expostulated. "You call that 'easy'?! Big ones here! Little ones there! Decisions! Decisions!"

I shudder to think that what I have said to you about your happiness being up to you may produce dozens of simpering male and female clones of Pollyanna, Pippa, or Rebecca of Sunnybrook Farm.

But I do submit that, as good a way as any to appreciate and be thankful for the gift of life is to decide to be pleased with what you *have* (your possessions); what you *do* (your occupation), and what you *are* (yourself).

The blessing I pronounce upon you at this dawn of the New Year is that you find the way to *choose happiness*. It may not be easy. I didn't say it was. I admit it can be effortful.

I submit that for most of us the cure for chronic unhappiness *exists*—and that it is *inside* each of us. As a first simple step, we might turn up the corners of our mouth, decide to smile. Then go on to make the resolve and exert the will to approve of ourselves, to enjoy what we *have*, and *do*, and *are*. And if you feel that what you "have, do, and are" are less than completely admirable, I hope you will begin to do all you can to change, in order to make them admirable, and that you will take pride and joy in that process.

כן יהי רצון, *Ken Yehi Ratzon*—May this be God's will and yours. 🌿

Rosh HaShanah, September 17, 1993

❧ Remembering What to Forget

Shabbat Zahhor **is a time** for remembering. It is the Sabbath before Purim when we celebrate the victory over Israel's ancient enemy, Haman, and when we read from the Torah the significant passage referring to Amalek, the ancient ancestor of Haman.

Jews are a remembering people. Indeed, one of our favorite religious practices is *Yizkor*, which means "remember." We are a history-conscious people. We understand the importance of remembering.

Memory does more than give us the ability to review the past. It also makes the present real and significant. Without memory the business of living would be utter chaos. Were we unable to remember from one moment to the next, the world would become a confusing maze. We could acquire no useful habits. We would be helpless infants.

Our days, to be coherent, must be strung together by the thread of memory.

On the conscious level, of course, it is impossible to remember everything. Even the best memories are able to retain only a small fragment of their experiences. Nor is it desirable that we remember everything. Quite the contrary. Important as the power of remembering is, no less important is the power to forget.

Life would be unlivable if we were not blessed also with the gift of forgetfulness. If we had to live each day burdened with the crushing weight of all our past griefs, failures, losses, and pains: if we could not banish from our minds our accumulated defeats, frustrations, and fears. If the wounds we have suffered on life's battlefield were always gaping and raw, life would be an intolerable curse.

There is a Jewish legend which tells us that when God finished creating the world and was about to release it, He suddenly realized that He had forgotten an indispensable ingredient without which life would be unendurable. He had forgotten to include the power to forget. So He called back the world and blessed it with forgetfulness. Then He was satisfied that it was ready for human habitation.

One of the commonest complaints of men is that their powers of memory are not as strong as they used to be, or as they should *like them* to be. What many of us suffer from, on the contrary, is that our power to forget is not as keen as it should be. As one poet put it:

This world would be for us a happier place
And there would be less of regretting
If we would remember to practice with grace
The very fine art of forgetting.

Just as we cannot remember everything, so it is impossible, if we are healthy-minded, to forget everything. Only the amnesia victim has complete obliviousness. The alcoholic and the drug addict can obtain temporary forgetfulness but only at an exorbitant price in health and human dignity.

If we can neither remember everything nor forget everything, how is it possible to know what we ought to remember and what we ought to forget? It seems to me that the answer is to make our memories selective so that we remember those things which are likely to make us better people and forget those things which tend to shrink us and weaken our character.

We ought to exercise the same discriminating care in furnishing our memories as we do in furnishing our homes. You may think that memory is automatic. And, as a rule, memory does not select and reject. It does not discriminate. It is not quite like a sieve which separates the wheat from the chaff. It is more like a barrel which catches whatever is poured into it.

That is true, but only part of the truth. Actually, memory never operates independently. Working alongside it is judgment. Judgment can *guide* memory.

The famous German philosopher, Immanuel Kant, was once jolted by the discovery that his presumably faithful servant, Lampe, whom he had trusted implicitly for long years, had in fact been robbing him steadily and systematically. Kant had no choice but to dismiss Lampe, despite his heavy dependence on him. Understandably, Kant missed him terribly.

The philosopher's diary reveals the echo of his sadness: For, in it, he wrote to himself: "Remember to forget Lampe." Kant was enlisting his judgment in the service of his memory, to help him reject Lampe.

Some years ago, a massive illustration of the importance of a Sabbath such as this came at a crucial juncture in American history. In 1941, the judgment of the American people decided that whatever else was permitted to grow dim in our collective memory, one thing that we would never forget was Pearl Harbor. In impassioned words over the radio and at mass meetings, the slogan "Remember Pearl Harbor" was hammered into our memories. And our determined prosecution of the war effort to its successful conclusion is evidence that the American people did "remember Pearl Harbor." Our intense preoccupation with strengthening our worldwide defenses at staggering cost ever since, so that we will never again be caught unprepared, is evidence that we still remember Pearl Harbor. This was a spectacular instance of the judgment of America guiding its memory.

This reality operated dynamically in Jewish history, as well. Early in our people's history, Moses decided that whatever else the Jewish people forgot, there was one memory they must always keep alive. "And thou shalt remember that thou wast a slave in Egypt." Again and again, this command, in one form or another, is repeated in the Torah. It is a fact that the Jew has always been in the forefront of those who fight for the oppressed, the downtrodden, the underdog. To this very day, the Jew has remembered that he was a slave in Egypt because the collective judgment of the Jewish people determined that Egypt was not to be forgotten.

And if, in our day, Israel has become an independent Jewish state, it is because the judgment of our people decreed twenty-five hundred years ago: "If I forget thee, O Jerusalem, may my right hand forget its skill."

Other nations, before and since, suffered enslavement and exile, too. For them, exile meant death and disappearance. The Jew not only survived, but he lived to rebuild and reconstitute his homeland. He accomplished this unprecedented historical feat because, in a thousand ways, he kept alive the memory of Zion—in his daily prayers, at the graveside of his beloved dead, under the wedding canopy. In every conceivable way, he remained faithful to his vow of Eternal Remembrance. Zion was not forgotten, because in the judgment of our people, its memory was to be kept continually alive.

Judgment not only molds memory but memory, in turn, molds behavior and character. This is true not only of nations, but also of individuals. To a large extent, we are what we remember. A keen student of human behavior, George Halifax once said: "Could we know what men are most apt to *remember*, we might also know what they are most apt to *do*."

What ought we remember and what ought we forget? Our Biblical ancestor, Joseph, faced this memory problem in one of the most dramatic moments of his colorful career. That moment occurred when Joseph, who had been sold by his brothers into slavery, found these same brothers standing as supplicants before him. But now he had become the Regent of Egypt and his brothers, driven by famine, appeared before him for food.

Joseph has them at his mercy. He can do with him as he will, but what *will* he do? The problem is fundamentally one of memory. What should he remember? He can remember how they beat him and cast him into the pit where he might have been left to perish had not an Ishmaelite Caravan fortuitously appeared. How they cruelly traded him off as if he were a camel or an ox.

Or he can remember how the young Joseph had provoked them. How he had brought malicious tales about them back to his father. How he had taunted them with his dreams of his destined domination over them. He can either remember the wrong he *suffered* or the wrong he *inflicted*. He can either exact vengeance or make amends.

Which experience shall he remember? The problem is not an easy one. Instinctively, Joseph appears ready to exact vengeance. In a variety of subtle ways, he torments his brothers, worries them and hurls accusations at them.

All this, however, is but the prelude which leads up to the climax—the moment when Joseph reveals himself to his brothers.

When that moment arrives, Joseph emerges in heroic stature. He has chosen to forget his brothers' misconduct, and to make amends for his own.

When he notices the fear that registers on their faces when he says, "I am Joseph, your brother," he reassures them: "Be not angry with yourselves that you sold me here. For God has sent me before you to preserve life. It was not you but God who sent me here." He then goes on to assure them that he will make arrangements for them and their families to live in Egypt where he will provide for them all.

It is in this way that Joseph solves his personal memory problem.

Maaseh avot siman libanim, "the actions of the fathers are a guide to their descendants." Joseph's experience can be highly instructive. It should teach us to forget those things which, if remembered, would bring out our worst traits. And to try to remember those things which, if forgotten, would suppress our nobler impulses. Many of us, at one time or another, have permitted ties of family and friends to be broken. There was an unpleasant scene, a heated exchange of words, an explosive moment. We chose to remember that moment, while we forgot all the unnumbered pleasant moments of family loyalty and the warmth of friendship. Would it not be wiser if we forgot the hurt and remembered the love?

All of us have suffered some wrongs and also inflicted some. Too often we recall the instances when we were the victims. We forget those where we were the offenders. Were it not wiser to reverse some memory systems: consign the wrongs suffered to oblivion and, where time yet permits, repair the wrong inflicted?

All too often we remember with bitterness the unfulfilled promises made to us. But we calmly forget the pledge we made and did not honor, the resolve we made and did not fulfill, the word we gave and did not keep. Were it not better that we forgot the first and remembered the second?

In our time, all of us have been both benefactors and beneficiaries. We have benefited others, to be sure, but, in more instances than we normally care to remember, we have also reaped the harvest of another's generosity, another's sacrifice.

If we enjoy the blessings of health, freedom, democracy, Judaism—it is because others have paid for these, our possessions, with their lives and their blood. Shall the little kindnesses we have shown make us arrogant, while there is so much that we have inherited which should make us profoundly grateful and humble?

Every day we see about us evidence of human pettiness, greed, self-centeredness and immorality. But if we observe carefully, we also see human nobility, generosity, self-effacement, genuine religious conviction and ethical action. The cynic remembers only man's faults—that is why he remains a cynic. The good man remembers his brother's virtues. Which shall we choose to remember?

Many of us have endured the anguish of final parting from a loved one. Parents and children, brothers and sisters, husbands and wives have tasted the bitterness of bereavement. Left with the choice of memories, they can either languish in pining as they dwell upon the death of their dear one, or they can find inspiration and ennoblement as they contemplate the life of their beloved.

They can either become bent under the burden of grief, or be braced by a sense of gratitude. From this loss, they can either distill an unending flow of tears, or derive deepened sympathies, clearer vision, nobler strivings. What ought to be remembered, the loss or the love, the death or the life?

These questions each of us has to answer for himself. In making our choice, we ought to remember that we *are* what we remember. Our memories mold our conduct and our characters. And what others remember of us, will be influenced, if not determined, by what we choose to remember.

The Sabbath of Remembrance is an occasion also to remember what to forget,

Let us forget things that vexed and tried us,
The worrying things that caused our souls to fret,
The hopes that, cherished long were, still divide us
Let us forget.

Let us forget the little slights that pained us,
The greater wrongs that rankle sometimes yet,
The pride with which some lofty one disdained us—
Let us forget.

The blessings manifold, past all deserving,
Kind words, thoughtful deeds, a countless throng,
The faults o'ercome, the rectitude unswerving,
Let us remember long.

Whatever things were good and true and gracious,
Whatever of right has triumphed over wrong,
What love of God or man has rendered precious,
Let us remember long.

So, pondering well the lessons it has taught us,
We tenderly may bid each day goodbye,
Holding in memory the good it brought us,
Letting the evil die.

March 9, 1979

❦ Drush for S'lichot

A *s'licha* is a prayer of penitence. It asks God to forgive the petitioners' sins. The root of the word is *salach*, a verb meaning "pardon." The plural of *s'licha* is *s'lichot*.

One thousand one hundred years ago, the name *s'lichot* was first applied to the kind of service we hold tonight by a great liturgist, the Gaon Amram. He was the renowned rabbinical genius who headed the illustrious talmudic academy at Sura in Babylonia during the third quarter of the ninth century.

Originally, the *s'lichot* prayers for forgiveness were composed to be recited on Yom Kippur, because asking God to pardon our sins is the chief purpose of the service on the Day of Atonement.

In ancient times, the Yom Kippur service used to be called *seder s'lichot* (Eliyahu Zuta 23), the *seder* or order of the service for repentance.

Then, because Rosh Hashanah, which was called *Yom Din*, "the Day of Judgment," was considered a preliminary event and an occasion to prepare for Yom Kippur, *s'lichot* petitions for God's mercy and pardon were felt to be necessary on Rosh Hashanah, too. Then the *Aseret y'mey t'shuva*, each of the "ten days of penitence" intervening between Rosh Hashanah and Yom Kippur were assigned *s'lichot*, these penitential prayers.

At various times in Jewish history *s'lichot* prayers were recited on the tenth of the Hebrew month of Tevet; on the seventeenth of Tamuz; on Queen Esther's Fast Day, the thirteenth of Adar, the day before Purim; and many other days of fast and mourning and commemoration of epidemics, massacres, droughts, and an assortment of calamities. It finally became customary for our people to recite such *s'lichot* prayers during several days before Rosh Hashanah.

Now what made Jews think they were such wicked sinners that they needed so many prayers so many times during the year to supplicate God to forgive their iniquities and transgressions. Were they so sinful, so much *more* sinful than their Gentile neighbors who did what they could to make Jews' lives a hell on earth? The truth is that our ancestors were perhaps far less sinful than their non-Jewish contemporaries or than we, their Jewish descendants. And the truth is that they suffered in ancient and medieval times far worse discrimination, exclusion, rejection, contempt, hatred, and horrible cruelty from their neighbors who were urged by their bishops and barons to believe that they were doing God's will in making Jews' lives as painful as possible.

As if the frightful pain of their daily existence were not enough for human flesh and spirit to have to bear, our tormented people suffered, in addition, from an incredible doctrine that was taught in traditional Jewish theology. A doctrine that is literally, and, in every way, incredible, which is to say, not to be believed.

You see, in addition to all that our people endured from persecution at the hands of their enemies, they carried the added burden of a punishing load of guilt. Where did that come from? From this very old theological doctrine, a belief and teaching which was already ancient in the days of the psalmist who wrote "from my youth to my old age I have never seen a pious person abandoned or his children begging for bread" (Psalm 37).

נַעַר הָיִיתִי גַּם־זָקַנְתִּי וְלֹא־רָאִיתִי
צַדִּיק נֶעֱזָב וְזַרְעוֹ מְבַקֶּשׁ־לָחֶם:

*Naar ha-yiti v'gam zakanti v'lo ra-iti
tsadik ne-ezav v'zar-o m'vakesh lochem.*

They had been taught to believe that whatever the immediate or apparent cause of their suffering, the real reason, the ultimate cause of their pain was sins which they had committed, for which they were being punished.

So what they were really praying for was relief from this pain. That was very real and present, and to get rid of that pain they were willing to confess having committed almost every kind of sin in all the long catalogue of confessions you find in the *Al Het Shechatanu* which we still recite on Yom Kippur. All this suffering, no matter from what evident source was, they believed the affliction of God. They were taught to believe that the *Kadosh Baruch Hu*, the "Holy Source of all Blessing"—*HaRachaman*, the "All Merciful One"—used every sort of misfortune, disease, disaster, panic, poverty, war, refugeeism, exile, fire, flood, famine, death, and bereavement as punishment for our sins!

This, I do believe, quite literally is an incredible notion, one that should never have been attributed to God, should never have been taught, or perpetuated and believed, taken as wisdom or truth. It is worse than unbelievable. It is abominable.

Personally I find it odious, revolting; as nauseous and appalling as the preachment of Jerry Falwell and his pious fundamentalist colleagues who self-righteously insinuate, for example, that the victim of AIDS, that horrendous, so far incurable, global plague, which threatens the lives of millions including babies, celibates, and other innocent persons, is God's way of punishing homosexuals and drug abusers, and thus discouraging others from following their sinful ways.

To believe and teach such a theological doctrine is itself damnable. It is blasphemous, among the gravest sins, a gross, blatant, flagrant insult to God. The problem of pain and the existence of evil is certainly the riddle of riddles in religion, the problem of problems in philosophy. But to dogmatically explain tragedy and suffering as God's method of improving human conduct is not a solution. It is a cruel cop-out, a blasphemous evasion—and an insult to God.

"Never have I seen good folk forsaken or their families going hungry,"—the person who wrote that had to be blind. Such crude simple-minded blind dogmatism is very old. However, it hardly squares with the grim realities of life.

But then, of course, the antiquity of an idea never did have any necessary connection with its truth. The obvious truth being that millions of innocents do suffer from countless mental, physical, economic, political and social sicknesses. The truth is that as Job (5:7) so rightly says "Humankind is born to trouble as surely as sparks from a wood fire fly upward."

From the womb to the tomb, suffering is the experience of *all* the human race. Suffering is something we can expect. Pleasure is a sometime thing.

Life begins with a cry of anguish which is the baby's response to the prolonged beating which every innocent infant suffers in the very process of being born. Life continues in a wail of protest against the world where every sensation experienced by the newborn child is torture by contrast to the soft warm peaceful security of its mother's body, from which it is suddenly and forcibly thrust out. Life begins with a sob of pain and disillusionment. It usually ends with a groan of agony at the thought or, in the process, of dying. And between that beginning and that end, each of us experiences thousands of aches, disappointments, afflictions, and frustrations.

We all sometimes experience pleasure and sometimes pain. Sometimes, but certainly not always, pain is a penalty for some violation of God's commandments. And sometimes, but by no means invariably, pleasure is a reward for ethical conduct. But there is no positive correlation, no necessary connection between all pain and punishment on the one hand and all pleasure and reward on the other. Why should there be? How much merit would there be in the virtue of an ethical person if he were invariably rewarded for good conduct—either here or hereafter, or because he feared punishment either in this world or the next? If goodness is not its own reward, if one does not serve his Heavenly Master without expectation of recompense, where is the glory of performing the mitzvah?

Why do the innocent suffer? Precisely so that neither they nor we will come to expect well-being and prosperity as our prize for good behavior, so that we will grow up and dissociate ourselves from the wholly infantile notion that prizes and penalties are God's techniques for stimulating us to good behavior.

"My ways are not your ways. Neither are your thoughts my thoughts," says the Eternal.

A donkey's master will hang a juicy carrot on a long stick in front of the animal's nose to get the beast to move, and hold in his hand a thick stick to use on the other end of the donkey—just in case…. But God patiently hopes that men are something more and something better than donkeys.

It is sinful, moral blindness to imagine that if a person is prosperous this is clear and positive proof of God's favor. Prosperity isn't a reward. It's a responsibility. On the other hand, where compassion was no more I doubt whether God Himself would care to continue the renewal of this gift of life.

Who knows? There may have been a time when only the wicked suffered but God saw that then no one cared. Therefore, He was compelled to spread suffering indiscriminately, letting it fall, like rain, on mountain and valley alike, not only upon the flowers but also on the weeds. Maybe, He reasoned, if the innocent also suffered it might arouse sympathy in the apathetic souls of the self-righteous. Apparently He was, at least to some extent, right.

The sin for which at *S'lichot* time we should ask for God's pardon is the sin of pretending to believe and presuming to teach that all suffering is punishment for the misdeeds of the suffering victim. And for the sin of philosophizing about the problem of pain, instead of reaching out a hand to dry the tears and heal the wounds of a suffering world—all humankind.

When we grow up to the idea that no matter who the victim may be, the ignorant or the innocent, the righteous or the renegade, the sinful scoffer or the saintly sage, suffering needs attention, compassion, help from us—God's partners in creation. Why, then, instead of loftily philosophizing about pain and the existence of evil, we will forsake our soft seats of security as spectators on the side of the road. We will let ourselves be rocked off our complacent centers of gravity and go out in the middle of the road where the going is rough, and be a friend to the people of our race—the race God favors—the human race. 🐾

September 1987

❧ Caring
The Mitzvah which Leads to Them All

Definition by Translation

The brilliant young anthropologist, Dr. Theodor Gaster, is leaving England to teach at distinguished universities in the United States. In parting, his wise and witty father, Britain's Chief Sephardic Rabbi, *Hacham* Moses Gaster, gives his son, Ted, this sage advice: "You will find Americans using certain expressions in odd ways: terms like 'shrink', 'complex', 'V.I.P.' You will understand these better if you translate each into Yiddish.

"For example, almost everyone there goes to a 'shrink'; that's an *eytzeh geber*. Many seem to suffer from some 'complex.' A 'complex' is a *kop dreyenish*. Individuals will be pointed out to you as being a 'V.I.P.' A 'V.I.P.' is a *gantzeh knacker....*"

Sin

Perhaps we might better understand the message of the holy days if we translate some of the old fashioned language of our prayerbook, not into Yiddish, but into more current American idiom. For example, key words like "sin," "repentance," "salvation". To many of us, these terms barely register as meaning anything. Not because they represent no realities, but because they belong to a bygone age, when people—my sainted mother was one—

would actually say of some reprehensible act: "That's a sin!"

Today, we would put it differently. We'd say of the same behavior: "It's insensitive, crude, cruel, self-defeating, counter-productive, unfeeling, stupid, boorish, mindless, or just sick."

We have no sinners today. Of course not! Only millions of delinquents; alienated, frustrated, hung-up, drug-addicted, sex-obsessed, anxiety- and guilt-ridden neurotics. That's all. But, certainly, no sinners. Perish forbid!

What is Sin? It is sickness of soul, whether conscious or unconscious, it's deep unhappiness with what we are doing with our lives: to ourselves and to those who share our life; the distressing misapplication of our talents and energies, our affections and concern, our physical, emotional, esthetic, financial, or spiritual resources to endeavors that bring us no sense of satisfaction or fulfillment, no feeling of achievement or joy in living. Consciousness of Sin hits us in the solar plexus of our minds with the feeling that we aren't doing what is right for us, or our spouse, lover, offspring, parents, siblings, friends, or our neighbor: humankind.

Repentance

And, translated into everyday language, what is Repentance? What, indeed, but the need, and maybe—hopefully—the longing, to *change*: the effort to heal ourselves, the quest for a cure for our sickness of soul; our wrong-headed, wrong-hearted way of conducting our life.

What does a skilled psychotherapist accomplish when he is successful? He turns his patient around. Or, rather, he gets his patient to accomplish this for herself. He redirects the sick way the patient feels, thinks, and behaves; helps her to exchange her chronically, pathologically unhappy

mode of operation for a different way—a way that will
make her regard herself with esteem rather than with contempt or deprecation.

To change, to *turn* from a bad to a better way, from a
sick to a healthy, wholesome kind of behavior, is precisely
the meaning of *t'shuvah*. "To turn" is the etymological de-
notation of *t'shuvah*, the Hebrew word for Repentance.

Salvation

For our present purpose, last: take the word "Salvation."
It's an old concept which means "being saved": rescued
from trouble, danger, disease, or death. Translated into
current speech, it means wellness, health, having a nice
sense of well-being, at peace with oneself and the world,
feeling right, so we can stand up and face our family and
friends, and perhaps, most especially, be able to look into a
mirror clear-eyed, unafraid, comfortable, at ease.

Sin is simply sickness of soul. Repentance is a prescription for the cure. Salvation is health achieved, wellness, the state of being and of *feeling* whole.

Two-Fold Triple-A

Now, to introduce and welcome you to the holy period it-
self: This observance is a "two-fold Triple-A": namely, the
Ancient Annual Assembly of Auditors, Accountants, and
Appraisers.

That is what we Jews are every Rosh HaShanah. This
is our twelve-monthly inventory time, the yearly occasion
when each Jew examines his spiritual assets and liabilities,
appraises his net human worth, audits his value as a *mensch*
to his family, his people, his world.

For this appraisal, accounting, and audit, our tradition
ordains a period of ten days, beginning on Rosh HaShanah.

For our personal inventory, the Talmud suggests a gauge for measuring ourselves as human beings. It says that one can judge a person 1) *b'Kiso*, 2) *v'Koso*, 3) *uv'Ka-aso*, meaning, "by his wallet, by his goblet, and by his anger."

ביסו, *Kiso* (Pocket)

Kiso ("wallet," "purse," or "pocket") implies that anyone can be measured by what he spends his money for: how he budgets his monetary resources. Besides paying for basics: food, clothing, and shelter, medical care and insurance, one's money buys labor-saving devices, air conditioning, and other cozy conveniences that make life comfortable. It also pays for luxuries: cosmetics, jewels, furs, liquor, smokes; second, third, and fourth cars, theater, opera, ballet, concert tickets, vacation trips, gifts, and all the other pleasures, extravagances, and status symbols that gratify the appetite for conspicuous waste, self-indulgence, ostentation.

It also, of course, supports charities, hospitals, schools, museums, synagogues, plus local causes, national institutions, and international agencies that enhance life worldwide.

To determine your spiritual size, to discover your worth as a human being—this is the first dimension. List in quantitative order the amounts you spend on furniture, vehicles, personal adornment, entertainment, art objects, books, music, gambling, liquor, etc., and you'll know how much you are concerned with vanity, amusements, aesthetics, education, thrills, "kicks," escapes.

Then list how much you voluntarily give away and to whom and for what; and you have one measure of how much you care for others and their concerns, and which others, and which of their concerns.

When a Jew protests the increase in his comparatively modest synagogue dues but promptly pays his far more

substantial country club dues without a murmur of com-
plaint, what more eloquently reveals just where his heart
is? What gratifies his soul? The club satisfies his appetite
for fun and games, for escape and display. To these desid-
erata, the synagogue offers no competition whatever.

You know the riddle—

Far vos darf. a yid fiess?
Why does a Jew need feet?
Tsu dem chupah fohrt men ihm.
To his wedding he rides.
Tsu dem kever trogt men ihm.
To the grave he is carried.
Tsu a shikseh kriecht ehr.
To a forbidden female he goes crawling.
In schul geht ehr nit.
To the synagogue he doesn't go at all.

Then, why indeed does he need feet? And if he does-
n't *go*, why should he *give*? Would he contribute liberally to
a museum of art and archaeology if painting and antiquities aren't his "bag?" Or to a symphony or opera company
if classical music isn't her "thing?"

And what if he cares little for his ancestral faith, his
people's sanctities, for the spiritual legacy which breathed
life into two hundred generations of Jews, sustained them
and brought him to this day? Then he will begrudge the
cost of its maintenance to this one institution which per-
petuates and inculcates this heritage.

כוסו, *Koso* (Cup)

You can judge an individual *b'Kiso*—by "his purse," by
what he spends his money on. And also *b'Koso*—by "his
cup," which is to say, his personal indulgence. We have the
same figure of speech in English, when we say of some

pleasure, hobby, or pastime that it is (or is not, as the case
may be) "my cup of tea." As *Kiso* refers to how we budget
our material means, *Koso* implies what we do with our leisure time.

And you can judge the size and nature of a soul—not
only its quantity but also its quality—by how much leisure
is spent at the TV set, the golf course, race track, gambling
table, beach, or swimming pool, theater, shopping mall,
travel—on the one hand—and on the other hand, how
much of it we use for serious study, for quiet contempla-
tion, for considering how one's life is spent, for enjoying
the beauties of nature, art, or music; what portion we devote to communal or congregational activities, philanthropic work, civic concern, and labor, gainful employment.

Even more than money (which is, after all, a replace-
able commodity), the way a man or woman spends time
(when not making a living) gives you a measure of his or
her individual spiritual stature, because time is an absolute,
utterly irreplaceable commodity. It is a basic measurement,
a fundamental dimension of life itself.

Still, there is more than longevity to life; more than
the quantitative length of time. There is the interior, quali-
tative dimension of intensity, of emotion, passion, interest,
concern, commitment.

בכעסו, *Ka-aso* (Anger)

Which brings us to the third component in the talmudic
prescription for judging a human being: *Ka-aso*, "his anger," his wrathful indignation—the measurement of how
much and how deeply he cares, particularly how intensely
he cares about the fate of fellow human beings.

Can we become excited and perturbed only by our
own personal inconveniences, frustrations, or shortages?

Only when external circumstances interfere with the cushy comfort of our own individual existence? For example, when our office or household help disappoint us—are late, indolent, or sloppy in doing their chores?

Do we become furious at rude sales-people, insolent cab drivers, at airline officials who blithely cancel flights, neighbors who do not have their lawns mowed or trash collected frequently or neatly enough, solicitors and trades-people ringing our doorbell or phone at mealtime, children or trash collectors who are too noisy and inconsiderate of our need for privacy and rest, and phone callers who disturb us only to discover they have dialed the wrong number?

Do all these and similar trivia irritate, annoy us, so exhaust our emotional energies that we have none left to spend, for instance, on the plight of millions of men, women, and children in these affluent United States who are homeless and hungry almost every day of their lives? babies all over this country who die before their second birthday for lack of sufficient, proper food? children who manage to survive this deprivation, but who suffer permanent and irremediable brain and body damage throughout their lives and consequently grow up perpetually tired, irritable, paranoiac, and mad at the world?

You don't believe in handouts? Very good! Apparently you are an informed and committed Jew; you believe that alms, doles, are the lowest, the most humiliating form of charity; that true philanthropy ought to make people self-supporting, with fulfilling jobs and adequate education to get those jobs. Well, what are you doing to see that this happens? What job opportunities, what job training are you offering?

You and your spouse sometime, doubtless, have wanted and therefore worked for a new car or a new house or a very special vacation. But have you ever wanted and therefore worked to find a job for an unemployed immigrant, an Afro-American, a Hispanic, a fellow Jew, a Holocaust survivor?

As long as you live, you will do something with your time, your money, and your energy. The question is, will you use it Jewishly, intelligently, religiously to ameliorate the lot of the poor, the weak, the denied, the wronged; or, like a callous pagan, will you ignore their suffering and react to their outbursts of violence, burglary, mugging, by corresponding bursts of brutal suppression, yelling, "Let's have law and order around here," "Call out the guards," "More cops, more jails." The choice is always up to you; which selection, dear friends, is yours?

Are you the kind of human being who says: "Somebody ought to do something about this; but why me?" or the one who says, "Someone ought to do it; why *not* me?" For between these two sentences lies all that the world knows of moral growth and human progress.

When that saintly old scholar, Von Hügel, lay dying, his niece bent over her uncle, because she could see his lips moving but could not catch what he said. She put her ear close to his mouth and heard the last words the gentle philosopher ever uttered, these: "Caring is everything: nothing matters but caring."

Justice is achieved only when those who are *not* personally injured feel as indignant as those who are: When one human heart feels others' ills as if it were personally *responsible* for them. And if you do nothing at all to cure them, then patently you are responsible for them—having stood by and let them happen; as responsible as you would be if you did nothing to prevent a child walking in front of a moving vehicle or a blind man stepping over a cliff.

The Great Evil

There is this great evil in the world which most of us condone and many of us are guilty of: indifference to evil. We remain neutral, impartial, unmoved by the wrongs done to other people. Indifference to evil is more insidious than evil itself, it is more common and more contagious and more dangerous. The tragedy of our time is not the glaring noisiness of bad people, but the quietness, the appalling silence of the so-called "good" people. Our generation will have to repent, not only for the diabolic action and vitriolic words of the men of darkness but also for the crippling fears and tragic apathy of the children of light.

Thus, the real evil in our world is not the occasional, spectacular, vivid catastrophe; the real evil is our neglect of causes, our indifference to conditions, our unwillingness to give the time, the money, and the effort to stop preventable disasters. Ask yourself when was the last time you were furious enough about some social evil to lift your voice and most especially reach out your hand to do something to cure it.

We are worth as much as the things are worth about which we are concerned, and we show our concern in what we do *b'Kiso, v'Koso, uv'Ka-aso*—with our money, our time, and our emotional energy.

These are the dimensions by which you may judge how your life is spent. I pray that you may measure up well and that both you and God are pleased with your inventory. 🌺

Rosh Hashanah, September 14, 1996

❧ Was Genesis 22 the Test Abraham Failed?

Every Rosh HaShanah the *baal korey* repeats the *Akeda* story, beginning:

> After the foregoing events, God tested Abraham, saying, Take your son, Isaac, whom you love, to the Moriah region and offer him there as a sacrifice on one of the hills I will indicate. Next morning, taking with him his son, Isaac, Abraham cut wood for the altar and set out for the place God would designate as the scene for binding Isaac in preparation for sacrifice....

About fifteen years ago, in a clever homily composed by a newly-ordained HUC-JIR colleague the point was made that the first Patriarch "flunked the test." As proof, the young preacher adduced, *inter alia*, that one of the significant "foregoing events" was Abraham's challenge to God at Sodom (Gen. 18) where, addressing Him as Judge of all the Earth, who must do justice, Abraham insists that justice demands that God renounce His decision—and save the wicked city—if at least ten decent people are found in it.

Abraham was faulted by our young colleague for the alacrity with which he responded to God's request to sacrifice Isaac. Not a word of protest against his having to slaughter his innocent, beloved son, whereas, only four chapters earlier, in Genesis 18, there was the Patriarch's vigorous protest and dispute with God over the justice of destroying the sin-steeped city of Sodom.

The idea does seem reasonable. Then why *didn't* the father of our folk stand up to God in defense of innocent Isaac, when our first Patriarch had been so very brave and bold about defending altogether evil Sodom? I submit that it was, in fact, at Sodom that Abraham failed the test. It, too, was a test. Why else would God confide in Abraham what He was about to do to Sodom, except to elicit some response from the man divinely chosen to become a great and mighty nation? And God got Abraham's response there, and Abraham discovered how wrong and futile his defense was. Ten righteous souls? Indeed! There wasn't even one; not a single worthy human being in that loathsome city.

To prove the point and have it penetrate, God sent angels to help Abraham's relatives, residing in Sodom, to escape. With what result? First, God's messengers were unable to persuade the men, affianced to Lot's daughters, to leave Sodom. Next, Lot and his wife and daughters didn't want to leave and had to be forcibly pulled out of the city. They were forbidden to look back, yet Lot's wife did just that. In nostalgic regret at having to forsake the forbidden pleasures of that wicked town? or in sinful gloating over the plight of her erstwhile neighbors, by contrast to her own safety? Whatever her motivation, in punishment for her disobedience, she was transformed into a pillar of salt.

Then Lot asked permission to stay in a place as close to Sodom as possible, so that the angels of destruction had to delete that area from the list of settlements scheduled for annihilation. When everything in the region was being obliterated, Lot and his daughters spent the night in a cave in the hills. The elder said to the younger: "Let's get our father drunk" (with a holocaust impending, they'd evidently managed to sneak some intoxicating beverage out of Sodom) "and tonight I will be a wife to him and tomorrow you will take my place." That's how Moab and Ammon were conceived. Each of these incestuously engendered bastards fathered a nation which, for centuries, was inveterately hostile to Israel. These four—Lot, his wife, and their daughters—were apparently the best residents in all of Sodom. Imagine what the rest were like.

So much for Abraham's misplaced sympathy for the iniquitous denizens of Sodom. Thus, it was at God's announcement of Sodom's obliteration that Abraham failed the test. However, there he did learn a lesson. And that is why he kept a prudent silence in response to the order that he was to take Isaac up to Moriah. At Sodom, he learned that you don't question the decisions of God. YHVH's decrees and demands are invariably just and right. As the Yiddish lyric puts it:

> *Gott vayss vos er tit*
> *umzist shtroft er kaynem nit*
> *Gott, in zein mishpot, iz gerecht.*

> God's aware of what He does,
> punishes no one without cause;
> in His judgments, God is [always] right.

At the testing in the *Akeda* story, God wanted to see whether Abraham had picked up what he was supposed to have learned from the Sodom experience. Clearly, our first Patriarch had profited from his failure at Sodom. However, there probably was more that God wanted to prove, in asking Abraham to offer up Isaac as a sacrifice. YHVH had no need to learn what Abraham's response would be if He ever asked for child-sacrifice, as the pagan deity Moloch, for one, demanded of Abraham's heathen neighbors (or so they said, when their practical problem was too many mouths to feed). Thus, they developed a pious, if extremely cruel method of reducing the number. Near the site of ancient Carthage there is a cemetery filled with the tiny graves of neonates that had been thus disposed of. YHVH didn't need to discover what Abraham's response would be to His request for Isaac's life. Being prescient, He knew. But He apparently believed that Abraham needed to know how absolute was his trust in YHVH, who was no Moloch. Apparently, Abraham had to be reassured of that, so YHVH arranged the test—for Abraham, who may have wondered … and who, perhaps, welcomed the opportunity to prove to himself his utter faith in God.

We are aware, of course, that these are biblical narratives, not realistic history or biography, but stories that make a moral point. In this case, the point that the founder of our folk always evinced complete trust in and obedience to YHVH his God, who abjures child-sacrifice.

You don't like the story? Blame the author. His skill as a theologian and psychologist may be flawed. You don't like having it repeated every Rosh HaShanah? Blame our ancient sages who ordained the schedule of scripture readings. Maybe the *hachamim* were as lacking in sensitivity as were the bible narrators before them and as they, themselves, were in other respects.

As one example: There was the centuries-old rabbinically-ordained practice of *Bar On'shin*. This was the precursor—from antiquity to some time in the fourteenth century—of Bar Mitzvah. *Bar On'shin* ("son of punishments") shares clumsy nomenclature with Bar Mitzvah ("son of commandment"). For centuries, when a boy became *Bar On'shin*, he began to be responsible for his own ritual mal-, mis-, and non-feasances; he became a medieval Jewish adult.

How was the occasion observed? When he showed he had reached puberty by having grown two hairs on his *mons veneris*, his father took him to be examined by the town's elders and exposed for their scrutiny. That was the centuries-old practice, until the 1300's of the Common Era, when parents and elders both became sufficiently civilized to realize how shamelessly cruel and stupid the practice was. What if the boy didn't grow any pubic hairs at all, was a *tum-tum*, "sexless"? The whole community got to know this. It was not only his, but also his family's disgrace. Yet, it took until the very late Middle Ages for this wise and understanding people, the merciful sons of merciful forbears, to decide to end this shameful crudity and substitute for it what I once harshly called a maudlin version of Priapic worship: Bar Mitzvah.

To get back to the *Akeda* story: We cannot expunge it from the Torah; and, perhaps, we shouldn't, even if we could. We need to know whence we came. But we can certainly quit rubbing our cultivated, sensitive, civilized people's noses [ears?] in it every Rosh HaShanah. Perhaps, by substituting the Creation story in Genesis 1. You have a second day service, and need another reading? Why not the Eden story? It is colorful, charming, obviously a narrative, not a factual account with its talking reptile, definitely not a snake. A snake is not punished by having to crawl on its belly: that's how snakes normally move. The creature that tempted Eve must have had legs at the time. They were removed in this myth, as penalty for the reptile's tempting Eve, who, in turn, tempted Adam to share the fruit of the tree of knowledge—which was definitely not an apple. The word "apple" occurs nowhere in the story. As a food, it appears nowhere in the Pentateuch or in the

Prophets. We find it once in the Song of Songs (2:5) and in Song of Songs 7:8, there is a quaint, somewhat amusing reference to its fragrance.

To reconnect with our text, and to conclude, anyone who initiates a movement to remove the *Akeda* story from its place as the Rosh HaShanah lection, has a willing—no, an eager, even generous, subscriber to the worthy cause: me. A successful campaign would save rabbis the annual earache from having to listen to worshipers' complaints about their having to listen to this "dreadful" story every Rosh HaShanah, a *shandeh far die goyim un die kinder*, "an embarrassment for gentiles and children" attending a traditional Rosh HaShanah service. How very much more appropriate to celebrate *Hayom Horat Olam,* Rosh HaShanah, the anniversary of the day the world was born, by reading from the first pages of Torah the lovely legend of how it all began. 🙕

Revised, 2003

Some Spiritual Insights

✿❀ Moral Courage

Physical courage is not the Jew's chief pride. But he does have a past, distant and immediate, rich in fearless warriors. And, if the hour calls for something other than sweet reasonableness, he does have that tradition of prowess to fall back upon.

It is moral courage, far rarer than the vulgar sort, that is the Jew's more characteristic trait. The courage of the simple Jewish farmer, Naboth, who faced King Ahab himself when that monarch demanded Naboth's vineyard to add to the royal gardens. And Naboth replied: "The Lord forbid that I give the heritage of my fathers to you!" The courage of the prophets who dared to face prelates and potentates with the terrible: "I accuse!" and who risked their lives speaking unwelcome truths to the populace.

"What nation," Macaulay asked, "ever contended more manfully against overwhelming odds for its independence and religion? What nation ever gave such signal proofs of what may be accomplished by sheer bravery?"

It is difficult not to recall the conditions under which this people has survived centuries of the bludgeonings of fate whenever we see in mountain districts one of those amazing trees which cling in solitary defiant tenacity, thrusting its roots into the unyielding granite, living despite all. Such trees are a sermon in courage. So is Jewish history.

The future may be dark. But not so the manner in which we must face it. We shall find courage to bear each day's burdens, not by escapist hopes that the future will be easier, pleasanter, brighter than the past or present, but by the quest for contact with the source of strength that filled the hearts of our people and its heroes in all ages.

What is that source? Reflect. We have not supplied a world merely with sublime examples of courage. We also gave that world God. 🕎

✿❀ Chanukah

In classical antiquity, the hearth was sacred and its fire was kept religiously alight. We are told that when Aeneas left Troy he took with him the holy hearth fire, carried it, and kept it burning through seven years of wandering, finally bringing it to Rome where for a millennium it was never permitted to go out. Guarding it were the vestal virgins, priestesses of Vesta, goddess of fire.

Even more ancient is the Greek legend of Prometheus, bringer-of-light. Prometheus was a Titan, one of the mythical giants who ruled before the gods came and overthrew them and carried them captive to Olympus. Then fire was the jealously guarded possession of the gods. So, for long ages men's homes were dark and cold until Prometheus, the friend of man, stole some of the celestial flame and brought it down to earth. For this offense, of defying the gods of Olympus to bring light to man, Prometheus was chained to a rock and condemned to perpetual torture.

Older than any of this is the Bible account of the origin of light. So far from being withheld by God, it was He who commanded, "Let there be light." And there was light, God's first gift to man. Light in the darkness of this earth was, from the very beginning, the evidence of God's presence and His providence.

So it was in the light of a burning bush at the foot of Horeb, a wondrous fire which illumined but did not consume, that Moses beheld a vision and heard the voice of God summoning him to his liberating mission. Then, by a luminous cloud by day and a column of fire by night, God led His people through the wilderness toward the Promised Land. And from that day to this, in every synagogue (*shul*) in the world, there glows an eternal lamp, the *ner tamid*, above the holy ark. It is a light we keep forever burning: the light of man's faith in God and of God's hope for man.

It was this light that was extinguished more than two thousand years ago by the idolatrous Syrian King Antiochus, when he overran Israel and his soldiers desecrated the Temple of God. It was to rekindle this lamp that our people waged the first war in recorded history for the freedom of the human spirit. It is that struggle which Chanukah commemorates. In that struggle no battle is ever the last, no victory is final. ❧

✿ Invention, Discovery and Creation

Religions are expressions of men's attitude toward existence and their behavior based on those attitudes. Not all religions are sweet and noble. But does that justify our willingness to set up science as a suitable replacement for religion—something it is utterly ill-suited for and never professed to be?

No professional scientist thinks his science is a religion. But some amateurs do. Why? The amateur's overweening faith, in science, and his tendency to put his trust in it, as a substitute for religion, is based, it seems to me, on a widely prevalent error in thinking. This error mistakes discovery and invention for creation. With little or nothing more than this error for its foundation, some of us cherish the belief that we can dispense with religion, now that we have all the discoveries of science and the inventions of technology—with the promise of many more to come.

What this notion overlooks is the simple fact that no scientist, or technologist, or artist, or magician (not even the best advertised and most expensive Paris dress-designer) has it in his power to produce a "creation." No man or woman is capable of creating anything. Not if we understand the true meaning of the word "create." To create is to bring into being something which never had any kind of existence before. We use the term "create" properly when we speak of God's creation of the world from nothing. No human being can, or ever did, create a single atom of any substance, a single unit, or erg of energy that did not exist before.

To "discover" means simply to uncover; to lift or remove a cover, and thus to reveal something that has been there, but just never before been perceived. Newton discovered the law of gravity. He did not create this force. Ben Franklin conducted electricity from a bolt of lightning down his wet kite string. He did not create this power. Each of these men learned something of how these primal energies operate; and other discoverers and inventors taught us how to deal intelligently with them; how to use them for our purposes. Discovery is not creation.

And invention is not creation. To invent is to form useful combinations of already existing material and energy, or to use previously known combinations for some novel human purpose. The discoverer, the inventor and designer always begin with something already given. And among the things given are the scientist himself, the human being, and his brain.

The question remains: Given by whom and for what? The religionist basing himself, it is true, only on faith—believes that all that is was given by God; given to men for the perpetuation and enhancement of all human life. He cannot prove this, any more than you or anyone can disprove it. But he believes this and he conducts his life as if this were so, He believes this on faith. 🐾

☙❀ What If ...

Like many a college student today, having been exposed to a smattering of scientific knowledge and some accompanying skeptical philosophy, a young man from a pious Hasidic family had become an *epikoros* ("unbeliever"). He had lost the faith of his fathers. However, still a dutiful son (like many today who proclaim their disbelief in God, yet religiously and inconsistently enough obediently go to say *kaddish*—to sanctify God's name in God's house in memory of their revered parents) this *epikoros* obeyed his father who asked him to go and have a talk with the rabbi about his religious faithlessness.

Coming into the old *tsadik*'s study, the young man found the rabbi looking out of the window in deep meditation, his back to his caller.

The *epikoros* waited in the painful silence, what seemed an eternity. Then, quite suddenly, the rabbi turned to speak and uttered two words: "What if…" The words tolled like a knell in the young man's brain and sank their penetrating shafts of meaning into his soul.

"What, young man, what if you are right in your belief? What if this world and its life has no meaning, no plan or purpose, no design and no destiny?

"You know, of course, that neither you nor any other atheist can prove beyond a reasonable doubt that this is so; any more than I as a man of faith can positively prove the contrary; namely, that 'life is real, life is earnest, and the grave is not the goal.'

"But, say that you are right; what then? Your stay on earth can have no more significance or satisfaction than that of a forest beast or barnyard animal. Assuming you are right, you will never even have the gratification of proving it, of saying to us simple, believing souls in some after life, 'You see, we cynics knew the truth all along, and we told you so.' You will not even have this satisfaction because, if you are right and there is no God, and no sense to it at all, no intelligent plan and no purposeful design, then there is no soul and no spiritual life.

"On the other hand, what if you are wrong, and this life is full of rhyme and reason, of spiritual beauty and glory, to which you have been willfully insensate, deliberately deaf and blind? What if you have squandered your brief stay here, behaving like a mouse in a museum, or like a cow at an open-air concert, physically present but spiritually oblivious—with no sensitivity to, nor appreciation of, Creation and its Creator? You have lost everything there was to be had.

"What if I am right and there is a God and you are His cherished child, made in His own likeness, with a soul capable of relating to all spiritual experience and a holy mission here? If that be so, then you have lost everything, human and divine, worth living for.

"On the other hand, what if I am wrong, what have I lost? Only what you have and what you know: your doubt, your cynical pessimism, your sense of meaninglessness, frustration and futility—certainly nothing worth having or knowing.

"Consider the advantage of religious faith over the misfortune of enduring a purposeless existence. If you cling to the faith that your life has eternal meaning as part of a cosmic plan—you have everything to gain and nothing whatever to lose. The choice is always yours."

✿ Faith and the Law of Probability

Science is presumably limited to the certain, the demonstrable. Religion, because it must be coterminous with life itself, goes beyond the limits of science. It encompasses both the certain and what must be taken on faith.

In a very fundamental sense, however, even science is founded on faith. In the first place, real scientists no longer speak dogmatically of the law of cause and effect; but diffidently, tentatively of the law of Probability. They now say two quantities of H and one of O in certain circumstances will probably produce water. In the second place, every scientific experiment, discovery and invention depends ultimately on the human senses. Even the results of the most complicated computers must be observed by human eyes and other organs of the human body. And who is any longer so rash as to contend that these senses of ours are infallible? Even if a thousand scientists and a hundred million ordinary citizens testify that they have observed the same phenomena, what absolute proof is there that they are not all deluded, that their perception truly corresponds with reality? None! There is no way of perfectly proving this.

Indeed, for how many centuries did scientists generally believe that the earth is flat, that spontaneous generation actually occurs, that the way to cure lunacy is to exorcise (by incantation or by flagellating the victim's body) the demons which allegedly inhabit it?

But, far deeper than this go the foundations of science built on faith. The depth of the dependence of science on faith is superbly illustrated in the biography of Elisha ben Abuyah as told by Milton Steinberg in his beautiful book entitled, *As A Driven Leaf.* Elisha had been a rabbi who almost 2,000 years ago forsook Judaism in quest of a way of life that would be altogether scientific, utterly logical, entirely provable. He searched the civilized world for such a philosophy. Toward the end of his life in Alexandria, Egypt, he listened enthralled to the lecture of a sage who explained all the phenomena of life and the universe in terms of mathematics, the most perfect and absolute of sciences.

At the conclusion of the lecture, Elisha rushed up to the teacher, embraced him, and wrung his hands in all-out admiration and tearful gratitude, for the inspiration and the insight he had just gained—at long last. It was what he had been seeking all his life. "There is only one question I have," he said. "Perhaps I missed the preliminary lectures in your course; so I don't understand one term you used: the word 'axiom.' What are the proofs for these axioms on which all the rest of your philosophy is reared?" The philosopher looked at him in amazement. "My dear friend," he said, "you obviously know little about mathematics, the purest of sciences. For, if you did, you would have learned that the axioms, on which the whole structure of geometry rests, are fundamental principles of faith." Axioms are assumed, taken on trust; there is no way to prove them. That is precisely why they are called "axioms"—self-evident propositions, something we believe worthy of acceptance as truth, but cannot prove. 🐾

✿ On Breaking the Glass
Advice to Bridegroom and Bride

The act of stamping upon and smashing a glass, which you have asked permission to do (no part of a beautiful modern marriage service) is a medieval practice as benighted in its origin as it is uncouth in its present performance. Let it represent for you a break with anything unfortunate, unhappy, and unaesthetic in your past which you should like to be expunged from the record and obliterated. ✿

❦ This Is Yours

The Supreme Court has decided that it is unlawful to read the Bible as a religious exercise in our public schools. To this reasonable and well-anticipated decision there was some protest. Not quite as vehement and vociferous as that which erupted after the court struck down the regents prayer—but some.

One newspaper artist responded to this protest with a trenchant cartoon. He drew a foursome of golfers out on the fairway. It is obviously the Christian Sabbath, for, in the immediate background the bell of the Church next to the golf course is tolling loudly. But evidently not loudly enough to drown out the voice of the pious soul who interrupts his swing at the ball to declaim: "I'll be damned if I let any court keep my kids from hearing God's word!"

But this God—and this Bible he doesn't want his children deprived of—are they truly his? Does he venture to go near them when the church bell pleads with him to do so? In his home, does he ever disturb the dust on the covers of the sacred volume? Or, is it so very sacred that it is never touched? No, it isn't his at all, really.

But it is yours. And it can be very truly yours, if you will. It is in the first place yours, because it is the personal history of your people; the story of your fathers' travels and travails; their birth and their covenant and their conversation with God, their labors and experience, their hopes and dreams for your life, and for our future. These are your people whose record is inscribed here, your sages and singers and seers speaking to you of your God.

Not in public schools (where they have enough trouble teaching our offspring how to spell) but here in this place, where such study belongs, these words of wisdom, solace, and inspiration can be very truly yours if you make the small effort to come and learn, on Sunday morning, or Sunday evening, or Thursday morning or Friday night, or Saturday morning, or afternoon, or almost any other time you find convenient—they are yours to console you in your tribulations, to share in your joys, deepen you with knowledge, give wings to your dreams. 🕮

❧ The Bible: Textbook on Evolution

Consider the story of the youthful Jacob who first took advantage of his brother's hunger to obtain the coveted Birthright, and then took advantage of his father's blindness to get the coveted Final Blessing. Or take the story of the young, pampered, vain, conceited tale-bearer, Joseph.

If we are studying these altogether remarkable stories with adults, we can speak of the great message of the Hebrew Bible, which is a message of the evolution of the human spirit, the growth of the soul of men and nations. We can see how the Bible heroes are thoroughly human, subject to all the weakness that flesh is heir to.

But they are divine spirit, too, as well as mortal flesh; and despite their weaknesses, which they share with the rest of us, they matured in time and ultimately attained the stature of spiritual giants.

The Bible teaches one lesson above all others: Evolution. It can teach this to mature minds; but a child's notion of evolution is about as profound as his concept of Einstein's theory of relativity.

To adults, we can speak of what scholars term "the inconvenient traditions of Scripture." The mind of a grown-up can understand that such inconvenient traditions as that of Hebrew slavery in Egypt, or the Hebrew law of eye for eye and tooth for tooth is a proof of the veracity of the Bible. No one would invent such unflattering early history of his people. The very absence of touch-up, of white-wash; the plain, unvarnished account of our humble beginnings—is a sign of candor, the hallmark of truth.

Surely, as a band of uncouth slaves, we had a rule of retaliation. Aren't there Kentucky mountaineers of our own day who still live by that law; "feud'n" they call it? Indeed, many modern nations have not risen even to that low level of morality. But thirty-three hundred years ago, the law of retaliation was a distinct advance over the rules by which Israel's neighbors lived.

And within a few centuries, this same people had arrived at a stage of ethical development where one of its thinkers, Amos, could interpret all of life as one long quest for justice. Hosea could speak of God's relationship to His people as one of infinite and unwavering love. Isaiah could envisage a world where, at the end of days, such peace would reign in the world that even the lion and the lamb could lie down together.

What the Bible teaches the mature mind is that with persons, as with peoples, it is not whence they came that counts; what matters is how and to what spiritual heights they grew. 🪶

❧❀ Security

Parlor psychology has made popular many new words and new meanings for old ones: neurosis, frustration, complex, rationalization, subconscious, regression, identification.... The current fad has also made certain other words unpopular, or emptied them of their meaning: God, religion, sin, guilt, morality.

Today, through much of the amateur conversation on mental hygiene runs the magic word: Security. We must achieve "security" for ourselves and for those whose lives we guide and influence.

But where shall we find this security, this feeling of confidence in the world and in our ability to cope with life? In the tortuous maze of definitions of inhibition, projection, transferences sublimation? In the notion that life's values are subjective and relative? Not likely.

Competent professional psychiatrists perform a needed task in our society when they attempt to heal sick souls. It is necessary to treat minds when they become twisted and pathologically unhappy. It is also important to understand that they got that way because they, and usually their parents too, have strayed so far from the enduring roads built by ages of life-tested wisdom, that they have lost sight of the religious values, and standards of faith and codes of conduct that make our personal life human and our society civilized. ❧❀

❧ Child Archaeologists?

> The Yllis is a weird fowl. It flies tail foremost.
> Caring very little about where it is and even less
> about where it is going, it wants only to know
> where it has been. —Joh. Bleau, *Mythic Ornithol-*
> *ogy.*

Every year, during religious school registration, we hear:
"This *is* a Reform Temple, isn't it? ... Good! ... Because
neither my husband nor I are religious. We just want our
child to learn the Bible stories and history." The language
may vary, but not the "idea."

Patiently, we explain that our goal is not to teach the
young about the origin and colorful career of a peculiar
people once known as "The Hebrews." We are here to educate them, and all the members of their family, in the
practice of Judaism, how to live as religious Jews in America today.

This means personal attendance and participation in
worship and study and social life in the synagogue. It
means the possession and use of Jewish books, periodi-
cals, music, art and ceremonial objects in the home. It
means Jewish ideals taught there as well as in our school,
and practiced there as well as in the community by adults
as well as by children. It means not only knowledge of the
history, but identification with the destiny of all Jews everywhere.

It is sometimes surprising to parents that Judaism, as the Reform Temple teaches it, is not a course in curious antiquities, but a contemporary way of living. But it is always a delight to us when parents, who intended "to settle" for so little for their school child, can be persuaded to do all this for their whole family.

✣ The Ark which Carries Those Who Carry It

The word "ark" (*aron* in Hebrew) can mean either a receptacle or a vehicle. It may be a box or chest in which things are kept and carried; or a vessel, a conveyance that can carry you. The Torah, say our sages, is both kinds of ark: "It is an ark which carries those who carry it."

To illustrate how the Torah can be either a load or a carrier, the ancient rabbis tell this story. Coming down from the top of Sinai, Moses held in his arms the tablets inscribed with His word by God Himself. Such was the power of the sacred letters engraved in fire on those stones that Moses did not have to carry them. He had only to cling to them and they carried him down gently over crags and crevasses.

But, when they had brought him down to the foot of the mountain and God's words came face to face with the golden calf which Moses' people were worshipping in his absence—an awesome thing happened. Instantly, the holy letters vanished from the stones on which they were engraved. All that was left in Moses' hands were two blank, massive rocks, impossible for any man to hold. Moses didn't fling them to the ground, say the rabbis; it was all he could do to get out from under them quickly enough to avoid being crushed.

With the letters on them, the tablets carried Moses; without the holy words, they were too great a load for him

to bear. What are our sages trying to tell us? With a knowledge of Torah and a love for our faith, Judaism lifts and
sustains us. Without such knowledge and love Judaism is
an unbearable burden. ❧

❧ I Am My Brother's Brother

The answer to Cain's question, "Am I my brother's keeper?" is "No. I'm not. If my brother needs a 'keeper,' he ought to be committed to some institution—a jail or an asylum, where they have keepers. I'm not my brother's keeper. I am my brother's brother!" Isn't this obvious? Then why does brotherhood have to be preached? Indeed there are many who insist that interfaith meetings are without meaning or value because they merely persuade the already convinced.

Personally, I am convinced that it is not only useful, but quite necessary constantly to persuade the persuaded. And I am convinced that every preacher and teacher agrees with me. Why else would priests, ministers and rabbis preach every week and teach every day? That is how they *keep* their people persuaded. They know that, like the body, the spirit too must be constantly nourished.

I can think of at least one other benefit which interfaith meetings confer. They commit the participants in the program to the ideal of brotherhood.

I am ever mindful of the wisdom of the bishop to whom the young pastor came, discouraged and begging release from the burden of his ministry. "Why do you want to quit, son?" "Because I have no faith, Sir." "You have no faith? You call that a reason? My boy, go back to your pulpit and *preach faith*."

The man who has the obligation to teach something may fail to convince others. But he will probably do a good job of persuading himself. Is there some important public figure whom you feel needs to be persuaded of the brotherhood of man? Invite him to be a speaker on your program. In his effort to influence you, chances are he will at least convince himself. It will be harder for him to return thereafter to his former irreligious way of thinking and unbrotherly behavior. ✿✾

❧❧ What We Mean by Faith

Is the task of religion—the attempt to answer the question, "Why? What is the meaning and purpose of life?"—too difficult even for the most valorous and intrepid? Difficult?! It is probably impossible! Doubtless, we can never fully succeed. And yet, if humanity is to survive, someone must be willing to try. We cannot stop the flow of information, discovery, and invention; and *should* not, even if we could. We must learn to live with and, if possible, to benefit from all that any research can teach us. Indeed, if we are to survive, all of us everywhere must constantly make the effort to put the pieces of understanding together: to see life whole, and to deal with it as a unity.

No one knows all that he needs to know in order to enable him to live his life perfectly. For that matter, no one can even imagine what a perfect life would be. Not all the accumulated knowledge in the world is sufficient to enable even one individual with certainty to live out his life in complete bliss. Yet, if we are to live at all, we must do so with just the means at our disposal. That is, with knowledge which is incomplete and resources which fall short of total adequacy.

We must make the best use we can of what we have and what we know; and, employing our best intelligence, make the best possible guess as to the meaning of the unknown. We can do no better than to act on our most educated hunch, until better knowledge proves that hunch to be false or unreliable. This reliance on our best guess as to the unknown is what we mean by faith.

All of us live, in very large part, by faith. Columbus had no absolute, guaranteed certainty that this planet is a globe—curved round in every direction—that land lay west of the Azores, any more than the Wright Brothers knew beyond a shadow of a doubt that heavier-than-air craft could fly.

You and I do not know for certain that we will be here tomorrow, or that people we love are trustworthy; or that pledged promises will be fulfilled; or that when we flip an electric switch a light will glow or a motor whirl. We accept all this on trust, we believe this because it has happened thus in the past: it is reasonable to assume it will happen thus again. We accept all this on faith, because this is the only sane way to live; namely, to accept what we know for certain, and to have faith where we have no such certainty. ✠

✿ The Wisdom and the Will

The same human intellect which unraveled such awesome mysteries as the calculus and the force of gravity,
aerodynamics and nuclear fission, when applied to problems that human beings face in living peaceably and help-
fully together, ought to accomplish similar wonders if
similarly, enthusiastically, zestfully, hopefully applied.

They tell of a man who visited hell and was astonished
to find it a rich place, abundantly provisioned with fine
food. He was even more amazed when he saw how pathet-
ically emaciated all the souls there were. He soon discovered why they looked like walking skeletons, even while
they moved hungrily through long rows of tables heaped
with delicious victuals.

Every one of these damned souls had a long spoon,
about the size of a canoe paddle, attached to each of his
arms in such a way that he could not bend them. It made
no difference how much food one could pick up, it was
impossible to bring any of it to one's mouth. So, there in
hell, they all starved in the midst of plenty.

Then he went to heaven which, to his utter surprise,
he found to be a place almost indistinguishable from
hell—in externals at least,—the same kind and quantity of
food everywhere and the same enormous spoons fastened
to everyone's arm.

The significant difference here, however, was that everyone was well-fed and happy. The reason was simple:

each soul in heaven understood that though he could not bend his elbow and put anything into his own mouth, it was simplicity itself for each one to feed his neighbor across the table.

You see, no one has to die to go to hell or to heaven. Hell is any place on earth where men refuse to use their brains, where they will stupidly hurt themselves for the insane satisfaction it gives them to be able to injure others. Heaven, on the other hand, is wherever men use their intelligence to gratify themselves by satisfying others.

Even with the keenest intelligence and the best will in the world, it may not be possible to convert this world from hell into heaven overnight. But we ought to be able to accomplish this in time.

✿✿ Worth What It Costs

Our Bible begins—not with Hebrews, but with humanity. Our most holy days celebrate the birth of the world—not of Abraham, father of our people, nor of Moses, founder of our religion, but of mankind.

The Talmud is quite as ecumenical as Scripture: "Trouble which Israel shares with mankind is trouble indeed. If it is endured only by Jews, it is no real trouble."

Can you imagine a modern Negro spokesman saying, "If it only bothers blacks, it is nothing to upset anyone else about?"

A Jew must stir himself to help his afflicted neighbor, even his enemy (see Exodus 23:4, 5; Proverbs 24:21). But no Jew is to assume that his gentile neighbor is necessarily under the same moral obligation.

Our best spirits and the finest strands in the tapestry of our tradition were broader, more world-encompassing, humanity-embracing in their scope than that of most modern preachers, Jewish or gentile.

The Pharisees (rabbis of the Talmud and Midrash) were closer than we, not only in time, but in stature, to the spirit of those brave, outspoken trumpets of God: the prophets.

Who but a Hebrew prophet could ever have uttered a statement like this:

"The Lord of Hosts said: 'Blessed be Egypt, My people, and Assyria, My creation, and Israel, My inheritance.'" (Isaiah 1-9.25)

Can you conceive a twentieth-first century Jewish preacher daring to utter such a *misheberach*: associating Egypt and Syria with Israel, all equally blessed by God? And remember, that in Isaiah's time, neither of these hostile neighbors of Israel was less of a scourge or menace to Israel than it is today.

Would any preacher at all in the United States, Jewish or gentile, say something comparable, for example: "Blessed be Russia, the Lord's people, and Red China, God's creation; and America, His inheritance?" You will agree, I think, that it takes more than a little imagination even to dream anything quite so fantastically incredible.

But the Hebrew prophets dared. So did the Talmudic sages, to whom the prophets bequeathed their glorious mantle and their broad vision. Judaism's founders were spiritual giants. They believed in, worshipped and spoke for a truly great God, a demanding, challenging. risk-exacting, task-assigning God. They understood that any religion which costs its communicants nothing in either soul-searching or in sacrificial effort, that demands no mental exertion, or material treasure or risk of personal security, is worth what it costs—nothing. 🌺

✿ Waking the Sleepers

The Nineteenth Century, overwhelmed by the discoveries of biological science which shook their thought-world, asked the question, "Is God dead?" The Twentieth Century, frightened out of its wits by the development in nuclear physics, faced the question, "Is man dead?" Or about to become extinct through self-destruction?

Yet, the roar of the concussive winds, the convulsions of earth quaking and the desolation of the fires which could be set off by someone pressing a button, need not affright us if we rouse ourselves to perform our function as fully human human beings.

The rabbis tell of a man sleeping in a burning house. His anxious neighbors rushed to his bedside and attempted, unsuccessfully, to carry him out through the door. They tried to lift him, bed and all, through a window, but failed. Finally one of them stopped all this futile, frantic activity with an idea. He said, "Let's wake him up. He'll find his own way out. He will save himself."

Salvation cannot be bestowed. There is no magical formula for it. Each man must seek and find it for himself.

That is the purpose of the *shofar*-call of the holy days: to rouse our slumbering spirits, to awaken unto the meaning of living humanly, to help us take this gift of a new year from the hand of God—fresh from the mint of Time—and use it in such fashion that the very way we live this year, the very use to which we put His gift, will express our grateful thanks to the Giver.

✿✿ The Deserter

The Hasidim tell of a rich *hasid* who habitually came to services early and stayed on late to pray long before and after all the other worshippers had gone. The *tzadik*, his *rebbe*, one day tapped him sharply on the shoulder to interrupt his devotions and said: "You can stop now. What I have to say to you is more important religiously than what you have to say to God. You are a deserter from the army of the Lord of Hosts. You imagine you are doing your proper duty by all this praying. I assure you that this is not so. You think that a deserter is only a coward who flees from battle to go home or to hide, or a traitor who sneaks off to join the enemy. That is not so.

"Let me tell you that one is just as AWOL who shirks his assigned task in order to take up one that suits his personal preference—like forsaking his job with the artillery to march off and drill with the infantry, or quitting his assignment in the Judge Advocate's department to do a stint with the Quartermaster Corps.

"God's forces are similarly deployed. He assigns to each of us the tasks He has equipped us with a capacity to perform. For profound Torah study, He has scholarly experts. For probing the problems of theodicy and the nature of man and Israel's relationship to God and our mission to mankind, He has philosophers and theologians. For intense communion with Him through prayer, He has pious mystics.

"Need I tell you what specific task He has in mind for rich men like you?"

✿❀ The Reconversion of Chaplain Goldstein

Rabbi Herbert Tarr wrote a delightful novel called *The Conversion of Chaplain Cohen*. This book grew out of his experiences as a military chaplain.

The Conversion of Chaplain Cohen is a conversion to the most fundamental kind of Judaism; namely, to the realization that God's great concern is not for Jews but for people—for human beings, for all of mankind; that to serve God is to serve His children: black, brown, red, yellow and white—no matter what their cult or creed, or lack of either.

The *Hasidim* tell a story about two Russian peasants drinking in a tavern.

"You say you love me," said Ivan to Mischa.

"That I do," said Mischa.

"Do you know what gives me pain?" asked Ivan.

"How do I know that?"

"If you do not know what makes me suffer, what does your saying you love me signify, what does it mean, what does it do for either you or me?"

Have you ever tried empathetically to understand the daily humiliation of what it means to endure existence as a Negro in the United States, the home of the brave and the land of the free? Have you ever pondered the awful horror of the statement of the fourteen-year-old Harlem girl who was asked during World War II: "What would you do to

Hitler if you had him in your power?" Others who had been questioned had said they'd boil him in oil, let rats eat him, drop him head first in quicksand or lye. She said, "I'd just paint him black and send him here."

The Hebrew Bible begins not with the Jews but with the world and man. God did not labor in the sweat of his brow to produce Abraham or Moses—but Adam. The only absolutes on earth are people. They are an end in themselves—all other things are means. The fundamental immorality and irreligion is to regard and use people as means. The basic morality and essential religion is to be concerned about the injustice, the humiliation, the hurt, the rejection, the defilement of someone else. To sense the other man's pain and fear and suffering and lift up your voice and your hand to do something for him as if his injury and unhappiness were your own. It is to this religion that Chaplain Cohen and Chaplain Goldstein and every man of God must be converted or, perhaps, only reconverted.

And all of us are men of God, or at least children of God, created in His image. Does it cost something in effort, is there risk to stick your neck out for someone else? Certainly it does! There is! But whoever said that religion was easy, or morality cheap? Any morality, any religion, which costs its practitioners little or nothing, is worth what it costs—little or nothing. The conversion of Chaplain Cohen and the reconversion of Chaplain Goldstein is a conversion that must happen to every man of God and every woman and child of God, if religion is to be meaningful in our lives and effective in our world. ✤

❧ Joy and Wonder

It isn't true that "youth is wasted on youngsters." It is grownups who waste the precious experience of their own childhood, sloughing it off like dead skin. Our childhood was intended to teach us lifelong lessons.

Pure joy, for example. The ecstatic look on the face of the little girl as she receives an unexpected gift from a visitor. The light in her eyes, the dancing of her little body, the shriek of delight: "For me?!" We do not miss the word "thanks". We are more than thanked by the vision of a whole being transported with simple pleasure.

We learn in time to say "Thank You", promptly, politely, quite automatically. But never so joyously. Gone is the capacity for spontaneous and exquisite joy in the small pleasures of life.

And the thrilling sense of wonder. The perfect, religious awe with which a small boy beholds the magic of a toy balloon, a kaleidoscope, a spinning top; the mystery of wind swaying the treetops, the marvel of heat applied to a mess of dough to produce a miracle—cookies! To say nothing of the wonder of fireworks, stars, locomotives, babies, movies, flowers ....

The child is father to the man. Childhood's sense of wonder is intended to educate the adult heart. Yet so many of us are like the proverbial cat in the museum: present in the midst of a million marvels, but apparently unconscious, unaware, insensitive to it all.

The world is full of thought-teasing, soul-stirring magic for a child. To have "out-grown" the high sense of wonder which is the heritage of our childhood is to have re-nounced a good part of life, perhaps the best part. ✿

✿ Outside—the Sword;
Inside—Panic

In his farewell message to his people, Moses warned us against the worst possible fate we could bring upon ourselves: *Mihhutz tshakel haherev; mayhhadarim ayma*, "Outside your camp—the enemy's bereaving sword; inside—the panic of dissension."

Let this not be history's judgment upon us. Against the callousness, hostility, or cynical indifference of the nations to Israel's fate, world Jewry must stand steadfast as one people: united in thought, feeling and action; in mutual moral and material support.

When the psalmist sang, *Ma tov ... shevet ahhim gam yahhad*, the word *gam*, meaning "also" or "even," is superfluous, if all he meant to say was, "How good ... it is for brethren to dwell together in unity."

The psalmist was not wasting words. He did mean to say, "How good it is when even brethren live unitedly together"—especially Jewish brethren with our remarkable critical faculty, our predilection for argument, disagreement, fault-finding.

Remember Ben Gurion's assessment of his fellow countrymen: "A nation of two and a half million prime ministers." Disunity is one luxury we Jews cannot afford.

In his farewell message to his sons, Jacob-Israel also warns them before he blesses them, in these words: "Gather yourselves together that I may tell you what shall befall you in days to come."

Unlike the psalmist, with his (only seemingly) superfluous *gam*, Jacob leaves it to us, his people, to supply a requisite *im* ("if") thus: "If you get together"—behave as a united band concerned for each other and your total destiny as a people, you will have taken the first quintessential step to ensuring that—"you will have a future."

☙ The Window of Our World

Of God as man's employer, two thousand years ago Rabbi Tarfon said, "The day is short, the work is vast, the Master urgent. He does not expect you to complete the task, and does not permit you to stop trying."

Are parents disheartened by their tribulations in rearing children? Are statesmen and diplomats discouraged by the obstacles in the way of peace and freedom? Do educators deplore our uncultivated tastes and perverted values? Do ministers lament our religious indifference and moral laxity? Well, what are their parents and leaders, and teachers and preachers for? Is it not so that each day they may spend themselves, all their heart and soul and mind, to accomplish the difficult jobs immediately before them? And then, using the skill and power developed by such constant, all-out exercise of their spiritual muscles, go on to attempt the impossible tasks still waiting to be mastered.

Is there suspicion and fear, hatred and assorted forms of ugliness in our world? If life were all bright and beautiful, what use would God have for our intelligence and energy? But if we are intelligent we will strive to make life beautiful.

There was once a young king who rubbed his magic lamp, and the jinni appeared who, at the king's command, built for him a wondrous palace. All of a long day the youthful monarch wandered from room to room inspecting this exquisite marvel of architectural splendor. At dusk, he found the only flaw: a window bare of ornamentation.

The jinni explained: "This casement, Sire, was purposely left unadorned so that, in completing it, you may share some of my own pleasure in creating this structure. Also, it will give you deeper pride in possession if you contribute some part of the building yourself."

Need I say that the royal youth spent the rest of his life trying to finish that one window? And each day, as he worked, he gained a deeper appreciation of the work that had gone into this magnificent palace, the gift of the jinni.

This is true. Those who labor longest and hardest on their own small area in the mansion of life best appreciate both the wisdom and beauty of the total plan, and the value of their own devoted effort. 🐾

❧ The Examined Life

The unexamined life is not worth living.
—Socrates

In Norse lore human life is pictured as the flight of a bird through a banquet hall. Out of the night the bird comes winging through a window into the bright festive room and flies out through an opposite window back into the black night.

The night is eternity, dark with mystery, from which, without our asking, we are hither hurried, always puzzled by the questions, Why? and Whence? And again, without our asking, willy-nilly we are hurried hence.

The womb opens to permit our entrance into the lighted dining-hall of this world which, for a brief span, we experience with all our senses and emotions. The tomb opens to receive us on our return to the shadowed endlessness of the unknown.

Life, like a dome of many colored glass,
Stains the white radiance of eternity.

Eternity, to Shelley, was not utter blackness, but the whitest light which we—each a tiny prism in the great arching dome of the world's life—break up into its components: a rainbow spectrum of hues—from deepest, darkest indigo to gayest, gaudiest red.

"We spend our days as a tale that is told." To the Psalmist each man's life is a story. And what is the purpose, meaning, value of a story? Almost an infinite variety of purposes, meanings, and values. One thing to the author when he conceives it, another while he writes, still another one when he finishes, and another again when the critics and the public respond.

From the aspect of eternity, the story each of our lives tell, the brief bird's flight we make through this earth's banquet-hall, is like the quick burst of colored light from a photo-flash bulb. Considered, that is, *sub specie aeternitatis*, from the point of view of eternity, of endless time ... but considered humanly—that is, finitely—the days of our years are long enough to be lived, long enough to be worth studying, to understand, to know that they can be lived more deeply, more richly, more significantly, satisfyingly.

And this is the function of religion: to help us to make our existence count as a meaningful, fulfilling experience—meaningful not only to us, but significant also to the world we live in. 🐾

❧ Recharging Our Batteries

You have heard people say, "I am Jewish but not religious. I can be just as good a Jew without going to *shul.*" They are putting together syllables that make sound—but no sense. The first generation of the de-synagogued may still be looked to for contributions to Jewish charities. Their children usually are uninterested even in that. Their grandchildren dislike having the words "Jew" or "Jewish" mentioned in their presence.

The same holds true of other faiths. The first "emancipated" generation says it can pray anywhere: the woods and seashore are places just as holy as churches; Plato and Beethoven are more inspiring than the Bible. As for morality, "my ethics are just as high as the ethics of those who go to church to pray and listen to sermons." The second generation scoffs at the idea of prayer. As for ethics: "aren't they, after all, relative?" The third generation says that Jeremiah and Jesus were psycho-neurotics, that Nietzsche and Ayn Rand have the right idea, and the sooner we slough off the whole "Judeo-Christian slave-morality" of compassion and social sensitivity, the better.

In prehistoric times, before man attained the first glimmer of a conception of a God of justice or mercy, he would not hesitate to eat his neighbor when he was temporarily out of other food. In our own day, men have resorted to wholesale cannibalism, or genocide, when they have eradicated from their thinking the idea of the fatherhood of God, on which, alone, the brotherhood of man is based. We needn't imagine what the world would be like when men forsake God. We have had samples: Nazi Germany, Soviet Russia, Red China.

Painful recent history has proved to all, but those so blinded by prejudice that they refuse to see, that detached from religion, no morality ever survives. Destroy religion, and even the vaunted "goodness of heart" perishes in the New Order, where sympathy is a vice, helping the weak a crime; where only ruthlessness is admired.

Cut flowers look pretty for a little while after they are severed from their roots in the soil. They do not last very long; they rot. Morality has roots deep in religion. Separated from those roots it dies.

To change from the botanic to an electronic figure: Even the most efficient household appliance is useless unless it is plugged in to a power-source of electricity. The cordless appliance, which is useless detached from direct contact with the current, needs to be frequently reattached for recharging. To recharge human batteries, spiritually and ethically, is the function of organized religious institutions. ✦

❧ You Are His Witness

In some intense emotional crises, when the veracity of a statement is doubted, we may exclaim: "As God is my witness!"

Far more often, however, it is the other way around. You and I are His witnesses.

Isaiah said it: "'You are my witnesses,' saith the Lord, 'and I am God.'" Rabbi Isaac explained this to mean: "If you are My witnesses, then I am God. But if your conduct and character give no evidence that I am present and functioning in your life, then for all practical human purposes, I am not God; I might just as well not exist."

God needs our testimony; the evidence our lives can bring to bear in proof of the truths of religion. Certainly, there is much documentary proof; the evidence of Scripture. But living witnesses are better, more persuasive evidence.

The presence of a living, loving child, whom you can exhibit with pride, is a rather more gratifying and persuasive evidence that you are really a parent, than (let us say) a certificate from a hospital, or the Bureau of Statistics, or a document from any other institutional source.

So it is with you and your Creator, you and your faith, you and Judaism. In the last analysis you are the witness.

To your neighbor, Jew or Gentile, to all the members of your family, especially to your children, you are the evi-

dence of the influence that religion can have on human behavior. Willy-nilly, you are God's witness.

When our people were commanded to build the tabernacle in the wilderness, God said its purpose was so
that He might dwell among them. He did not say: "Build
me a sanctuary so that I may dwell therein", but "so that I
may dwell *among them*", in the midst of this people.

The Jewish sanctuary was never meant to contain
God, but to *radiate* Him. The true sanctuary is the individual, the man who becomes a dwelling-place of the Divine,
who witnesses by his conduct and character that he was
fashioned in the image of the living God. ❧

❧ Thought for Memorial Day

It takes more than the external paraphernalia of constitu-
tions, congresses, juries, and voting booths to make a true
democracy. Have not many totalitarian states, including
the former Soviet Union, all of these outward appurtenances of a republican form of government? Yet, can we
seriously think of them as democracies?

It is not political forms, but the spirit in the people
which alone can keep a nation free. That spirit is com-
pounded of certain familiar ideals: justice, the sanctity of
the individual personality, consideration for the weak, the
stranger … to mention but a few.

The Hebrew Bible, and the Synagogue which taught
its message, kept alive these moral ideals and the goal of a
world of brotherhood and peace. The faith of our fathers,
and the institution they founded to perpetuate that faith,
nourished the aims and hopes of democracy for more than
twenty-five centuries.

The Synagogue is the age-old school and present-day
citadel of democratic ideals. Weaken it and you loose the
props undergirding what is noblest in the structure of
western civilization.

No religion is worthy of the dedication of our lives
which consists merely of shrines—no matter how costly
and magnificent; or sacred volumes—holy scriptures and
prayer-books exquisitely bound and carefully preserved—
or ethical pronouncements eloquently intoned in echoing

sanctuaries; or reverence for the dead, however poetic the memorial service.

The noblest religion is consecrated men and women. It is people paying respect to their martyrs and saints by perpetuating the best in their way of life. Religion at its best is human beings adding the strength of their numbers, their intelligence and their energies to the spiritual power-house which continues to inspire that way of life in our day as it has through the long centuries.

✿✿ Adversity

Frederick the Great of Prussia is reported to have once remarked to the Rabbi of Mannsbach at *Sukkos* time: "Why don't you Jews ask the four questions now rather than on Passover. At the *Seder* table you are all seated comfortably around a beautiful banquet table and you ask, 'Why is this night different from all other nights?' Isn't that a more appropriate question when you're commanded to take your meals out in a leaky hut in the damp and cold of autumn?"

To which the rabbi replied: "Physical, social, political and economic insecurity are so normal for our people and have been for so many centuries, that we just don't think of asking 'why' when we break bread alone—out of doors—exposed to the elements with the flimsiest kind of roof over our heads and almost no wall at our backs at all. But when we feast like kings together in the warm, comforting glow of security among loved ones and friends, that is so unusual a circumstance that it prompts us to ask the question." ✿✿

❧ Recollections

I remember when we were children and the three of us took a bath in a big bathtub. Sarah was eight. Toby was about two. I was about five.

The tub was a large copper tub with wood on the outside. It had to be heated from the outside, underneath. There was a long pipe. You had to get out of the tub to light the fire.

There was a dance floor in the attic. It took up about half of the attic. Above the dance floor, there was a large chandelier made of brass and porcelain. The other part of the attic was used for storage. There was also a number of horsehair couches and chairs.

Sarah worked and bought me the very best clothes for college. I was the best-dressed freshman on campus because of her. My mother bought only the finest materials for our clothes.

Once we had company and the topic of discussion turned to artists—great artists; and my mother spread out her hands towards us and said, "These children are my works of art." ❧

On the Rabbinate

❧ The Rabbinate
A Job for a Nice Jewish Boy or Girl?

I want to talk to you about everyone's favorite subject: himself. So I am going to talk about myself, about my job as a rabbi.

About you, too, of course, dear friends, because if I deserve the title and office to which you have elevated me, I am your teacher. Very truly yours. For that is what you are saying when you utter those two syllables, *rabbi*—you are saying "my teacher."

Which reminds me of the young starlet who has been told by her mother and by her psychiatrist to try to break her bad habit of monopolizing every conversation by always talking about herself. Out on a date one evening, she finds herself doing this again. So she stops and, throwing a dazzling smile at her escort, she says: "Now, let's talk about you. What did *you* think of my last picture?"

It is the custom of a colleague of mine, out in California, to stride from one end of the *bimah* to the other, whenever he is addressing any audience. On the occasion I have in mind, he was delivering a eulogy. Up and back over the platform he walked, his eyes closed as if in communion with the spirit of the departed, rolling off exquisite phrases in tribute to the decedent. Then he paused at the casket which was open—Hollywood style—to display the artistic handiwork of the mortician's craft, and, for the first time, opened his eyes. He looked into the casket and gasped: "Good Lord, this man I *know!*"

Rabbis are people. I know. I've been one and know rabbis as colleagues for seventy-four years. So I think I know what it takes to be one and also what sort of person can, if she/he chooses to, become a competent one.

Is the rabbinate a job for a nice Jewish boy or a nice Jewish girl? The answer is a qualified "No." If he or she is nice, affable, sweet, gentle, agreeable, kindly, amiable, pleasant, genial, and if that is *all* that he or she is, the answer is "No." The rabbinate is not for him, not for her. Just being pleasant, pleasing everyone who comes along isn't the rabbi's reason for being, the prime purpose of his existence. Pleasing all-corners is the function and aim only of members of the world's oldest profession. If you don't know what occupation that is, then you are too young to be told and to have your innocence ruined. But most emphatically, the rabbi does not belong to that guild.

Nevertheless, one Hasidic rebbe, the eighteenth-century Naftali Zvi Horowitz of Galicia, jokes about this business of the rabbi having to please everybody. In his autobiography, he slyly writes: "At first I did not want to be a rabbi. Because I was told that a rabbi had to flatter his flock. So I thought I'd be a tailor. Then I saw that even a *schneider* has to flatter his customers, too, and so does a *shuster* ("cobbler"), and even a bathhouse attendant. So I said to myself, 'In what way is a rabbi worse off?' That's how I became a rabbi." This is what the *zadik* Naftali Zvi Horowitz writes. But he writes with his tongue in his cheek.

This rebbe was anything but a sycophant. He was everything a rabbi ought to be: a scholar, a mensch, a man of vast courage.

The word rabbi is derived from the biblical Hebrew, *rav*, meaning "great." With the first person singular possessive suffix, "my," added. Literally, it means, "my great one, master, teacher." It is a title of respect or honor for a teacher or doctor of Jewish law. And doctor, of course, means not a physician or surgeon or healer. It is derived from the Latin *docere* which means "to teach" and is related to such other Latinate-English words as "doctrine," which, of course, means "teaching," and "docile," which means "teachable." Doctor is a title originally signifying its possessor is so well-versed in a department of knowledge as to be qualified to *teach* it.

Historically, fundamentally, originally and primarily, the rabbi's job is to teach the doctrines of Judaism to teachable people, to Jews certainly and, of course, to any others willing to learn.

The earliest form of the title was first used in Babylonia. It was *rav*. It referred to a *hakham*, a "sage," one learned in Torah and in the oral traditions of the Talmud. One who taught what he knew to his disciples in classrooms, to the congregation from synagogue pulpits, and who acted as a Judge in the *Bet Din*, ("Jewish Court of Law") to which Jews brought all their litigation for more than two thousand years until the Twentieth Century.

For most of Jewish history, it was sinful, forbidden, unthinkable and virtually unheard of for Jews to sue each other in civil courts. Most everywhere in the world until almost the Twentieth Century, in every Jewish community its rabbis were the executive, legislative, and judicial branches of the government for Jews and recognized as such by the civil authorities. In every department of life, to Jews, the rabbis were *the* authorities.

We have in the Talmud the statement: "It is a religious duty to obey the rulings of the rabbis. He who does so is a *tzadik* (a 'righteous person'), he who does not is a *rasha* (a 'miscreant').''

The second-century sage, Helbo, says: "The rule you hear from the lips of a rabbi, regard it as though you had heard it from Mt. Sinai." "A decision of the rabbi's is law," says the eleventh-century scholar, Eliezer ben Isaac. The sixteenth-century Isserlein says, "No one may contradict the rabbinic teaching."

From the editor of a nineteenth-century edition of the Talmud, Chajes, this dictum: "Obedience to the authority of rabbinic tradition is binding on all Jews. Whatever the rabbis ordain, must be."

For approximately twenty centuries, until this present (very different) one, the rabbi was a scholarly teacher and an authority who wielded very real power over his people.

Not that all this exercise of authoritarian power went without protest from the most protestant people the world has ever known—the Jews. No, indeed. More than two thousand years ago, the earliest rabbi whose name we know, Shemaya, the teacher of Hillel, protested this hunger for power which attracted some young men to the rabbinate. To them he said, *Ehav et ham'lakha*, "love work"; *usna et harabanut*, "hate the rabbinate"; *v'al titvada larashut*, "do not lust for power [for authority]."

And as late as the eighteenth century, one Jewish scholar, Jacob Emden, when he came to the prayer in the Orthodox morning service which says: *Baruch ata Adonai Elohanu melech haolom shelo asani isha*, "Blessed be He Who has not made me a woman," recited instead, *shelo asani rav*, "Blessed be He Who has not made me a rabbi!" By way of explanation, he said: "I chose the way of humility and I hated the thought of becoming a rabbi."

In addition to being learned teachers and communal administrators, legislators and jurists, rabbis were considered saints and among the Hasidim were actually called that: *tzadikim.*

The Talmud, for example, asks: "Who are the *Malakhay HaSharet* ("the ministering angels of God" who are mentioned in the Sabbath hymn, *Sholom Aleykhem*)? The answer given is "The rabbis."

The Midrash says of the teachers of Torah: *Torat Adonai tmima*, "The law of the Eternal is perfect—when it is taught by a rabbi, a saintly man striving for perfection."

The eighteenth-century Hasid, Simcha Bunim, says: "The rabbi is one who embodies in himself, in one harmonious synthesis, the Heavenly and the Earthly, the spiritual and the material, and integrates these into one organic whole. He is the neck which joins the head to the body."

A sage, a justice, and a saint. A rather tall order. The requirements for the rabbinate today are not fewer than they once were. On the contrary, they have multiplied. They are less demanding in some respects but now more numerous, varied and burdensome in others.

Today, the rabbi wears more than just these three hats. One of the old ones is still his. He is still the teacher. Some of us wish we could limit ourselves to that one function alone. We wish it were true, what Isaac Mayer Wise, the founder of American Reform Judaism, said a century ago, namely: "The rabbi is the teacher of Jewry. No more and no less."

What may be a little closer to the truth is what Kaufmann Kohler, President of the Hebrew Union College, said: "The rabbi is primarily a teacher. This is the consistent tradition from all our past and must be our aim and purpose now."

David Philipson, the late Dean of American Reform Rabbis said: "The rabbi's first concern is learning and scholarship."

A rabbi's first and holiest duty is to disseminate Torah. But even this is an immensely difficult task demanding
considerable oratorical, literary, pedagogic, and public relations skill to make it relevant to the contemporary scene.
But even more important, it calls for prodigious courage.

It is easy to make Judaism palatable with pleasant plat-
itudes. But it takes enormous valor to make it pertinent
with prophetic insight and daring. Yet this is the rabbi's
mission: to hearken to the command, *Kra v'garon*, "Cry
out," *kashofar harayn kolekha*, "spare not your voice, raise it
loud as a trumpet," *vhaged l'ami pisham*, "declare unto My
people their sins" (Isaiah 58:1).

This isn't easy. It is very hard, indeed, to teach this
people, all of whom are, themselves, teachers. Ben Gurion
once told President Johnson that his being Prime Minister
of Israel was a far more difficult job than being President
of the United States. He put this question to Mr. Johnson:
"How would you like to try governing a nation of two million Prime Ministers?"

Well, the rabbi's job is to attempt to minister to a
mamlekhet kohanim, "a kingdom of priests," *vgoy kadosh*,
"and a holy nation," an *am hakham vnavon*, "a wise and understanding people." This is our people's great problem,
and, as rabbis, it is ours amplified.

Jews are like other people only more so. And rabbis
obviously are Jews only more so. The Jews' difficulty is
that they were put on earth to teach Torah, they are supposed to be an *or lagoyim*, "a light unto the nations of the
earth," a bright-burning example to mankind of justice and
righteousness, piety and brotherhood, mercy and love.
And rabbis are expected to be *or la-yehudim*, "a light unto
Jews." All Jews are expected to be teachers of Torah, of
God's will for man's life. And rabbis are expected to be
teachers of these teachers.

And who loves teachers? Who wants to hear that what he is doing is wrong; and who wants to hear what he ought to do to be doing right?

You know what happens to men who try to teach others how to live? Everyone knows the schoolboy's one-paragraph biography of Socrates: "Socrates was the wisest man in Athens. He went all over Greece telling people how to live. The Greeks killed him."

No teacher's life is a bed of roses. "He that accepts a rabbinic position," said one authority, "must be able to live by the commandment (Deut. 1:17) *Lo taguru mipnay ish*, 'you must not be afraid of any man.'" And he went on to say that the rabbi whom the *baale-habatim* never had the urge to run out of town, isn't a rabbi. And the one whom they actually succeed in driving out of town, isn't a man.

"Judaism in these days of skepticism, of religious apathy, of mammon worship, of wholesale apostasy requires men of spiritual power and undaunted bravery, men with the zeal of an Elijah and the tongue of an Isaiah if they are to be worthy, trusted guides amidst the perplexities of life; towers of strength when all things seem to be giving way and falling apart"—so spoke Kaufmann Kohler, President of Hebrew Union College. The year was 1904.

Hasidism ("pietism") is an old concept in Jewish life. It is a word which not only designates three specific movements in Jewish history—one in Palestine in the first century, C.E., one in twelfth-century Germany, and the most recent movement beginning in East Europe in the eighteenth century, and still going strong from Jerusalem to Brookline. The term *hasid* also is used for any rabbi's faithful disciples. In both senses there are *hasidim* who believe that all they need is a rabbi, and there are not a few anti-religious rabbi-haters—some of whom occupy lofty positions in the Jewish community—who are just as convinced that they need no rabbis. Doubtless they are both wrong.

It has been said that in the world to come, the *hasid* will be called to account for saying, "I have a rabbi who tells me what to think, say. and do; in a word, how to live; therefore, I don't need a book or anything else." And so will the anti-synagogue, anti-rabbinical intellectual who says, "I can read books by myself. I don't need a rabbi."

Ever since the French Revolution, which initiated the crumbling of the ghetto walls and the beginning of the assimilation or acculturation or integration of Jews with the general Christian population in the Western world, the function of the rabbi has become much broader than it once was. And, in many ways, quite different from what it used to be.

Today's rabbis are not only teachers and priestly functionaries (marrying and burying and unveiling and invoking and 'benedicting') preachers (formerly the function of a magid), temple administrators (which was once the function of the *shamash*), public relations persons, ambassadors to the goyim (which once was the function of the *shtadlan*), and officiants with a surgeon at circumcisions (a job once reserved exclusively for the *mohel*)—but most especially his job now is that of pastor, which is to say a psychiatrist without fee on twenty-four hour call, handling cases of disaffected spouses and sibling rivalry, counseling the troubled, visiting the sick, comforting the bereaved, and ever so much else besides.

All these non-scholarly activities take up so much of the time, energy, and peace of mind of the rabbi that there is little left for study and instruction. Admittedly, these additional functions are in imitation of the practices of Christian clergy. Jews who do not attend services or classes in Judaism (which once were the chief rabbinic function), now demand multitudinous services which, in former ages, were never the province of the rabbi.

Willy-nilly, these have become the expected functions of the rabbi in our time. And the tide and course of this proliferation of function is not easy (and perhaps not possible) to stem, let alone to reverse.

So, in addition to erudition and piety and courage and eloquence, of today's rabbi is required skills in all these multifarious departments—plus patience with criticism which he must learn to consume with his daily bread—plus insight and understanding of human weakness and crotchetiness and discontent with whatever he does or says or is.

No, this isn't a job for a 'nice' Jewish girl or boy, if niceness, amiability, affability, and gentleness is all the prospective candidate for the rabbinate has to offer. But if he or she has a good part of these other qualities and enjoys challenge, this might be just what the doctor ordered as a career—and by "doctor," I mean only what the word means: "teacher." 🔯

✑ The Quite Imperfect Tribute

Of the First Congregation of Jews to the First Sermonic Effort of the First Rabbi in the World; or We Can Stop Envying Moses

As new rabbis, in the 30s of this century, my young colleagues and I used to envy Moses. To use an expression popular among G.I.'s in World War II, he was, we thought, a 'goldbrick,' in that he had a job that didn't involve any work. For example, did he ever have to wonder where his *kehillah* was? On Shabbat or any other time? They were always there. All 603,550 of them (Exodus 38:26). In Sinai they turned out even for this stuttering preacher. What alternative did they have? His was the only show around.

Did he ever spend sleepless nights wracking his brain for a titillating title to blazon on his *mishkan,* Tabernacle, bulletin board or to advertise in *Itton Ha-Midbar,* "The Wilderness Times," in order to attract an audience?

Long after the world's first preacher had stammered his last "Amen" and was interred in Moab, a prosy posterity titled his talks unenthrallingly: "Words…," "If Then…," " See…," "When You Enter…," "Standing…," "He Went…," "Listen…," etc.

But so long as he lived, the first of all rabbis never had a moment's concern about the possibility of his flock being seduced by more enticing sermonic fare offered elsewhere. There were no competing preachers in nearby rival pulpits.

As for his own assistants and/or associates, those he picked personally, consulting no one—no Search Committees, no Pulpit Placement Consultants. His successor, too, he selected himself, without benefit of the advice or consent of any *baalei ha-batim*—no expert laymen. Moreover, he took his own good time choosing his replacement. He became emeritus only when he reached a decent age for retirement: 119.

During his active incumbency as *Rabbeynu*, "Our Rabbi," he never bothered to develop any novel, clever gimmicks—celebrity series, sherry hours, fashion shows, door prizes, rock festivals, Las Vegas nights—either to bring out a crowd or bring in the money.

Fund-raising was no trouble at all—a piece of cake. He simply invited voluntary contributions to the Tabernacle Building Campaign. The response was so overwhelming that the chief artisan at the construction site was impelled to leave work to come and complain to Moses that the gifts were excessive. *Moshe Rabbeynu* had to stop the traditionally generous Jews from bringing more (Exodus 36). Nor is there any evidence that donors' names were inscribed on their gifts—or anywhere else in the sanctuary. They weren't paid for their gifts by personal advertisement. That's how they were taught: That if you get paid for it, it isn't a gift. It isn't a *mitzvah*. For a contribution to be a *mitzvah*, doing it must be its own and only reward.

When *tzo'r'rim* (not "enemies" really, but "troublers"; folk who loved to give him *tzores*) had the foolhardiness to attack Moses, he never stooped to any sort of self-defense. Why should he? It wasn't necessary. He could leave them to God. He did.

When one racist faulted our teacher for marrying a black African woman, condign divine punishment was meted out to this denigrator. She was afflicted with leprosy. Poetic justice! So proud of being white—was she? Now she was leprous: the whitest! (Numbers 12).

On occasion, obstreperous parishioners impugned Moses' motives, accused him of exceeding his office, sought to supplant him. Did their revolting behavior embarrass *Moshe Rabbeynu?* Ever to the point where he hoped the ground would open up to swallow him? Not he. He preferred that the earth yawn and swallow them. It did (Numbers 16).

Among his most unspeakably intense joys, Moses had the delicious soul-satisfaction of burying all his perverse and pernicious parishioners, a whole generation of them (Numbers 32:13), while none of his critics or deprecators had the pleasure of attending his funeral (Deuteronomy 34:5f.).

In one detail of his career, however, today's rabbi is luckier than his ancient ancestor and aboriginal model. In the thirty-two or three centuries from Moses' time to our own, the attention span of Jewish congregations has increased appreciably. The average twentieth century Jewish *kehillah* is more patient and long-suffering, will endure more long-windedness from its rabbi than Moses' first congregation would take from him.

This is all the more remarkable, considering that ours is preeminently the Age of Speed. No longer does everything have to be bigger to be better. It has only to be faster. This is the era of the quick lunch, begun with instant soup and concluded with instant coffee. Swift relief from the sudden indigestion which immediately follows this speedy meal is promised by a wide variety of remedies, all guaranteed to be fast, f-a-s-t, *FAST*.

A vast array of tempting drugs or treatments offers, among other benefits, quickly expanded consciousness, removal of unwanted hair, new growth of much-wanted hair, renewal of robust masculine vigor and vitality, health, wealth, and wisdom, and complete happiness—*NOW!* Some people may even risk exposure to religion—so long as you "Make it quick, Doc."

There's hardly a rabbi now alive who hasn't been subjected to such painful exhortations (variously phrased, depending on the general character or current mood of the critic) as the trite, "Brevity is the soul of wit," or the similarly stale, "No speech has to be eternal in order to be immortal," or the blunt and banal, "Keep it short," or the brazen and brutal, "If you don't strike oil in twenty minutes, quit boring."

Rabbis, who are annoyed, hurt, furious, or just sick and tired of being needled on the score of rabbinical wordiness, should reread the record of Moses' first attempt at sermonizing. It occurs in the first paragraph of our *parasha* for this Shabbat.

As you probably know, the sermon is of Jewish origin. Our prophets invented it. Moses was the world's first preacher-prophet. He was, understandably, less than eager to take the job. Maybe he anticipated the thanklessness (to make no mention of the uselessness) of *darshanut* ("the practice of preaching"). Perhaps he foresaw the results of his first effort in this utterly new human(?) enterprise.

But it is unlikely that his worst nightmarish premonition of the event came anywhere close to the dismal reality of his congregation's actual response to his maiden sermon, a world premiere of the genre.

It was the tiniest of *droshelach*, a "mini-sermonette," really—only five sentences long. Exactly fifty-two Hebrew words.

Prophetically, Moses had anticipated all the excellent rules that would one day be devised: for example, "Speak to the point and quit when you reach that point"; "Use your words like focused sunbeams so they burn deeply"; etc.

To what effect? His audience's instantaneous response was stunning: *lo sham'u el Moshe*—they hadn't listened to him at all—hadn't heard anything he'd said! Why? Because of *kotzer ruah*—"shortness of mind," that is, of attention span (Exodus 6:6-9). Impatience caused by suffering as slaves.

Even in the mouth of a stutterer, a hundred words could have taken only about a minute to utter. But even when the sermon topic was of first importance—having to do with their own security, survival, and freedom—so minute was the listening capacity of that first congregation exposed to the first sermon of the first of all preachers that Moses wasn't able to engage their minds even for one whole minute.

Colleagues who can—if not regularly or often—at least occasionally hold the attention of their flock for as much as ten minutes can stop envying Moses. By now you may be suffering from *kotzer ruach*. Well, relief is near. In fact it's here. *My* ten minutes are up. 🍃

❧ Prescription
For Epidemic Pernicious Anemia
(Spiritual Type)

I was awakened from deep sleep by a startled cry in the night. It was followed by the dull thump-thump of a body falling down a stairway: the cruel sound of tender flesh, covering brittle bone, thudding against bare hard board. Then—after a brief breath-catching pause—a wail of pain: "My head! Oh, my head!"

Recognizing the voice, I surmised what had happened. Our small cousin, spending his first night with us away from home, groping in the dark, unfamiliar hall, had toppled down the flight of stairs leading to the first floor.

When I came down (this time very carefully) there was my mother on the bottom step holding him to her bosom, rocking him gently, softly stroking a little lump on his noggin, and crooning in soothing sing-song Yiddish: "It's only a little knock on your sweet little head..."

But the anguished sobbing did not cease, for the child was not comforted. I could see why, though my mother could not. She neither saw nor yet felt the blood which streamed from that side of his lacerated scalp she was pressing to her shoulder. By the time the doctor arrived to take stitches in the injured little *kepeleh*, her lovely pink dressing gown was drenched with the warm red stuff.

Although this incident happened more than eighty years ago, I recall it vividly. I have had frequent occasion to conjure up that scene, as an analogy to so many tragi-comic situations. Often I think of the picture the two of them made: my concerned and well-intentioned mother, confident that she had discovered the cause of the discomfort and was applying the appropriate remedy; certain that the injury was superficial and the cure simple—rubbing the wrong spot—and neglecting the right one, which needed much more radical therapy than gentle words and soft caresses.

I think of it now, when I see congregations attempting to cure the chronic sickness of the synagogue—its emptiness from one Yom Kippur to the next Rosh Ha-shanah—by pleasant esthetic touches: Let's brighten the Sanctuary with blond mahogany paneling, let's cheer the heart of the worshiper with brilliant stained glass abstracts, with clever mobiles for lighting fixtures, with embroidered damask drapes for the *Aron Kodesh*, and state-of-the-art public address system or wall-to-wall washed-broadloom floor-covering, and acusticon tile ceiling, streamlined *bimah*, pulpit, and choir loft, or electronic organ, rheostats, electric-eye door openers, and up-to-date a-tonal, quasi-traditional *chazanut*. Let 's get some avant garde poets to dress up the language of the prayer book, use computers to accumulate and correlate data on what kind of weather, news items, display ads, and sermon titles produce the biggest turn-out for late Friday evening service. Let's see to it that the decorum of the service matches the decor of the Sanctuary: that the ushering is appropriately poised, polished, professional, perfect.

Alas, to what avail these gimmicks? Why do we put our faith in such external appurtenances of piety? Is it only inertia: or is it sheer desperate escapism that impels us to hope for a renascence of spirituality in such superficialities as the newness, size, shape, color, or architectural proportion of our temple, the sound of its music, the format of its hymnals and prayer books, the wording of its liturgy?

I am probably as sensitive to esthetics as the next man. The fact is that I have personally designed a series of stained glass windows and silver Torah ornaments, and a set of bronze Temple doors, and the elaborate matching pair of outdoor bulletin boards—an elegant masthead for my Temple news bulletins, rich velvet ark curtains with tri-dimensional Hebrew letters in gold affixed thereto, a gadget on wheels for re-rolling the Torah, brass brackets for holding the scrolls on the *bimah* rail during Kol Nidre—and much else in the same vein—all still in use.

For years I have been a working member of the Liturgy Committees of the CCAR. At their urging, I have contributed materials for a forthcoming prayer anthology and the projected newly-revised *Haggadah,* and other prayers and services for the J.W.B. and the Synagogue Council of America. This by no means exhausts my efforts at beautifying our worship service. I gladly engage in this work because I know (Matthew Arnold to the contrary notwithstanding) that Hebrews, as well as Hellenes, are moved by the holiness of beauty—currently perhaps even more than they are by the beauty of holiness.

Nonetheless, I suggest that the most exquisitely poetic prayers, printed on the finest vellum or India paper, bound in the supplest Moroccan leather, intoned in the midst of gorgeous pageantry, dramatically lighted by the loveliest stained glass windows, to the obligato of a flawless choir chanting impeccably Jewish music, will all together fail to evoke the religious spirit within the soul of a man who will not come to synagogue to pray, simply because he does not believe in God, or in public prayer, or in any prayer. Who is he; where is this man? You will find him in your congregation. In fact, he represents a substantial

proportion of the membership of your congregation—
and mine.

This, I believe, is our real problem: How to persuade
our people that God is, and that He answers prayer. Failing
this—with all our passion for the peripheral, our engross-
ment with ritual, liturgical, organizational, architectural,
and sonic esthetics—we are like one who is utterly ab-
sorbed in making sure that the bandages are pristine white,
absolutely sterile, neatly wrapped, and securely taped around
the body of a man dying of pernicious anemia.

A modern Johanan ben Zakkai could also, and as
truthfully, complain to God: "Your people have forsaken
You." Our people have not indeed relinquished all that
goes by the name of "religious Jewish practice." But do
most of them relate their favorite pious observances to
God? For instance, the very popular *Yizkor*? Are those who
come to recite *Yizkor* primarily motivated by love or fear
of *God*—or only by fear or love of the spirits of the *departed*? Was not *Yizkor* originally innovated in the hope of
luring mourners back to the practice of regular synagogue
attendance? With what success? Our modern "Jewish"
counterparts of Chinese and Egyptian ancestor-worship-
ers telephone the temple office to inquire: "When are the
services for the dead?" Why do they insist on knowing the
precise hour? Lest, *has v'halila*, they arrive too late, or too
early, and are exposed to a service devoted to worship of
the living God, rather than exclusively to reverence for the
ghosts of the dead?

Now, what spiritual response would be evoked in our
people if suddenly *we* summoned them all (say, by tele-
gram) in the middle of a busy weekday to make the momentous announcement, "There is a God in the world!" as
we are told Levi Yitzhak of Berdichev once did. Why
would this not be effective with our parishioners? May I,

ever so gently, suggest that an important reason is because *we* are *not* Berdichevers.

How did Levi Yitzhak, and the Salanter, and the Besht teach the elements of deep Jewish religious spirituality— *dvekut, kavanah, hitlahavut?* Was it not by the example of their own universally recognized piety? I submit that they were able to do this because each of them held deep, clear, and strong theological convictions. They were constantly, irresistibly drawn to the Shekhinah, ever seeking the living God. They were completely convinced of the efficacy of prayer, and its specially increased efficacy when uttered in a sacred place, at a stated time; in concert with God's holy folk. Being so spiritually constituted, they had less difficulty communicating their belief and getting their people to imitate their practice. What techniques did they employ? All that there are.

The spiritual leader communicates religion not by academic proof for the existence of God, by formal classroom theological syllogisms, but by *all* that he *says*: from the pulpit, in prayer and preachment, in the classroom, the press, the civic rostrums, in synagogue bulletins, in private conversations, in letters to his congregation; by *all* he *does*: openly and in secret, in his study, his home, the living-rooms of his parishioners, the public places in his community; in a word, by what he *is*. Is he a splendid, palpable, emulable example of the faith that there is a God in the world, in his world, in his personal life? Is he living, visible proof that prayer works; that it can transform a man's conduct and character, can transfigure him?

To coin a maxim: Religion is not so much taught as it is caught. It is a benign infection that can become a contagion as it leaps from soul to soul. There is no other therapy for the spiritual lethargy (bordering on catatonia) which besets our people in our time. There has never been any other prescription for this ailment in any age. I submit that it is at least naive and at most indolent to lean on esthetic gimmicks and gadgets to effectuate the cure for this malady: indifference toward worship. It is futile, sinfully irresponsible, and false to point the finger of blame only at our people, at *their* apathy, *their* impiety, *their* obtuse spiritual callousness and blindness.

After all, we are their teachers, so the fault, dear colleagues, lies not quite so much in them as in ourselves; and in this indictment I make no Fifth Amendment appeal. On the contrary, I do—unequivocally and most emphatically— include myself.

If you, my dear colleagues, are innocent on all counts; if you are religionists whose creed, conduct, and character are all of one piece; whose belief, behavior, and very being all combine to tell your people, "There is a God in the world, One Who hears and answers prayer! How can you doubt it; you can prove it by me!"—then, you are far above needing any apology from me (though you have it herewith; indeed, of the most profuse, abject variety). If you are clear of any blame or fault in this, your fundamental responsibility, you are the Rabbi our people need to heal them of this religious anemia. Indeed, I do more than merely apologize to you: I love, honor, cherish, and bless you; for you will do more than give them good doctrine, making wise the simple. You will restore their soul and rejoice their heart—and mine. 🪷

❧ Aspects of
Reform Judaism

♫ More or Less Ritual
(An Essay on the Place of the Ceremonial Motif in the Total Symphony of Jewish Life)

Everyone knows the anecdote of the three men, each of whom claimed membership in the world's oldest profession.

"Surgery," the doctor insisted, "is the most ancient calling. Genesis records that God caused a deep sleep to fall upon Adam, removed a rib and closed the incision with flesh. Obviously an operation performed under anesthesis, complete with cosmetic suture."

"Quite so," replied the engineer. "But that was God's final act in Creation. God's first was to bring order out of chaos; clearly a job of engineering."

"True, true," the politician said. "But who do you suppose created all the chaos?"

There the story ends. Here our discussion begins. For bringing order out of chaos is indeed the work of God. And we give evidence that we are made in God's image when we take the formless stuff of existence and fashion it into meaningful and esthetic designs for living. In fact, that is how civilizations are born. For the difference between Cro-Magnon man and the cultivated citizen of, say, Cedar Rapids is not one of native intelligence or of instinctive emotions or behavior, but of intrinsic culture patterns, the accumulation of long processes of integration and organization. It is analogous to the difference between a yard full of stone, brick, lumber, glass, cement and metal on one side of Main Street and a functioning building on the other. On both sides of the avenue the material may be the same, but the form is different. Intelligent, purposive organization and labor have brought order and efficient function out of a chaotic heap of stuff. That is the goal of civilization.

Now a ritual is a form. It is a patternful way of doing something, a way that has a symbolic significance, a meaning beyond the act itself. Sophisticated folk no longer believe that rituals have magical power as primitive people think. But all of us indulge in rituals of one kind or another, and depending on our temperament, some of us even enjoy the indulgence. And we don't have to be religionists to do this. For we find ritual not only in religion but in every department of civilized existence.

There are the simple rituals of greeting, like saying "Hello" and "Goodbye," tipping a hat or rising for a lady, beginning a letter with "Dear Sir" and ending it with "Yours truly." There are the elegant formal ceremonies of place cards, receiving lines, thank-you notes, guest towels, and the ritual of dress: white tie, chesterfield coat, corsages and gowns that achieve formality when they are worn at half-mast.

Rituals are like the poor—we have them always with us. Like death and taxes we cannot escape them. They are the trappings of cultured social living. They do not constitute the foundations or girders or the cornerstones of the structure of society, but they are the graceful inscription over the entrance, the impressive burnished bronze on the doors, the marble dadoes in the corridor, the clever ventilation gadgets on the windows, none of them absolutely essential to the functioning of the building, but all of them very nice. They are indeed the niceties, the amenities, the good forms in the architecture of civilization.

Neanderthal man knew them not, neither did the Piltdown savage understand such niceties. But they betoken the shift from the jungle to Park Avenue. No well-bred society is without them. They serve as the lubrication in social intercourse. They also have an additional, related function which brings us up to the ritual of religion and back to the story with which we began.

You see, God is more than the Engineer of the universe. He is the Architect of Creation; the cosmic Artist. He is concerned with order not merely because it is functional, efficient; but because, without form, there can be no esthetics. And God did have a dream of beauty when He conceived the universe. And the religious man accords God the sincerest form of flattery. *Imitatio Dei*—the imitation of God, is religion in essence. For religion is an art—the art of living.

The difference between the religious and the irreligious life is the difference, for example, between a fine painting on canvas and a mess of paint on an artist's palette. The pigments are the same on both surfaces. It is their arrangement which makes all the difference. Inspiring the arrangement on the canvas is vision, a dream of perfection, and directing the hand of the artist is intelligence, talent, perhaps genius. As a result of all this we have … what? Perfection? No. Not that, ever. But a masterpiece, something to stir the imagination, to kindle the spirit of the beholder. In a word, a thing of beauty. And that precisely is what we have in the *tzaddik*, the *hasid*, the pious, saintly soul: a bit of living, human art.

All great art is the expression of man's delight in God's handiwork. Whether it be a sunset or a snowscape, a still life or the representation of the human form art is reverent imitation of Divine creation.

Historically, all art had its beginnings in religion. The earliest examples of architecture were temples and tombs. Primitive sculptures are of the gods. The first songs were psalms and the oldest literature, scriptures.

Religion itself is art on the grandest scale, using the most colorful and dynamic of media: human life, in the midst of the vast ever-changing panorama of the universe.

In the physical world, religion has sought to invest with sublimity all the cyclic changes of nature. New moon and New Year ceremonies spiritualize the lunar and solar phases. The ritual candles of Hanukkah, the winter solstice festival, bring spiritual light and beauty to the life of man when the sun's light wanes. The Passover Seder heralds the spring with the bright, joyous hope of freedom and redemption. Sukkot greets the autumn with the lovely symbols, prayers and offerings of thanksgiving. The solemn observances of the Fast of Atonement lend spiritual meaning and dignity to what otherwise might be only a neurotic's feeling of guilt over sin and life misspent.

To the cycle of our personal careers, too, religion comes to bring dignity and grace. By the ritual symbolism of circumcision, confirmation, marriage and memorial ceremonies, religion sanctifies and ennobles the biological cycle of birth, puberty, mating and death. It is religion which provides the means for transforming the raw materials of existence into the esthetic and significant patterns of an art-full way of life. This it does not entirely, but as we shall see, partly through ritual. Yes, it is religion that brings to life all the elements that go to make beauty: perspective, proportion, harmony, symmetry. Not nature in the rough, but nature idealized, nature plus spiritual meaning, nature plus the beauty of holiness and the holiness of beauty—make art.

Now, our peculiar "art form" is Judaism. But if we are to get the proper perspective and understand what proportion ritual should play in the total symphony of Judaism, we must look at the complete score. Only so, can we decide whether we need more ritual or less. When we examine the composition of our way of life as a whole, we can make up our mind whether greater emphasis on the ritual motif will or will not create imbalance and distortion.

So let us now examine the five themes which, together, comprise the symphony of Judaism. We will find the best concise statement of those themes in that glorious summary of our faith, the *Sh'ma*.

1. First, there is the theme of *theology*. "Hear, O Israel, the Lord our God is One." Expressed here is the epitome of our belief that we live in a *uni*-verse, a *uni*-tary world, under the law and government of *one* God; that His children are *one* family, members of a *single* race—the human race. This unique idea of one-ness gave new direction to science and philosophy and brought them both a long way forward in their quest for truth. It represents the nucleus of Jewish theology.

2. Second, there is the theme of Jewish *mysticism*. "Thou shalt love the Lord thy God with all thy heart and with all thy soul and with all thy might." What motivates human action is not so much the intellect as it is the emotions, as the word "emotion" itself suggests. Without a passionate commitment to their beliefs, even the most scholarly philosophers and scientists have been known to change their minds in order to save their skins—as did many a European professor, persuaded by the "high" logic and truths developed in the laboratories of Hitler's Brown House and the Kremlin.

It is an imperative of our religion not only to understand that both God and His creation are one, but to cling to this faith with all our heart and soul and might; to transform mere belief into an unshakable conviction that it is this faith which makes life worth living, and worth fighting and suffering for and, if need be, worth dying for. This is the mystic motif in Judaism.

3. The third theme is learning, or Jewish education. "These words which I command thee shall be upon thy heart, and thou shalt teach them diligently to thy children." Our conception and our love of God are not to be jealously guarded secrets. Torah means "teaching." It is not a static body of knowledge, but an educational process in which we are the eternal students and the appointed teachers of our children and of God's children—mankind. That is why learning: books, school, lectures, classes, symposia, play so supremely important a role in our way of life.

4. The fourth theme is ceremonial: "Thou shalt inculcate them by outward signs on every hand. They shall be as symbols before thine eyes, upon the doorposts of thy house and upon thy gates." Jewish fundamentalists, with narrow literalness actually cramped these very words into little boxes and hung them on their persons and their homes. But, intimated in this commandment is the whole rich realm of ritual. Implied is the awareness that concrete forms, visual aids, auditory, sapid, tactile, kinesthetic and even olfactory experiences, ceremonies that involve not only the intellect but the sensory organs—these, too, are pedagogic technique.

There was religion long before there was language. Words are not the only instrument of instruction—as every lover knows. Every faculty of sense is a door to learning, a way to stimulate feeling and believing.

The sight of the *mezuzah* and the *menorah*, the sound of the *shofar* and *Kol Nidre*, the touch of *kiddush* cup and the taste of *matzah*, the smell of an *etrog* and of the *Havdalah* spice—all these instruct us in our faith, inculcate reverence and the beauty of holiness and the holiness of beauty. This is the motif of *ritual* in our religion. But neither it, nor any of the other three is an end unto itself.

5. Fifth, and finally, there is the theme to which all the other four are subservient. It is the themes of the *Ethical Conduct of Life.*

All the foregoing you shall observe and perform, says the *Sh'ma*—"*L'ma'an tizk'ru v'asitem et kol mitsvotai.*" "*V'h'-yitem k'doshim*"—to the end that you may remember to do all My commandments and be holy.

Believing in God, loving Him, teaching His Torah, concretizing it in ritual—unless all this eventuate in the enactment of the commandments in our lives and in our world, why then we are like one who hinges lovely doors to a beautiful vestibule, that opens upon a fine foyer, from which gorgeous corridors lead to an abandoned shack.

For the end, the goal of all our religious thinking and feeling and teaching and symbolizing is but this: to do the commandments that make one holy as Judaism understands holiness; to seek peace, to feed the hungry, clothe the naked, care for the poor, to love mercy and your neighbor as yourself.

Theology, mysticism, education, and ritual—each has its place—as a means toward an end, as preparation for moral action, for the ethical conduct of life.

And I believe that the early nineteenth-century Jewish Reformers had this in mind when they set about clearing a path through the tangled underbrush of superstitious beliefs and practices which had grown up and overrun the

214 Albert S. Goldstein

garden of Jewish life during the centuries when it was shut in behind ghetto walls.

It is all too easy, with the wisdom of hindsight, to say now that some of those pathfinders were perhaps a little over-zealous in their selection of road-clearing equipment. The eager beavers among them seem, indeed, to have used flame throwers and demolition bombs to do the job, especially when they went to work on the ceremonial growths. And when they finished, their scorched earth tactics left us not a road, but a blasted wilderness, a burnt-out wasteland.

Let us in fairness to the founding fathers of Reform, however, credit them with putting first things first. They were keeping their eye steadfast on the goal. They did have singleness of aim. They were intent on preserving and perpetuating the essential message of Judaism, the ethical commandments, the doctrine and faith of the prophets. In their ears there rang the prophets' warning against the age-old orthodox belief in ritual as an end in itself, the belief that *ritual* is *religion*.

Ritual, says Reform (echoing all the prophets from Moses to Micah and the last Isaiah)—ritual may be a means toward the good life, one of several means. But none of them is worth much if the end is forgotten. Ritualism is no substitute for righteousness.

Doubtless the early Reformers who started out to prettify the ghetto Jew by trimming his beard overdid it when they ended up snatching him bald. But let us not go to the other extreme of imaging that whiskers, or their ceremonial equivalent, are a sure sign of inner spiritual vigor and a sovereign cure for the religious debility of which it is currently fashionable for Reform Jews to complain. Our Conservative brethren wear hats and *talitot*, and the Orthodox still cherish their beards if not their side curls, but I wonder, with all the ritualism, whether a thorough check up would show them spiritually more healthy than we?

Religion, as I have said, is the art of living; and our particular art-form is Judaism. The most sublime expression of the dynamic art of Jewish living is not to be found in our prayer books or our holy writings, not in our oral pronouncements, whether from the pulpit or the trustees' board room, and also not in the sensual beauty of synagogue furnishings and the drama of ritual.

The great art potential of Judaism inheres rather in the moral commandments. To sit in gorgeous sanctuaries and recite ancient poetry, or listen to sonorous prose and watch, or even participate in, exquisite ritual pageantry, is not religion—unless it leads to the beautiful deed: the effort to transform the ugliness of cruelty, injustice, poverty and pain into a spiritually esthetic social order.

The art of living is a giving of one's talents and means and strength to this task: it is consecration, the joyous acceptance of life as a mission.

If we remember this and begin to do it, then whether we accompany our conversion to religion with much ceremonial or little will hardly matter. 🪻

✿ Should We Give a Get?
Reform and Jewish Divorce

In 1962 our colleague, Rabbi Paul H. Levenson, posed the question to Dr. Freehof. The maestro's *tshuvah* was (characteristically) prompt, a model of erudition, close reasoning, and lucid prose. It (uncharacteristically) concluded with a completely unequivocal No. We should not give a *Get*. We should continue content with civil divorce.

Freehof's responsum adduced history, *halakha*, sociology and *sechel*:

It noted "the new mobility of Jews in the modern era ... emigrating, inaccessible husbands ... civil divorce was an emancipation proclamation to *Agunot* ... accepted by at least 80% of world Jewry ... Those who insist upon a *Get* are a dwindling Orthodox minority."

It cited *halakha*: "Unlike marriage, divorce is not really a religious ceremony ... marriage has blessings, divorce has none ... Divorce is primarily civil law (*diney mamonot*) ... In divorce *dina d'malkhuta dina* does fully apply."

However, while our Reform acceptance of the validity of civil divorce has become "a virtual consensus among Jews all over the world, [even those] who have no connection at all with our movement, some of our own people now feel that a civil divorce is not sufficient, that we should [like the W.U.P.J. member, West London Synagogue] give some form of Reform *Get* ... There have been debates in the Conference on it … It is almost a classic question in Reform …"

Why now? How account for the persistence of this question *dafkeh* now, in this generation of Reform rabbis? For a clue, turn back to 1948, date of the establishment of The New State.

From its inception, Medinat Israel incorporated Orthodoxy into the structure of its politics and government: A "Religious Bloc" in the electorate, Knesset and Cabinet; a Ministry of Religions over marriage, divorce and inheritance: a federally appointed Chief Rabbinate. This integration of "Church" and State is, of course, a hangover from the *'halakha'* of the late unlamented British Mandatory period. Nevertheless, Orthodoxy makes the most of this authority over the lives of all Israelis, most of whom—like the rest of world Jewry —are non-Orthodox.

The achievement by their brethren in Israel of such impressive power—a heady brew—intoxicates certain Orthodox elements here in the United States. It has produced a rash of truculence with the attendant syndrome: throwing their weight around, making frightening noises and threatening gestures. Symptomatic is the threat to disqualify remarriages of couples divorced without benefit of clergy, as well as the issue of such remarriages, labeling the offspring *mamzerim* and refusing to solemnize their marriages.

Intimidated by this sound and fury, some colleagues urge us to give a *Get* too. Some suggest that we send civilly divorced persons to the Orthodox Bet Din; others, that we provide our own make Reform-style *Get* ; still others, that we establish C.C.A.R. *Battay Din* for this purpose.

The arguments mustered for Reform *gittin* have to do with *halakha*, "logical consistency," and *akhdut*. As for *halakha* with or without *gittin*, to the Orthodox none of the

marriages we solemnize are *halachically kosher kiddushin*—
e.g., we have no truly *halakhic ketubah,* and no proper *chupah*
(not canopy, but consummation is the real meaning and
requisite).

If we are to follow traditional *halakha in toto,* wherein
are we Reform? Yet if we make exceptions, how will whatever we do be acceptable to the Orthodox? (Will not the
Bet Din refuse a *heksher* to the caterer who is not *shomer
Shabbat*—regardless of his scrupulosity in separating milk
from meat dishes?) No halfway measures will satisfy the
constitutionally implacable. Each concession encourages
their self-righteousness, whets their appetite for all-out,
unconditional surrender.

Assuming that we put aside considerations of logical
consistency and resort to the Orthodox *Bet Din* just for
gittin, not only do we then abdicate our authority in this one
respect (which must inevitably lead to other abdications)
but we run the risk of subjecting ourselves and others to
what can be distasteful consequences. Have you ever sent
an Orthodox divorcee to a *Bet Din* because her legally divorced ex-husband refuses to give her a *Get* unless he is
paid for the inconvenience? Occasionally, I have been able
to confirm her story from the very lips of the pious chair-
man of the *Bet Din* himself, *viz.,* that that ecclesiastical
body will do nothing to make the recalcitrant and vindictive husband grant the "religious" divorce, or rebuke him
for his avarice. On the contrary, I have even heard this:
"Her new fiancé is plenty rich: what will it hurt him to give
the former husband the few hundred dollars he wants?
This new husband can surely spare it; the old one can certainly use it."

Or do we contemplate asking the *Bet Din* to invite us
to sit in on their deliberations when a Reform Jew's case is
being heard?

On the other hand, if we institute our own Reform procedures for *gittin*, a local or regional C.C.A.R. *Bet Din*, how-will that help *akhdut*? Would any decisions or documents of a Reform ecclesiastical court be *kosher* to the Orthodox? We do not have to speculate as to the reaction of Orthodoxy to Reform *gittin*. Some liberal Jews in Britain do have their own form of *Get* and, as Freehof says,

> The results have not been an increase of Jewish unity. On the contrary, the *Bet Din* has been infuriated at them and has issued a special pamphlet against them for presuming to meddle in matters that do not concern them ... If we think of increasing Jewish unity, the plan will fail, because no variation from all the detailed laws of *gittin* could be countenanced by the Orthodox. To them, our *Get*, if we give one, would be a travesty.

Then why do it at all? Because it is *halakha*? Because traditionally, it was the function of the rabbi both to initiate and to dissolve marriages?

We live in an age of specialization. In the era when it was appropriate and necessary for rabbis to officiate at divorce proceedings, the *Bet Din* handled all Jewish legal matters. This is no longer the case. There was a time when the only record of marriage, divorce, birth or death of a Jew was that in the archives of the Jewish community. That situation no longer prevails. There was a time when Jews had no attorneys, judges or legal officers other than rabbis. This is no longer true.

I do not lament these changed circumstances. In our day, I cannot see it as the function of the rabbi to participate in the dissolution of a marriage, particularly not as the *halakha* conceives *gittin*. A man may divorce his wife on any excuse at all—even for one as trivial as her incompetence as a cook. If he finds her so objectionable that he can no longer endure her presence, of course he ought not be required to remain married. But as Reform Jews, committed to the equality of sexes, must we not grant the female partner to a marriage equal rights in matters of divorce? This is plainly un-*halakhic*: the *halakha* accords the right of divorce only to the male partner to a marriage.

It is true, the *halakha* provides that if the husband has a disgusting disease or occupation (leprosy; gambling with dice or racing doves), she may appeal to the *Bet Din*, who may decide to flog her reluctant mate until he voluntarily agrees to divorce her. Does any mid-twentieth century *Bet Din* have such persuasive power? Divorce, Orthodox style, is still very much a one-sided affair.

The rabbi in our day is no longer the juridical factotum of yesteryear; no more the all-in-one judge, lawyer, clerk-of-the-court, community archivist, which he once was. Like priest and minister, the rabbi is today a purely religious functionary. When the state licenses him, he may bind in holy wedlock a couple if the state has issued a specific license for their marriage. Without both licenses—his to officiate and theirs to be married—no valid marriage can take place.

No state authorizes rabbis to dissolve marriages. With the civil divorce decree, the dissolution of a marriage is complete. No *Get* adds a milligram to the weight or effectiveness of the civil decree. With that civil divorce alone, and a new marriage license, any Jew is now free to be remarried by any of hundreds of Reform rabbis. With only a *Get* and no civil divorce, no one can legally remarry and no one can legally solemnize such a marriage. For all practical purposes then, the *Get* is superfluous—a needless expense.

Assuming you set up procedures for Reform *gittin* ... would you grant them before, after or instead of legal divorce proceedings? If before, to what end? Your *gittin* will

not license them to be legally remarried. What if your ecclesiastical court orders the divorce and the civil court pro-
hibits it? Will your Reform court try the case after the civil
divorce? What if the state divorces them and your court refuses to? In either case, what an uncomfortable position
you have placed them in!

Or are you going to copy the current American Orthodox *Bet Din* practice—of being a rubber stamp for the
legal court's decision? To what purpose? Just so you can
force people through the process of coming also under
your authority, as well as that of the state? That is double
jeopardy! Will you hold over them the threat that you may
not grant the divorce, even though the state does? Is it pu-
nitive power that we seek or just any kind of power; even
the mere shadow of the substance of power?

What about the argument that rabbis who are involved in the process of solemnizing marriages should be
involved also in the process of dissolving them?

When a building needs to he demolished, you do not
recall its architect; any competent wrecker will do. Just because we are in at the start does not mean we must be in at
the finish. The obstetrician is not a mortician. And if we
say, "Yes, but do not rabbis officiate at circumcisions as
well as funerals…?" Of course, but in the latter case, the
rabbi officiates only to console the bereaved; he does not
make coffins, sell cemetery plots or dig graves. Similarly he
officiates at a *brit milah*—only to bless the new-born babe,
not to operate on the child's foreskin.

I submit that it is neither necessary nor advisable for
rabbis, who ought to be concerned with helping to build
family life, to participate in its destruction. Should we become involved in a threatening divorce? Yes, by all means—
long before the divorce takes place—to prevent its hap-

pening. But if we fail, we ought to take ourselves completely out of the way when the wrecking crew takes over.

Are we really worried about the threat of the Orthodox rabbinate: that it may refuse to recognize the legitimacy of remarriages we solemnized *sans Get*, and therefore the legitimacy of the offspring of such marriages? The refusing-to-recognize game is one which any number can play. If the Orthodox wish to climb so far out on the thin limb of their particular interpretation of Judaism, they are welcome to their role of twentieth century Karaites; (the *Shulkhan Arukh* their *Torah mi-Sinai*).

Non-Orthodox Jews, who constitute the enormous majority of contemporary Jewry, may very well let intransigent Orthodoxy wither on the vine. To conclude as we began—with Freehof:

> We had better continue as we are. History is on our side. We represent the living facts of Jewish life. I do not believe it would be helpful to us, or to the Jewish people, to proclaim that civil divorce is not enough, that some sort of *get* should be given, and that all the thousands of marriages and the tens of thousands of children born of a remarriage after civil divorce are illegitimate. 🐝

❧ Anent Mysticism...
A Personal Opinion

There are two distinct, drastically different, indeed, dia-
metrically-opposed intellectual biases. There is the positive
affirmation approving, even glorifying view that the verbal
statements of certain revered authorities or texts are not
only objectively true but constitute *The Truth*, are consequently, not only real, but the most significant reality. The
predilection for mysticism (Kabbalah) among Jewish thinkers is most natural. It is imbedded in the Hebrew language
itself. This classical tongue discovered by our people in Ca-
naan, epitomizes this predilection in one word: *davar*, which
means both "word" and "thing".

The negative, rationalistic view insists that words by
themselves must not be confused with things. Rationalism
teaches that mysticism is a confounded confusion of words
with reality. Bishop Anselm of eighth-century Italy, France,
and England averred: "In my mind is an Idea of God. It is
the idea of Perfection. In the very nature of perfection, it is
unflawed; it is lacking in nothing and is, therefore, not lacking in existence. How could that idea get into my mind if it
did not correspond to an objective, external reality outside
my mind, in the vast universe?" That "proof" of God's existence was accepted as valid by philosophers and their disciples from the time of Anselm (1033- 1109) to that of Immanuel Kant [Eighteenth Century], who thought, "In my
head is an idea of one hundred gold dollars, but they do not

exist in my purse or pocket." Only God can say, "Let there be…" and the thing comes into being, is created by God's utterance—or so Scripture states. Only sleight-of-hand "magicians" do this, but they don't expect to be taken literally by anyone but young children.

In response to Anselm's preposterous "proof," Kant offered this simple refutation: "In my mind is the idea of one hundred perfect gold dollars: shiny, round, metal coins. Sadly, though the mental picture is quite clear, I do not find their substance in my purse or pocket."

When one repeats the cliché, "nothing is either good or bad, but thinking makes it so" we remain entirely within the realm of thought, language, words, ideas inside one's head. But those words, themselves, do not amount to substantive things. They are just thought inside the brain of the speaker and, perhaps, of the listener. But no material substance is created by the "idea". Only God's words create whole vast parts of the Universe; or, at least as we are told by the author of Genesis 1: "And God said, 'Let there be…' and it was so."

So with the *sefirot* of the Kabbalah: At the peak of the cone is God; one level lower are the angels, underneath them, the prophets, then the sages, etc. Or so writes the author of the Kabbalistic classic, the *Sefer Yetzirah*, the "Book of Creation." Like the rest of this mystical work, these are thoughts or ideas that are uttered, heard, and , perhaps, believed by the faithful. But unlike God's verbal utterances, which bring into being all the elements of the Universe, with the exception of man, no Kabbalistic statement creates any objective thing. They begin and end with thought, ideas, words; which, of course, may inspire readers of the texts to produce things of substance. But the words, themselves, are not objective, material, substance nor, uttered by mortals, do words, by themselves, create anything. ❧

✿ Ritual in Reform Judaism
The First 194 Years

There is probably no reader of this book who cannot identify David Ben Gurion. He was an Israeli General and his people's first Prime Minister. However, he was a poor sociologist and a worse philosopher. That wouldn't matter, considering his other great achievements, like ruling a nation, which he told Lyndon Johnson consisted of more than two million prime ministers. And like beating back the hordes of attacking Moslem Arabs, Israel's closest neighbors and fiercest and most ruthless and implacable enemies. Howsoever, his academic talents and judgment were close to zero; which wouldn't have mattered, except that he attempted foolishly to be both philosopher and sociologist.

Once he was invited to address the faculty, students, administration, and supporters of Brandeis University. How that audience would have appreciated hearing from him about his life and long association with Israel when it was only a Zionist dream, and his career as warrior in defense of the sacred soil and his testing and triumphs as the prime minister of *Medinat Israel* and its foremost spokesman to all the world. But to the astonishment of that academically elite audience he had the colossal *chutzpah* and faulty judgment to go maundering for more than an hour on what he fondly imagined was philosophy. Any Republican President of the United States could do that successfully. Every Republican president does it all the time. But, as everyone knows, these men have platoons of knowledgeable speech writers able to produce a literate, informative, inspirational address on any topic the president requisitions; but Ben Gurion had no such platoons and unlike Democratic Presidents, e.g. Woodrow Wilson, Franklin Roosevelt, Jack Kennedy, and Bill Clinton, who wrote their own material, Ben Gurion had no academic credentials; no intellectual qualifications for what he undertook on that occasion. Moreover, he didn't have the sense to realize he was no scholar. For me, he was an unforgettable embarrassment on that occasion. I was glad for, grateful to, and proud of, the Brandeis sophomores who refrained from derisive laughter at Ben Gurion's pathetic performance that day.

Early in Ben Gurion's stint as Prime Minister, while pondering the problem of the elementary right of all Jews to become citizens of Israel, he felt he had to have a clearcut definition of "Jew," a definition which, of course, existed and stills exists nowhere.

Perhaps the closest thing we have to a definition of who is a Jew is the legal decision, handed down by New York State's highest court. This was the end result of the suit brought by a world class medical scientist with a German sounding name (which I cannot remember). He sued *The Jewish Encyclopedia* for including his photograph and biography. Having converted to some denomination of Christianity, he sued the editors and publishers for (guess what?) "defamation of character" in identifying him as a Jew. He contended that this "false" identification damaged his standing with Christian colleagues and his relationship to his grown-up children, who did not know he was a convert to Christianity. Appeal after appeal, he lost his suit until it came to the high court, which decided that "He is a

Jew who says he is, or whom society generally regards and refers to as a Jew."

Undoubtedly, Ben Gurion was not aware of the case or the verdict. In any event, he went about trying to find the answer he thought he needed in order to decide which of the seekers of citizenship in Israel were to be admitted and which excluded. So he wrote to those he considered to be expert authorities asking each to send him a definition. I never heard what the answers were or what he did with them. I assume that the responses to his request were disappointing and discouraged him from publishing the results.

Whatever the views of Ben Gurion's expert authorities on the subject of defining a Jew, actually there is no such authority and there is no consensus beyond, perhaps, the verdict of the high court of the State of New York.

But while the search for definition made a newspaper item here and there, perhaps on a back page, Professor Abraham Cronbach, a great Jewish thinker, who taught social studies at HUC, deplored the whole quest. Cronbach was a scientific person, a philosopher, a social justice activist, a poet, a mystic, a humanist, a pacifist, a very gentle anti-Zionist, a Reform rabbi, an expert sociologist, as well as a Hebrew grammarian, a renaissance man, and one of two Jewish saints I have had the privilege of knowing. The other was Rabbi Leo Baeck, head of the Berlin *Gemeinde*, and, undoubtedly, the leading Jew in Germany; and clearly the most revered Reform rabbi in the world in the first half of the Twentieth Century.

Abraham Cronbach regarded the search for a definition of "who is a Jew" as a pursuit in which no rabbi should participate because it was exclusionary, intended to disqualify as a Jew anyone who did not fit the definition. Instead, said Cronbach, rabbis and all good Jews should be interested and involved in helping to make good Jews and he indicated the ways Jews could become useful, exemplary, admirable and precious.

He said, "A Jew is good in proportion to the number of Jews, Jewish ideals, Jewish causes, and Jewish institutions which he knows, understands, on occasion serves, and, if possible, loves." There are, of course, limitless possibilities of growth in this pursuit of Jewish excellence. There is no limit to the extent of one's knowledge of Jews or Jewish causes or to the frequency of the occasions for service or the depth, warmth, or sincerity of our love.

I wanted to say this up front so that you could carry away from this evening a positive message. From here on, my analysis of the roller coaster ride of ritual in the life of Reform Jews and synagogues may be less inspirational, informative, but perhaps not inspiring.

I'm going to talk about religious ritual, and my perspective is that of most of the prophets of Israel. The best of them, Amos, Joel, Micah, Jeremiah, and Isaiah, have little affection or esteem for religious rituals.

When I see people in the synagogue bowing and bending toward the holy ark, or standing higher and higher on their tiptoes when they say "*kadosh, kadosh, kadosh...*" what I think is that they are saying they have a low opinion of God's intelligence. They treat Him as one treats a small child or a feeble-minded person or a foreigner who may not fully understand English, to all of whom you make gestures to clarify the meaning of your words. I think it is an insult to God to have to show what you mean when you say, "We bow the head and bend the knee," by bowing your head, genuflecting, etc.

At the Hebrew Union College, in my time, there was a brilliant young professor of education, Dr. Abraham N. Franzblau, whom I recall for many reasons, but one especially—his statement, namely: "That before you can begin to teach a class anything try to *learn* them. That", he reminded us, "is not bad grammar." What he was getting at, of course, was the necessity to know where your students are coming from and where they are at; and to do that you've got to study them. I'm beginning the process now, with this class.

Now I'm sure most of you think you know a good deal about Judaism; but let's find out. To begin with, something simple: Would any of you care to volunteer to tell me what the phrase *Bar Mitzvah* means? From what language do the words *Bar Mitzvah* come?

No, they are not Hebrew. They're Aramaic, a cognate language several versions of which were widely spoken in a large area of Asia Minor in Bible times, about three millennia ago.

Literally, *Bar Mitzvah* means "Son of Commandment" not a very illuminating translation; actually, it refers to a boy of thirteen and it also designates a ceremony usually held in the synagogue, a puberty rite. It was a replacement in the Fourteenth Century for a somewhat more explicit practice that was perhaps a thousand or more years old at the time. The precursor of *Bar Mitzvah* was known as *Bar Ohn'shin*. This practice consisted of bringing a boy, when he showed signs of puberty, and exposing his genital region to the elders of the community. The minimal signs of oncoming manhood were two hairs on his *mons veneris*. This was the practice for a thousand years or more until the Fourteenth Century. Quite evidently, it took a thousand years or more for our self-styled "sages" to wake up to the realization that this was a nasty practice; inconsiderate and fundamentally cruel, embarrassing to the boy and otherwise totally stupid on the part of our medieval "sages." What if the boy never showed such signs? Why then the whole community would know that he was a *tum-tum*, (that's Hebrew; it means "a sexless individual"). He would probably become friendless and certainly spouseless after this knowledge was broadcast, which, of course, it would be, all over the *shtetl* in less than an hour. But after about a thousand years, our sages decided to drop the old practice and adopt a new one. They would no longer expose the private parts of a pubescent boy to the scrutiny of the town's elders. They would begin now to assume that by the time he was thirteen years old a Jewish boy had achieved the requisite physical condition and stood at the verge of manhood.

They called the new practice by an old name, *"Bar Mitzvah"*. (In Mishnaic times, until the Second Century CE, it simply meant a boy at puberty). When it became a ceremony, it was never a uniform practice and still isn't today; but it took place in the synagogue at a service where the Torah was read, which could be on Shabbat or Yom Tov or during the week, on Monday or Thursday. Bar Mitzvah began by being an opportunity for familial ostentation, for the family to show off, if the boy was really bright and could exhibit his familiarity with Torah and prophetic text. If he was an *illui*—a young genius in Hebrew lore—he might deliver a *pilpul*, an intricate lecture on some recondite talmudic theme. Why not? From the time he was about five, he attended school from sunup to sundown for eight years where the whole curriculum was exclusively one subject. (What?) Torah. (Some *Torah Shebichtav*, the printed text, but mostly *Torah Sheh B'al Peh*, oral Torah, i.e., rabbinics.) Midrash, Mishnah, Gemara and the various commentaries on them.

If he was no intellectual dynamo, but had a reasonably good memory, they could engage an instructor, who could get him to memorize a speech written by some impecunious scholar, who did this among a dozen other chores to earn a meager living. If neither of these were a possibility, but if the family was well heeled, they could show off by the elaborate party they could throw, not only for the boy's relatives and friends and neighbors, but for the whole community. It was an occasion for much celebration, jubilation, congratulation, and gift giving. I have called the Bar Mitzvah ceremony a sentimental version of priapic worship. But I don't think I told you what the title of its predecessor, *Bar Ohn'shin* means. It is about as poor a piece of nomenclature as Bar Mitzvah. It means "son of punishments" and refers to the fact that until he could show off those two hairs on his pubis, his father was responsible for the boy's ritual sins of omission or commission and would be punished vicariously; but after the youngster was able to exhibit the requisite signs of his imminent manhood, he was personally responsible to God for his ritual sins. In any case, you now know where Bar Mitzvah came from.

When, in 1924, I matriculated at the Hebrew Union College to begin my eight years of study in order to become a rabbi, there were, to my knowledge, no Bar Mitzvahs held in Reform temples anywhere. They were completely superseded and replaced by Confirmation for boys and girls. The impulse was, on the part of the Reform movement, to make Jewish girls religiously ritually equal to boys. That was the Reform Jewish way, from the beginning of the Nineteenth Century in Germany. It was in the middle of that Century that Isaac Mayer Wise (no relation to Steve, but father of Jonah Wise) brought Reform Judaism to the United States.

I was ordained in 1932 and held pulpits in Cedar Rapids; Davenport; and Sioux City, Iowa; in Rock Island Illinois; and in Joplin, Missouri, for a total of ten years. In all that decade, I never officiated at a Bar Mitzvah service. It was not until, after World War II, in 1945, when I came from my chaplaincy in the Second Air Division in ETO to the Eastern Seaboard, in the Bronx, that I had my first congregation with Bar Mitzvah.

Reform set the pattern in the United States for the other Jewish denominations, which, at the time, were the Orthodox and the Conservative. Orthodoxy, of course, was born the day that Reform came into existence. Before that, there were other divisions in Jewish religious life, going back to the beginnings of Judaism. In Bible times, there were the Rechabites, the Essenes, the Sadducees and the Pharisees, later the Karaites and Rabbanites, then the Hasidim and the Mitnagdim, and today, the Orthodox, Conservative, Reform, Reconstructionist, Secularist, Zionist, and the exclusively ethnic forms of Jewishness or *Yiddishkeit.*

And the years dwindle down to a precious few: two thousand five, two thousand six, and we'll be celebrating the conclusion of the second century of the history of Reform Judaism. Two more years! Two thousand seven, two thousand eight, and, if I'm still alive, I'll be observing the one hundredth anniversary of my one and only birth day, which, obviously, is the day, the absolutely only day, on which I was born.

In any event, in the first hundred years of Reform Judaism, (which was most all of the Nineteenth Century) blessed and directed by Reform rabbis, Reform Jews divested themselves, as individuals and as congregations, of burdensome ritual baggage most of it superstitious practices which our ancestors had been accumulating for millennia. We did that downsizing throughout the Nineteenth Century. During the next fifty years (the first half of the Twentieth Century) we relaxed and enjoyed the good, clean feeling of lightness and wholesome purity in being rid of so much rubbish that we never needed in the first place. But, inconsistently enough, during the last, most recent, half century, Reform has been busy re-ingesting almost all of the useless, worthless, needless stuff which it had spent a century (so much time and energy) unloading: grossly superstitious practices like smashing a glass by the groom at his wedding: This was in imitation of the antics of Polish and Prussian wastrels who were rich enough to be able to spend their days in their favorite indulgence, just drinking booze. They would finish their wassails by smashing the glass out of which they had been drinking by throwing it into the fireplace in the north wall of the banqueting hall. This was all part of their ongoing war with the spirits. These spirits were the ghosts of their dead ancestors who'd always come back to spoil the fun of their living descendants. Why? Because these spirits could no longer participate in these sensual human pleasures. Without bodies, they couldn't drink, or talk, or laugh, or smoke, or get drunk, or make love. Those pagan drunks wanted to get rid of these pesky spirits, so they offered them the last drops of wine they'd been drinking (after all, who knows how much wine, beer, or mead it takes for a ghost to get drunk and get lost. If the pagan boozer is lucky, maybe the glass will hit one or more spirits). Perhaps the noise of the glass breaking will scare them away. Anyway, the spirits are evil and enjoy destruction; so it may appease them to watch the glass being broken. Those primitive pagan boozers knew what they were doing; but I doubt whether the Jews, who imitate them today, have the foggiest notion what they are imitating and what non-orthodox rabbis tell them is usually pious, pretty, pseudo-poetic piffle.

When Jews began copying this pagan practice in the late Middle Ages, their rabbis excoriated them for imitating *prosteh goyim* ("vulgar Gentiles"). But when the religious leaders' protests didn't stop the practice, the Jewish holy men decided to convert the practice, make it Jewish. How? By getting their parishioners to believe that this pagan folk-custom was in memory of the destruction of Jerusalem and the Holy Temple there. To reinforce the Jewishness, the rabbis insisted that when the glass was broken, all the wedding participants and guests would begin to sob, weep loudly, and recite the 137th Psalm, with its words, "If I forget thee, O Jerusalem, let my right hand wither. May my tongue stick to the roof of my mouth if I set thee not above my chiefest joys" (and what could be a chiefer joy than a *chatunah*?). However, have you ever seen this done at a wedding? So much for the inanity of nuptial glass breaking.

Then, there is the cutting of a garment you're wearing (or, minimally, a cheap substitute, a black ribbon pinned onto it). This practice was to persuade the ghost of the departed that with him or her gone, you'll never need or care to dress up again; you won't want ever to go any place any more, that's how grief stricken and woebegone you'll be now that your dear departed has departed from this earthly scene. Why do Jews do this? Why do they ignore what the prophet, says, "tear your hearts and not your garments" (and, incidentally, the prophet is Joel, not Elijah).

And, of course, there is the covering of mirrors in the house of mourning so that the image (which, to the primitive mind, is the soul of the decedent) is not caught in the looking glass and thus kept from being taken to the cemetery and buried with the corpse, but stays to haunt the house and scare people.

Then, there is our people's blatant, foolishness, (to say nothing of the involved immorality) in perpetuating the colossal absurdity of *Kol Nidre*: a musically lovely chant, consisting of a silly paragraph of Aramaic words express-

ing the desire that all the vows, oaths, pledges and promises one makes from now until a year from now be nulli-
fied, in advance, before they are even uttered.... And so
much other pious rubbish....

But, for our purpose, last, the lollapalooza of superstitious garbage: *tashlich*, when some Jews go to a creek, pond,
or other body of water and shake out of their outer garments the bread crumbs they put and carry there, food,
wherewith they feed the devil, who lives in a hole in the
bottom of the sea. They do this during the *Yomim Nora-im*
to pacify "Old Nick", because annually, at that time of
year, this nasty fellow is peevish, jealous of the Blessed and
Holy One, who gets so very much attention and praise from
His chosen people, particularly at this time of the year. And
the pious Jew wants to take no chances, so he takes out accident, sickness, and life insurance by appeasing, in this
way—i.e., by food and flattery—this utterly evil character
who produces so much misery and pain for humankind.

I want you to know, without any doubt whatever, that
I am not making up any of this. I have all of it from studying the lifetime research of a renowned, world-class Tal-
mudist, who was also a scholarly expert in anthropology
and comparative folklore and religion. He was Professor
of Rabbinics, Dr. Jacob Lauterbach of HUC during all the
first half of the Twentieth Century.

Among his erudite writings was one book-length essay on the breaking of a glass at weddings and another on
tashlich. To anyone with a taste for close reasoning and
well-documented research in this area of Judaism, Lauterbach's work is as riveting as a detective mystery story is to
that kind of addicted reader.

Well, why have Reform Jews rejected the wisdom of
our Reform Jewish predecessors and renewed such practices as Bar Mitzvah, nuptial glass-breaking, and the rest,

including *tashlich*, and, God knows, maybe *shlog'n kapores* next year? *Shlog'n kapores* is an Orthodox *minhag*, a ritual performed before Yom Kippur in which a boy takes a rooster, and a girl, a young hen, each to wave about their respective heads as they recite a formula requesting that Death (the *malach hamavet*) visit the fowl instead of themselves this year. Yes, there are traditionalist Jews who still practice this not-very-pretty, primitive custom.

So … tell me, what do we envy in *minhag-* and *Halakhah-* laden Orthodoxy that some of us yearn so to retrace our steps? Orthodoxy's spirituality? Its esthetics? Its popularity with the masses? (Statistically Reform in the United States outnumbers Orthodoxy at least four to one.) What, then?

Are we reluctant refugees from the Orthodox *shtiebel*? Let those who are furtive fugitives now openly return. The old-time *shul'n* are still doing business at their old stands. Personally, I walked away resolutely and gladly eight decades ago and I suffer no regrets, no nostalgic hankering to return. What I rejected in Orthodoxy then, and still reject, is precisely its obsession with externals, with routines and formulas. What appealed to me in Reform then, and what I still feel is Judaism's chief glory, is the vision and faith of our prophets. Are we disturbed by the behavior of jaded Jewish intellectuals, who, weary of their flirtations with strange flames at alien altars, now seek "peace of soul" in the dark embrace of catholicism—Christian, Jewish, Buddhist, or what have you? Shall we then attempt to lure such wayward spirits back to the synagogue by offering them the same kind of escape from reason and from the moral-social struggle … and call that Judaism?

Admittedly, there is much that is cold and empty in some contemporary synagogue services. But wherewith shall we fill the frigid void? Why, with the ritualism of Isserles? (Isserles was the *Ashkenazi* partner of the *Sephardi*,

Caro, as compilers of the *Shulḥan Arukh*). Why not with the glowing spiritual insights and the ardent moral fervor of Isaiah who exclaimed:

> "The Lord said, 'Because this people approach me with their mouth and honor Me with their lips, while their heart is far from Me, and their worship is mere empty forms devised by men and learned by rote, therefore, will I do an astonishing thing to this people: The wisdom of their sages will vanish, and the intelligence of their wise men will be confounded.'"

This prophesy of Isaiah (29.13) fulfilled many times in history, has today, amazingly enough, befallen the sages of that branch of Judaism—our own Reform—which pays the most pious lip service to the teachings of the Prophets.

It is certainly true of our times that men "wander from sea to sea" (and continent to continent) "thirsting for the word of God". They ask, 'Wherewith shall I approach the Lord and bow before God on high? Shall I approach Him with silken skullcap and prayer shawl made of Acrilan? Doth God take delight in a streamlined *Yizkor* service, or in myriads of gaily-colored *Chanukah* decorations? Shall we offer Him exquisite ritual pageantry as atonement for the emptiness of our souls, the fruit of our committees on ceremonies, as substitute for religious inwardness and moral-spiritual sensitivity and progressive social action?

Go to Bethel and sin, and to Emanuel and sin more, in that you bring Me, one year, your oratorical or operatic Confirmation spectacle, and the next your klieg-and-rheostat-lighted *Neilah* service, and march around your sanctuaries carrying My Torah whose contents your congregations cannot read.

For so you love to do, O Israelites, saith the Lord. I loathe, I despise your high-church antics, I cannot abide your episcopalianisms. What is the multitude of your rituals to Me? Who has required this of you? It has been told you what is good and what God wants of you: "To do justice, to love compassion, and to walk humbly with God."

When the Roman Empire was coming apart at the seams, soul-sick, its people dispirited, unhappy, the best its Caesars could manage was bread and circuses. With what remedial effect? Do we expect better results from "*Yiddishkeit*": from *tayglakh, latkes, hamentashen,* blintzes, knishes, *cholent, tszimess,* and the dramatic processional synagogue circling of *hakafot*?

Religion ought to be the expenditure of quantities of human effort to rise to some appreciation of values higher than the enjoyment of the pleasure of the senses, to an interpretation of life holier than materialism. But is not the enjoyment of show, of ecclesiastical ritual and sacerdotal pageantry precisely as sensual an experience as any other? Why, then, can we not see what the prophets saw so clearly? That all this is no less a sensual expression merely because it is performed at the *bimah*s of synagogues rather than on the stages of theaters.

For our present purpose, finally, I am saddened because of what I feel to be two reasons for the special interest in "*Shulhan Arukh* Judaism" just now. One factor, it seems to me, is the emergence of the State of Israel as a *fait accompli*. While Zionism was still only a hope and a task, it offered some Jews, who had never felt quite at home struggling with the abstract imponderables of Jewish philosophy and theology, liturgy and mysticism many comfortably concrete, practical things to do and talk about: *dunam*s of land, statistics of immigration, fundraising. Now these Jews have discovered an acceptable *ersatz*: dealing with tangible ecclesiastical paraphernalia: *tsitsit, mezuzot, b'samim* boxes, *kashrut, slichot,* the revival of Tisha b'Av *kinot,* and *tashlich.*

The other possible incentive (negative and disheartening) is the menace of war not only with the totally evil Taliban and Al Qaeda but with the whole deadly hate-poisoned hordes of the Islamic Moslem world, more than a billion strong. In such an evil time, the cowardly wimps and nerds of the Judeo-Christian world keep silent and fill in the silence with ceremonies.

They redundantly repeat tired old rituals instead of mustering the energy and exerting the enormous effort needed to translate prophetic vision from a pleasant manner of speaking into tireless and effective religious action; action that will move social justice beyond being a noble, but static, ideal into its rightful sphere of operation as the world's meaningful and vibrant way of life. 🌺

Paper presented at the Brotherhood Meeting of May 21, 2002, at Temple Ohabei Shalom, Brookline, MA

✿✿ What We Can Do
To Build a Better Union of American Reform Jewish Congregations

When I consider what is wrong with the way the UAHC [now, Union for Reform Judaism, "URJ"—ed.] operates I call to mind the conversation between a lawyer and his client during a trial in a courtroom. The client says to his attorney, "I need another lawyer."

"How come, " says his lawyer, "Don't you like what I'm doing?"

"Oh," says the plaintiff," You're all right in your way; but, you see, my opponent has two lawyers and while one of them is in front of the jury talking, the other one is at the table with the defendant, thinking; but when you're up there talking, there's no one doing any thinking."

When I was ordained, just seventy years ago, this coming May [2002], the Union was run by several colleagues who hadn't done very well as leaders of small congregations, and needed jobs. To save salary costs, it would be necessary to attract outstanding men in the rabbinate, the Union Board engaged these men of less than sterling leadership qualities. And, of course, they got what they paid for: Mediocrities who unproductively presided over the same dull routine patterns year after dull year. Until one year, at the Union Biennial, a brilliant colleague of ours blasted the organization to a state of wide-awake alertness with a master buglers' reveille call to real, radical reform.

He titled his message "While the Union Slept." That ringing alarm brought about the advent to successive Union
leadership of two charismatic colleagues: Maurice Eisen-
drath and Alexander Schindler. Their inventive programs
brought the Union up to date—their date—the Twentieth
Century—which, of course, has just passed into history.

It seems to me that what the Union needs today are
ideas, techniques and plans that might light up the road we
begin to travel now in the new century. I readily admit that
I am blessed with neither the prescience nor the *chutzpa*
that would enable me to outline even sketchily the shape
that such projects and programs might take. What I am
calling for is the selection by the wisest among us of the
best thinkers in our movement, people endowed with the
rare combination of brains and intense concern not just
for Jewish continuity , but endowed with a resolute determination to make Jewish knowledge and Jewish action
flourish and fulfill our people's potential.

We need to develop and encourage the growth of
think tanks or task forces that will, for example, experiment with methods of communication. These methods
have evolved over the ages from sign language to articulate
speech, to formal oral, literary production, to printing, to
convey thought and feeling by verbal message, then by
telephone, telegraph, radio, and, now, by multiple media,
including cinema and television and the internet.

Instead of producing printed records of successfully
tried and potentially useful information or inspirational
material or preserving them only on sound cassettes, we
might bring at least the high points of plenary session debates and the enlightenment and inspiration revealed or
developed in workshops at conventions. More than that,
and, perhaps more appreciated and effective, might be

video tapes of extraordinary, specially impressive projects successfully completed in individual congregations.

I can think, for example, of memorable shul-ins at Ohabei Shalom, some involving as many as 300 kids; sometimes tots with their parents, spending whole weekends inside the synagogue experiencing intriguing stuff for them to hear and see and do during all their waking hours. Had we put this all on video tape, it might be helpful to other congregations. I also recall dramatic productions entirely put together by synagogue members: Words and music, choreography, scenery, costumes, lighting, direction, the whole works and week-long combinations of art exhibits and concerts, all the painting, sculpture, ceramics, woven fabrics; and the duets, quartets, orchestras, choral groups, solos, vocal and instrumental music produced and directed by members of the congregation. Videos of these presentations could very well be useful as entertainment and as examples for other congregations to follow.

Competition for excellence between interest groups within a congregation and between congregations would surely improve the quality of these video productions. These tapes would compete regionally and nationally for the privilege of being part of libraries which would circulate such material to member congregations.

I am quite sure that better, more clever and inventive minds than mine could think of far more fascinating projects than these. All I am doing here is to suggest that such minds be brought together, organized, and encouraged to try. It just might awaken new life in the Reform movement in American Jewry. 🌼

❧ God and Synagogue

✿ This Crucial Ḥour

Judaism forged out of its experience a peculiar and price-less concept, namely, Divine Law or Torah and man's sub-jection to its rule. That idea became the dynamic essence of the ethics and religion of the Western world. To fortify the ideal, Judaism evolved through the centuries, a unique institution, the synagogue, as the instrument of Torah.

This ideal, envisioning God's will in the world as the supreme and sole standard of conduct, is threatened today on every battlefield. The names of the contemporary com-batants are new, but the alignment is as old as history.

Whether the legions of darkness call themselves Bab-ylonians, Romans, Germans, or Japanese, their purpose does not alter—to destroy the humanizing work of reli-gion, to substitute faith in power for the power of faith. The battle which began with the Mosaic challenge from Mt. Sinai has reached the zero hour in our time.

The synagogue stands then as an enduring symbol of what decent men in every age have fought to preserve against the destructive will of pagan brutes.

One of the greatest English scholars, Professor R. Travers Herford, wrote that the Jewish people, in all its long history did nothing more wonderful than to create the synagogue. "No human institution," said he, "has a longer continuous history, and none has done more for the uplift-ing of the human race."

The synagogue came into being as if by divine providence. Even while the Temple at Jerusalem still flourished on its holy hill, obscure groups of humble teachers gathered simple followers about them in tiny villages and great cities throughout the land of Israel, to expound the Torah, the moral law of God.

With the exception of a few titanic prophets, scourged as harbingers of doom, none foresaw that the proud Temple would soon be level with the dust.

Yet while priests sacrificed and Levites sang, the synagogue grew in the rich soil of Israel's longing for God and truth and prepared itself for the day when Priest and Levite would be silent.

Who could have foretold, that these tiny groups of poor students, their voices tense with intellectual and spiritual eagerness, were being designated by history as the saviors of Judaism and religion among men, as God's arm into the future?

According to our sacred lore, the synagogue had to be built on the highest elevation in any town. A community whose dwelling places or pleasure palaces towered above the sanctuary, courted ruin. The smallest village, if it contained but ten males, was required to build a house of worship. It is written, "Whoever lives in a city which contains a synagogue and fails to join it is not a good neighbor."

Why did the synagogue exercise such sway? Because it was for generations the pulsating center and heart of Jewish existence. Because it was the power-house which generated every energizing impulse in the religious social, cultural, philanthropic, and, in a larger sense, even the economic life of Israel. Because within its walls, Jews gathered to marry, bury, study, practice charity, plan their policy toward their secular masters—and pray.

The synagogue was the life blood of the Jewish people, the Ark of the Covenant which they built and rebuilt tirelessly, lovingly on every spot to which their exile-weary feet impelled them. It was the first thing which they constructed and the last thing they forgot on their pilgrimage throughout the centuries.

When we consider, therefore, the role of the synagogue in today's world, we cannot evade the striking comparison with its function up to a few generations ago. It would be futile to deny the unfavorable balance.

We are living in a secularized world, a medley of countless interests. In the place of one all–embracing highly-concentrated unit, the scientific, emancipated society of today has spawned a thousand specialized organizations.

When the ghetto walls crumbled in the nineteenth century, the Jew began to share in the "larger" world. He thought he no longer needed the synagogue. It cramped his style. To a very large extent, the disintegration and dilution of modern Jewish life stem from the diminished vitality of the syanagogue. Like a lighthouse from which the waves have receded to other shores, the synagogue still flashed its beacon light—but there were few to see and seek its guidance. And Jewish life foundered or, at best, found itself in strange ports.

When the world beckoned him, the Jew was so anxious to heed its invitaion, that he threw off what he deemed was the "dead weight" of the synagogue, like a runner doffing his outer garments.

In his unseemly haste, he made two fundamental errors. He believed that mankind wanted him without the synagogue, and he believed that he himself could live without it. Neither of these assumptions has met the trial of this, the most critical period in the modern history of Israel.

The crux of any intelligent view of the world's plight today is that Totalitarian anti-Semitism did not launch its brutality against the Jew alone, but against the whole religious fabric of the Western world, of which Judaism and the synagogue are the matrix, the underlying foundation.

It is an oft-repeated truism that Fascism exploits man as a soul-less tool of the idolized state. Religion looks upon each man as the child of God, endowed with dreams to be fulfilled, aspirations to be reached, potentialities for perfectibility.

This view of man *b'tzelem Elohim,* as "the Image of God," lies at the very core of Western Civilization. For one thing, it has bred democracy. Almost every statesman in the great democracies, especially President Roosevelt, has taken occasion to picture the democratic ideal as a religious doctrine. Why? Because the basis for man's equality consists in this: that every creature is endowed with a divine spark, breathes the breath of God.

In fact, all the progress mankind has made in the "humanization" of relations between people, whether they were rulers and citizens, or employers and workers, has issued from the insistence on the sanctity and therefore the inviolability of the human being.

This crucial attitude was the elemental mother of Jewish thinking. It began with "creation" in the first chapter of the Bible, and its clear light has rested on the brow of every Jewish sage—a vision of matchless grandeur, infinite application, and saving power. And the thrilling story of mankind is the record of the struggle of this idea against the doctrine of brute might.

Today this conflict is crystal clear. With negligible exceptions, the spokesmen of decency confess that victory in the peace as well as in the war will mean a return to the great elemental religious truths, which alone can redeem the world from collapse.

To be a real German, in the Nazi sense, it was necessary to have broken all connection with the synagogue—yea, to the third and fourth generation.

But to prepare for citizenship in tomorrow's world, a world where humanity and justice and morality will be respectable again, where men will again believe in Divine Love and Divine Law, it is more than ever necessary that we cling to our faith and the synagogue which enshrines it.

The renegade Jew who forsook the synagogue, to embrace a wider cause, no longer hears (if he ever did) the flattery of his neighbors. He has succeeded only in weakening the spiritual forces of survival in a desperate hour. As one whose forebears lifted up the standard which men must save if they are to save themselves, the de-synagogued Jew is like a leader who deserts his army in the day of battle.

The synagogue is not a barrier but a vehicle to the larger life. Israel confronts a new alternative. A generation ago, our liberals assumed that they were selecting the world *or* Judaism. Now they must decide between the world *and* Judaism, or the extinction of the common inheritance of morality and beauty whereby the best in man may some day conquer the beast in man. The choice applies especially to our American citizenship. Louis Brandeis said, "There is no inconsistency between loyalty to America and loyalty to Jewry. The Jewish spirit, the product of our religion and experience, is essentially American. Not since the destruction of the Temple have the Jews in spirit and in ideals been so fully in harmony with the noblest aspirations of the country in which they live." Loyalty to the synagogue is more than merely compatible with patriotism.

It is a moral obligation, a pre–requisite to the kind of patriotism which goes beyond mere flag worship to the fundamental ideals which the flag embodies. Democracy without religion has no sustenance.

The synagogue can quicken Israel to its obligations to the outer world. It can also enrich immeasurably the inner world, both as a Jew and as an individual.

What makes us Jewish? Do we inherit the prophets and sages and saints in our blood? Not at all. The magnificent heritage of our past must be re-won by each of us through our own contact with the thoughts and ideals of our ancestors.

The glorious vision of Isaiah who heralded an era when swords would be beaten into plowshares and spears into pruning hooks; the humility and gentleness of Hillel, who admonishes us to refrain from doing unto others what we would not have them do unto us; the God-enthralled courage of Akiba,who perished on a Roman rack, literally torn to pieces, because he would not desist from teaching the Law; the flaming heroism of the Maccabees, who purified the Temple of the pagan profanation; the intellectual genius of Maimonides who united faith with reason in quest of God; the mystic longings of Halevi and Gabirol, who soared to God on the wings of poetry—an unbroken chain of sages and martyrs and warriors and lawgivers and psalmists, from Abraham to Einstein, from Moses buried in an unknown grave to Joseph Trumpeldor, whose humble mound overlooks the colony in Palestine which he shielded with his life—thirty centuries of striving and searching and hoping. There is our Judaism. We are proud, genuine human beings, we are self-respecting Jews by virtue of our wish to learn our heritage and continue it, to absorb the spiritual strength of our fathers and to preserve it, to know the example of our saints and to send it on undimmed into the future.

Nothing can crush a people fortified by the infiltration of an ancient cultural treasure into its bone and sinew. Whatever armament we Jews may fashion for self-defense, our most impregnable bastion remains within—the knowledge and recollection of our past as a people. The most dangerous hurt that can come to us is the loss of pride and inner dignity. Once we sever our connections with self-knowledge, once we have no roots, we are a beleaguered army cut off from its source of supply. An informed, self-integrated Jewry, conscious of its mission and its spiritual aristocracy, will be above time and fate, partner to eternity and victor over dictators who strut and have their hour and cease to be.

Finally the synagogue's function, more now than ever perhaps, is to strengthen and deepen our faith in God. Collective ritual, communal prayer are a medium, a means to that end. Their significance and effectiveness depend, however, on what we bring to them. They can only be the external voice; it is the heart which must speak.

Despite the criticism which has been directed against the synagogue service—and some of it comes from earnest and sincere persons—the chief fault lies not with the prayers, but with the pray-ers.

Faith is what we need. Science has constructed the most complex material civilization that has ever been put in human hands, but only faith can fashion it into a thing of beauty. How shall we come by faith? Well, God is not so much defined as experienced.

Often He comes as but a moment's sacrament, a luminosity that flashes across the pathway of our lives—and then departs. In the remembered radiance of that insight we pass our days, and each of them bears a ray of its gleam.

Never was our spiritual need greater than it is today. Peril and insecurity have sharpened our hunger for the Divine Assurance. Prayer in synagogue, if we would only release our inhibited souls to its message, will usher us into the Divine Presence.

The classic statement of the synagogue's aim is threefold. It is a *beth hakneses*, a "house of assembly"—in what fellowship can we more fruitfully assemble than in the fellowship of service to the idea of man's inborn divinity. It is a *beth hamedrosh*, a "house of teaching"—what can we more needfully teach to the world and to ourselves, than the inspiration of Israel's past. It is a *beth tefilah*, a "house of prayer"—for what can we more profoundly pray than faith, faith in the eternal loving care of God, in the essential goodness of man, in the ultimate victory of right. 🌺

♣❀ The Ḥallahs in the Ark

I want to tell you the story of *hallah*s in the ark. Most of you know about raisins in the ark at Temple Ohabei Shalom. There is no mystery or humor involved in that. Someone puts the little red boxes of raisins there during the day on Friday and on *Erev Shabbat* and on Shabbat morning, when the congregation recites *Aleynu*, children are invited up to the *bimah* to stand before the ark and Rabbi Lipof gives each child a box of raisins.

This is about *hallah*s in the Ark. It happened five hundred years ago. The place is Israel; the scene is the quaint village of Tz'fat and its little *shul*. Half a millennium ago, when the Jews of Spain and Portugal were expelled from the whole Iberian Peninsula, they scattered over all of Europe and North Africa to France, Germany, Poland, Greece, Turkey, Morocco, Algeria, and Egypt; some went to the Holy Land. Among them was Jacobi. Jacobi was a shoemaker, not just a cobbler who repairs shoes. He made all kinds of shoes from all kinds of leather. He was a careful skilled craftsman who enjoyed his trade. He was a round man, with a round face, a round body. He was even a little bowlegged. A kind man; but the thing that everybody said about Jacobi was that he was very religious; so pious; so devout.

He would attend services every Shabbat and listen intently to what the rabbi was saying, which was a little odd, since Jacobi spoke a sort of Spanish called Ladino, while the rabbi spoke Hebrew. But still, Jacobi would screw up his face and squint his eyes and listen with all his might trying to hear and understand every word. On three successive Sabbaths—*Shabbat Trumah, Shabbat Va-Yak-heyl,* and *Shabbat P'kudey*—the rabbi in his sermon spoke of *lechem panim,* the twelve loaves of bread which were put on display each week on a table in the sanctuary when the holy temple still stood in ancient Jerusalem. Jacobi understood *lechem,* the word for bread, and *Elohim,* for God. He also used his imagination to fill in the rest. He got so excited that he ran home to tell his wife the amazing news.

"Esperanza," he said, "Guess what I found out today? God eats bread! You are the best baker in the whole country. So this week make some *pan de Dios,* 'God's bread,' and I'll bring it to God."

That week, Esperanza assembled the very best ingredients. She mixed them all together and added her own best skill. Then she kneaded the bread with love, and baked the loaves with patient, painstaking care.

Jacobi proudly carried these loaves to the synagogue. "*Senor Dios,*" he said, when he entered the *shul,* "I've got Your bread. You'll love it. My wife, Esperanza, she's a wonderful baker. You'll eat every loaf, enjoy every slice, every crumb." And with that he took the bread and put it into the *Aron Kodesh,* the "Holy Ark" and left.

Some time after he left, the *shamash,* the synagogue's caretaker, entered. "*Ribbonno shel olam,*" he said, "you know I love working here in this lovely holy place. That's what I want most in this world. But it's seven weeks now that I've been working, and I have not been paid anything yet. I need you to do something—maybe a miracle! Yes! You should make for me a miracle, and I'm trusting you to do it. Maybe you've done it already. Maybe if I open the ark the miracle will be there." The *shamash* walked to the ark and opened it, and there, indeed, was the miracle he'd prayed for: twelve loaves of beautifully baked fresh bread—two for the first Sabbath meal, two for the second, two for the third, and one loaf left for every day of the rest of the week.

The next day when Jacobi and Esperanza opened the ark and saw that there was no bread left there, you should have seen the look of love that passed between them. The next week it was the same, and the week after that it was the same. The *shamash* learned to have faith in God, but if he stayed at the synagogue too much or came to work too early there was no miracle, no bread.

So thirty years went by. One day, thirty years later, Jacobi came to the synagogue with his load of bread. "*Senor Dios*, I know your bread has been lumpy lately. Esperanza's arthritis. She can't knead the dough the way she used to. Maybe you could do something for her. If you did, you'd eat better." Jacobi put the bread in the ark and started to leave, when suddenly, the rabbi showed up and grabbed him.

"What are you doing?" the astonished and angry rabbi demanded. "I'm bringing God his bread", Jacobi replied.

"Blasphemer! God doesn't eat bread or anything else!"

"Well, God's been eating Esperanza's bread for thirty years!"

The rabbi and Jacobi hid to see if they could figure out what was going on here. No sooner did they hide than in came the *shammas*. He began to mutter, "I hate to bring this up, Lord, but you know your bread's been lumpy lately. Maybe you could talk to the angel who does the baking." But he reached in anyway to take the bread, when suddenly the rabbi jumped out and grabbed him. The rabbi began to yell at the two men, telling them how sinful they were. He went on and on scolding them until all three of them began to cry. Jacobi cried because he wanted only to do good to earn the reward for doing a *mitzvah*. The rabbi cried because all this happened as a result of his sermons about the *lechem panim* on display in the ancient temple. The *shamash* cried because suddenly he realized that the miracle was at an end. There wasn't going to be any more bread.

Over the sound of their weeping, the three men heard loud laughter coming from the corner of the *shul*. They turned to see who that was laughing. It was the great mystic scholar of Tz'fat, Isaac Luria. He was shaking his head and laughing. He said, "Oh, rabbi, these people are anything but sinful. They are pious, devout models of religiosity. You should know that God has never had more pleasure than watching what goes on in your *shul* on Shabbat. For He sits with his angels and they all laugh with pure pleasure. I mean this man brings the bread and that man takes the bread and God gets all the credit, and you, rabbi, are guilty of inspiring it all with your sermons about display bread.

"Rabbi, you must beg these men to forgive you." Then he looked at Jacobi and he said, " Jacobi, you must do something even more difficult than what you've been doing for thirty years. You must bring your bread straight from Esperanza's kitchen directly to the *shamash*'s house; no detours to the Ark in the *shul* on the way, and you must know, understand, and believe with perfect faith, that God will be just as pleased. He will have just as much, if not more, pleasure than having you put it in the Ark." And so it was, and so it is.

Now what does this story tell us? That you should not put raisins in the ark and pretend that they are a present from God but instead let the ushers pass them out to the kids as they pass out of the chapel after the service? No. The story reinforces the teaching that just as you cannot do very much for an emperor because he's already got more of everything than everyone else, but you can please even an emperor by being kind or helpful to his children. So it is with God—only more so. There's nothing you can give directly to God because everything there is, is all His. He created it all. But you can please God very much by being kind and generous to His children, who are in need of your kindness and help. You want to say thank You to God for your blessings, share some of those blessings with His less well-endowed children, who need your attention, concern, and care. Whatever it is that you have and can spare and would enjoy giving as a gift to someone who needs and will use it. Amen.

❧ Preaching, Prophecy, and Politics

There are parishioners who call it "meddling" when the preacher speaks of anything in any way connected with politics.

A rabbi knows that he would be remiss in his duty as a teacher of the Jewish tradition if he failed to call the attention of his congregation to the moral issues in any political campaign or in any proposed legislation, or if he were silent about any malfeasance, misfeasance, nonfeasance, on the part of anyone "whom the people have set in authority—the President, his counselors and advisors, the judges, lawgivers or executives, and all those who are entrusted with our safety and with the guardianship of our rights and our liberties." Judaism is concerned about what men in public office do. Every Sabbath we pray for them in the very words just quoted from our prayer book. In their capacity as public servants, we feel it is our religious duty to urge them to come up at least to some part of our expectations.

Communicants of other faiths may consider it reprehensible or indelicate for a preacher to speak censoriously of the chief executive of the nation. But our people do not consider it indelicate at all. Our greatest preachers always felt it was their duty to do precisely that.

When King David misbehaved, Nathan the Prophet shook his accusing finger at the ruler of Israel and cried:

"Thou art the man." Did the monarch's lofty political position excuse him in the eyes of the Jewish preacher from an offense that would have been reprehensible had he been merely a private citizen? Quite the reverse. Nathan thought his high office made the king all the more culpable. Nor was Elijah meek or gentle in his denunciation of his King Ahab and Queen Jezebel. Of course, these rulers called Elijah a "meddler," a trouble-maker, an agitator. But the conscientious preacher must learn to endure more and worse than merely being called nasty names.

In his first utterances in the Bible book bearing his name, Amos excoriates the governments of Syria, Philistia, Tyre, Edom, Ammon, Moab, as well as of Israel. He denounces them for their sins against people.

When King Jeroboam's hired priest, Amaziah, rebuked Amos, called him a conspirator against the King of Judah, Amos could readily plead guilt to the charge. He relied on the confidence that if this be conspiracy, God was his fellow-conspirator.

The prophet Isaiah never hesitated to upbraid his weak and ineffectual king, Ahaz. In 731 B.C.E., Ahaz was paralyzed with fear because two northern kingdoms had formed a coalition against Jerusalem; Isaiah told Ahaz in no uncertain terms that any normal woman had more sense and courage than the king.

This is how the prophet put it: "While you, the king, are trembling helplessly like a leaf in the wind, any healthy young Jewish female may conceive and bear a son and name him Immanu-el [a popular-enough boy's name meaning, 'God is with us']. She will choose this particular popular name in order to shame your panic by her confidence, and by the time such a baby is old enough to express his food preferences, those enemies of ours, of which you are so frightened, will have vanished from the world's stage.

Why, O King, haven't you at least as much sense of the realities and as much intestinal fortitude as such a normal,
healthy young Jewish woman?" [Isaiah 7].

Israel's great preachers—the prophets—concerned
themselves in public affairs whenever the political situation impinged on human welfare, which is, of course, prac-
tically always.

Unlike politicians, the prophets were not always poli-
tic, not always diplomatic, in the manner in which they expressed their views. That is understandable. After all, the
prophets were not running for office. They weren't seeking votes in a popularity contest.

Did those old Jewish preachers take risks in boldly
speaking out on critical issues? Of course, they did. But
whoever imagined that religious leadership is easy, that
great preaching is some kind of sinecure?

The Hebrew prophets took a dim view of prudence.
Amos said: "In evil times, the prudent seek safety in silence." But he wasn't silent, or prudent, or safe. Instead, he
was what a good religious leader must be: courageous and
honest.

When Israel dwelt in Egypt land, the first and greatest
of our prophetic preachers, Moses, demanded of Pharaoh:
"Let my people go."

The emancipation of an oppressed minority in any
country is fundamentally a political problem and achievement: whether the liberation is accomplished by civil war,
by revolution, litigation, legislation, or by wholesale emi-
gration. But in Jewish tradition, the Exodus from Egypt
has always been regarded as a religious achievement, and
to this very day, more than three thousand years later, it is
recalled on every occasion in our religious calendar.

Is it not significant that when the ten basic commandments were given at Mt. Sinai, it was this political emanci-

pation which was the preamble to them all? It is by no accident that the opening sentence of the Decalogue does not read, "I am the Lord, your God, who made heaven and earth," or "I am the Lord, your God; believe in me and be saved," but "I am the Lord, your God, who brought you out of Egypt, who redeemed you from political, social, and economic bondage." For these are matters of spiritual concern to the people of Israel and to the religion of Israel.

Freedom, justice, the well-being of peoples, and peace among nations—are all political ideals. But with us, they are more: with us, they are religious passions.

Our religion was never a matter of sacraments, never confined to the things that are said and done inside a shrine or sanctuary. Religion to us is what a man carries with him when he leaves the sanctuary, what he takes to heart and translates into the words of his mouth as he speaks in the forum and in the marketplace, what he transforms into the work of his hands as he strives to build a fairer community and a better nation.

When Abraham bargained with God for the salvation of the doomed town of Sodom, he said, "Lord, will you condemn the whole place to destruction if You find as many as fifty righteous people in the city? Forty? Twenty? Ten righteous people in the city?" And God agreed that He would save Sodom if He found even ten righteous people in the city. "Notice," say our rabbis, "that Abraham did not ask God to save the city if fifty, or twenty, or ten righteous people were discovered in the town's churches, mosques, temples, or synagogues. No," say our sages, "Abraham knew that God would not be taken in by any sanctimonious piety inside a sanctuary."

The religion that counts is the religion that gets out into the city, that manifests itself in the working of righteousness in our towns and states, between men and men, between nation and nation.

This is our concern with political principles and issues and men and parties, our concern as religionists, as American citizens, as parents of children born and reared in this blessed land. 🪶

❧ Reform vs. Orthodox
The Essence of the Difference

The difference is the attitude toward rituals. There are no hard and fast Reform rituals. There is a common notion that the non-observant Orthodox are Reform because they may call themselves such. It is not the number or even the kind of rituals that distinguishes between Orthodoxy and Reform.

This is the difference: If you identify religion with ritual, you are Orthodox whether you perform any or few or no rituals. If they are the end, the aim, the goal, the purpose, the content, and the meaning of religion, you are Orthodox. If they are merely a means, and I emphasize *merely*, merely a means, a method, a technique, a way of enhancing moral, ethical, spiritual, cultural, religious ideals in living, then you are Reform.

In the one instance, the Orthodox, their rituals are an end. In Reform, they are a technique.

There are two attitudes toward ritual that there were in ancient times toward animal sacrifice: one high, and the other low. The low attitude regards sacrifice as a technique to appease, to satiate, to bribe God, to pay for His favors.

For what shall a man or woman live? It is that for which they would willingly die.

Is this just another of those impractical paradoxes of religion? Rather, I submit, it is one of the most obvious facts of life. All of us show what we live for by what we are willing to die for. Not that all the popular ways we have of killing ourselves are intelligent or worthy uses of life. We may, indeed, shorten our lives by tensions and overwork in the scramble for money or *kavod*, "glory." We may die of overindulgence in food, drink, drugs, and other dissipations. But who would willingly die for any of these? Which of these indulgences ever inspired anyone to martyrdom?

On the other hand has any mother ever died for her child? Has a father ever dashed in front of an oncoming truck or train to push his youngster out of the way—or maybe some child *not* his own? Has a young driver ever swerved off the road, wrecking his car and himself, in order to avoid running over some stray dog in the street? Have men in a sinking ship or a burning building ever stood aside to let women and children escape, or ever gone back into the flames to rescue some helpless invalid?

Has anyone ever been willing to die for the sake of decency, justice, goodness, truth? To risk life for the health, happiness, or security of others—his family, his people, his land? Yes, indeed, millions have.

In crises, when we respond spontaneously, almost instinctively—how well we do!

When the stakes are life itself, we behave admirably, religiously; we are willing to die for the right reasons, for reasons beyond self, beyond personal safety and comfort.

In our finest hours, we show what we are willing to die for. They are sublime values: kindness, tender concern, compassion, love for humanity. In crises we prove that we are willing to die for them. What, then, keeps us from living for them day by day?

The Torah reading for Rosh Hashanah tells the momentous story of the testing of Abraham—how he was called to prove his loyalty to the highest and best in life; his devotion to his God. As demonstration of his love he was asked to sacrifice—not his own life—but someone far more precious—his only child. What then occurred? Abraham who had already resigned himself to Isaac's death, suddenly regains his son. He had thought him lost and now discovers him reborn. What joy can be compared with regaining a child already deemed dead? Not even the gladness that greeted the same child's birth. Ask some parent who had received word that his son was lost in action and then learnt that his son still lived. When you have been with such a parent, you will understand even better the profound significance of this Rosh Hashanah story.

By his readiness to give up what he most prized, Abraham gained even more than he gave. By our readiness to risk all for a cause that is dearer than life, we are reborn.

Do you know of any souls so spiritually regenerated? In Israel there are thousands of them: people who had already considered themselves dead—visualized themselves as carbon or bone-meal, fertilizer or parchment, or soap, emerging from the horror-chambers of central Europe during our lifetime. These men and women and children who re-took their lives from the very jaws of death, have since shown themselves to be the very exemplification of the simple fact that no one lives to his full capacity as a human being who has nothing for which he would be ready to die.

They share with one another and with their children a faith in the future, and hold fast to that faith—for themselves, for you and me, and for all who long and labor and pray for a world where men will live out their days in decency and dignity.

Israeli survivors of the Holocaust do not envy us, nor our abundance. Overwhelmingly, those brands plucked from the flame feel wealthy enough, rich in the inner glow of awareness that they serve a good beyond itself, and in so serving, have achieved this good *for* themselves as *well.* They have that for which to live. It is those precious values, precisely, for which they have proved themselves quite evidently prepared to die.

Often I think of them, and of myself, and of us all, Americans and Jews. For what do we live? For what are we willing to die? How often do we sacrifice personal advantage or gain for principle?

Where would any of us be if there were not men willing to risk life, indeed to relinquish life, for an ideal? If Moses had been willing to compromise with Pharaoh; if our people were willing to barter their conscience for the approval of some Pope, or Mohammed, or Martin Luther, instead of risking their lives and often enough giving up their lives—what then? Why then, there would be no single soul alive anywhere this Rosh Hashanah to recite the *She-he-che-yanu* prayer: "Be praised. O Eternal our God, who has blessed us with life, sustained us against all odds and in Your mercy brought us in triumph to this New Year."

Do we live lives less courageous and meaningful than Abraham's only because there never comes to us such a call as came to him? Does God no longer try us as he did the Patriarch—to prove ourselves equal to the challenge of our ancient faith—to be reborn, re-created at His altar?

Alas, we are tried more often than we are aware. When, for example, by every medium of modern communication we are told that for the price of a set of automobile tires, we could rescue from extinction a family still suffering torment in Yemen or Ethiopia or some other Arab land—is it not the God of our Fathers who is calling us?—the God of compassion, *el rahum v'chanun, erech apayim v'rav chesed v'emet*—calling us to make this relatively small sacrifice in His name?

When we are asked to invest in the future of our people, to become builders and guardians of Israel, do we seize the opportunity to dip into our surpluses and buy the Bonds which bind us to our people and build their hope and guard their future and, indeed, our own?

The challenge comes in so many ways. So many times we are called upon to make a sacrifice, to inconvenience ourselves for the sake of Judaism, for the sake of stemming Jewish ignorance, or assimilation, or apostasy—for God's sake. Ask yourself: How well do I respond to the call?

We are asked to espouse an unpopular cause: for example, the fight against the introduction of sectarian religion in the public schools, against discrimination in housing, education, immigration, the struggle for justice for non-conformists, or the defense of a man who has himself championed such a cause. Do we heed the mandate of conscience, do we hearken to the still small voice of God speaking to us in the inner sanctuary of the soul? Or do we cringe from the discomfort of speaking out for life in preference to death whatever the consequences may be?

God *does* call us; He tries us constantly. But do we have any ideals for which we would even *die*?

For what are we living? What goals beyond the preservation of breath and blood in our bodies stir us to strong action? What causes do we place beyond and above our narrow concern for self-perpetuation and personal pleasure?

Is not Rosh HaShanah the time for *cheshbon ha-nefesh*, a "reckoning of the ledger of the soul," an audit and accounting of the conduct that makes our character; a reconciliation of the goals we pursue, with the values that would make us fully human?

Let these days of penitence move us to live for those things which, if they are worth dying for, are certainly worth living for. ❧

✿❈ The State of Israel's Dependence on the Synagogue

It is the thesis of this essay on the relationship between. Judaism and Zionism, that, but for the synagogue, the State of Israel would never have been born in our time; and if, God forbid, the synagogue should come to an end, the State of Israel would not survive it by very much.

This dependence is clear and it is one way. It is not a mutual interdependence. The synagogue could survive without the reality of the State of Israel. The synagogue did live for nineteen centuries, which is about half of Jewish history, without the State.

Zionism

The word Zionism, as the name of a political movement, is less than a century old. But, as an integral part of Jewish theology, Zionism is as old as Judaism. The fiercely passionate love of our people for the land of Israel has been inculcated in Jewish hearts by the teachings of the synagogue for close to 2500 years, which is the approximate age of the synagogue.

The synagogue was invented by our people in Babylon, when they were exiled there. It was then that they spoke nostalgically of home, mentioning the holiest hill in the holy city of their holy land. The name of the hill was

Zion. To our people it stood for Jerusalem which, in turn, stood for all the land of Judah-Israel. Just as, sometimes, journalists use the term White House to stand for Washington and, what they really mean is, the United States.

Zion is the holiest hill in the holy city of Jerusalem, capitol of the Holy Land: Israel.

Holiness

Perhaps the holiest passage in Holy Scriptures is the *sedra Kdoshim*: Lev. 19. This Chapter is known as "The Holiness Code." It tells us how to be "holy as God is holy."

When the *sedra* is read on *Shabbat Kdoshim*, "Holiness Sabbath," during the spring of the year, there are two *Haftarot*, two prophetic readings, to supplement the Torah reading. A Sephardic *Haftara* and a different Ashkenazic *Haftara*.

The Sephardic *Haftarah*, the prophetic portion read on this Sabbath in synagogues of the Spanish-Portuguese tradition is this, from the book of Ezekiel: (20:3ff.) "Son of man! Give this message from the Eternal to the elders of Israel: tell them that on the day when I chose Israel, I swore to the descendants of the household of Jacob that I would bring them from the land of Egypt to a land that I had assigned them, a land abounding in milk and honey, the glory of all lands."

And in Ashkenazic congregations, those with German or other East-European roots, there is this reading from the book of Amos: (9.11 ff.) "I will raise again the fallen huts of David, repair and mend and rebuild them as in days of old. I will bring back the exiles of my people Israel to build waste towns and dwell in them, to plant vineyards, lay out gardens—eat their fruits, I will plant this people in their own land never more to be uprooted. This is the promise of the Eternal your God."

These are the prophetic readings on *Shabbat Kdoshim*, "Holiness Sabbath," when the Torah reading lists the commandments we must keep in order to become "holy as God is holy." Judaism (our religious faith) thus associates our people Israel's restoration in its land with the highest sanctities of our religion, with holiness itself.

It is an established historical fact that a people, vanquished by military might and dispossessed of its land, ordinarily loses its identity. Consider the fate of the Hyksos, Amalekites, Edomites, Moabites, Hittites, Ammonites, Kenites, Nabateans, Nuzi, Horites, Jebusites, Phoenicians, Philistines, Amorites, to mention only some of the nations who were Israel's contemporaries and neighbors in Bible times.

That we, of the household of Israel, did not come to an end as a people even after we were exiled from the Land of Israel is due, I submit, to three factors: 1. A unique Idea, 2. a unique Book, and 3. a unique Institution. ❧

❧ The Synagogue as Family

At our last annual congregational meeting, I spoke to you of love as it relates to Temple life. At the previous meeting I spoke of marriage in the same frame of reference. Some of you will recall that in that first talk I treated the relationship of the rabbi to his synagogue as a *shidduch*, a marital arrangement. In the other address I listed the ways in which various categories of members show their love for Judaism and Jewry by willing contributions of their time, talents and/or treasure to our faith and people.

We shall consider now the next normal development after marriage and love—namely, the family. A healthy, loving, married couple usually look forward to the blessings and the burdens, the triumphs and the tribulations of raising a family. It is the congregation as a family that will be our concern here.

One of the tense periods in the life of any married pair is the time when they await the coming of children. Children are expected, anticipated. And yet, emotionally, the advent of youngsters is a trial of the patience, strength, and skill of their parents. Often in each spouse's mind is the question: Will I still be first in the affections of my mate? Or, will this ambivalently welcome intruder steal first place in the heart of its mother, or perhaps, its father? In time, some more or less reasonable division of attention is effected between the trinity of father, mother and child.

Ordinarily, the firstborn in most congregations is the Sisterhood. Most often it develops into the strong, willing, and able daughter in the house, an energetic and highly competent maid-of-all work—a vigorous, junior *balebosteh*, taking care of fundraising, the Religious School, Adult cultural programs, liaison with other congregations, with the community as a whole, with world Jewry, and with humanity in general. And like many an only child, for a long while she basks serene in solitary splendor, the apple of her parents' eye.

But, like other families, congregations have a tendency to go on growing. In the course of nature, more children come along. Every set of sensitive parents knows the anxious care we take preparing the first child for the advent of the second, the apprehensions of the only child lest the new little interloper supplant the firstborn in the affection of the parents; or, at the very least, force the first child to get along on half the attention, whereas before he, or she, had all the glory. Sibling rivalry, the suspicion, fear, and resentment of the newcomer by its older brother or sister is a universal hazard in all families. Sometimes these tensions continue indefinitely.

Each family member has a need for self-expression and self-fulfillment, for response, recognition, and approval from parents and from the community. Offspring will vie with one another for distinction. In this competitive process, they have been known to grow reckless, not only of the welfare of other individuals in the family but often, in their excessive eagerness to outshine all the others, they will risk imperiling the peace, security, and happiness of the entire household. Time and again, it becomes necessary to remind them that each is a member of this family unit, and that upon the character of the relationship

276 Albert S. Goldstein

between them depends their individual growth and their united development as a family.

The human family is the world of mankind in miniature. It is there we learn how to become civilized members of society, how to get along with other people in our world. This holds equally true for the Temple family.

As religious Jews, this is, or should be, our primary concern: How to live in reciprocally beneficial relationship with all Jews and, ultimately, with all men everywhere. To attain this desideratum, much is required of us in the way of self-restraint, reciprocal respect, thoughtful consideration of the needs of others for self-expression and self-fulfillment, and that of the family as a whole.

Competition may or may not be the lifeblood of trade in a capitalist economy. But unrestrained competitiveness, uncontrolled rivalry, spells the death of any religious institution or enterprise. Mutual helpfulness, due regard for the opinions, the sensibilities, and the needs of the rest of the Temple family, are quintessential for the healthy survival and normal growth of a congregation.

In any very large synagogue, such as ours, the auxiliary groups, the Sisterhood, Brotherhood, Parents Association, Adult Club, Religious School, often become so big that any one of them may enroll as many members as you will find in other complete congregations.

To lead such immense temple affiliates requires people of a high order of intelligence and ability, of aggressiveness and organizational skill. Large synagogue affiliates need and often have leaders of a caliber equal to the task of running a whole congregation. With half a dozen or more such dominant personalities in one family, problems arise.

One leader may claim priority and special privilege for his or her group by reason of seniority, that is, because of its superior age; it very well may be as old as the congregation itself. Another claims first place because of the size of his affiliate. A third affiliate insists that it represents the most valuable segment of the congregation because its members are the intellectual, esthetic, or spiritual aristocracy, the elite of the synagogue. A fourth group tends to scorn the rest as a crowd of aged mossbacks, whereas their members esteem themselves to be the young, eager, active people—the youthful element in whose hands lay the whole future of the congregation.

The analogy with almost any man's large family is readily apparent. The eldest sister, for example, who wants to take mother's place, because she is the oldest. Big brother, who wants to supplant father, because he is the strongest. The smartest child, who wants to shine, because he is so brilliant. The youngest, because he is cutest. So it is that the big congregation, instead of having the customary number and kind of limbs it needs to be a normal organism, sometimes, instead, finds itself with a superabundance of tails, each of which would like to try to wag the whole dog.

It is therefore that I greet with the greatest enthusiasm a new committee just appointed to coordinate the complex activities of this enormous Temple family. For the past two years representatives of our Temple's affiliates have been meeting together to arrange their calendar of activities—to select the dates on which they will present their respective projects. Under the new system, however, they will do much more than merely clear dates. They will be asked to coordinate their programs to avoid substantive conflicts, so that two or more groups will not, for example, be soliciting the very same Temple membership to attend the same kind of function, whether it be a musical show, a lecture series, bazaar, class, outing, dance or theater party.

We shall now, at least formally and officially, be acting and moving forward as one large cooperating family.

But formal, official, paper cooperation will hardly suffice. Our heart must be in it. There must be mutual affection, sympathetic concern, and solicitude for the needs which each affiliate and the congregation as a whole, have for response, public recognition, emotional security, and new spiritual experience.

Like democracy itself, healthy family life is not made of agendas, formal committee meetings, and official pronouncements: Soviet Russia, for example, boasts a democratic-sounding constitution, periodic elections, polling booths, and ballot boxes—indeed, every external appurtenance of democracy. All that is lacking there is precisely what is most essential: Mutual esteem, concern for human values, and sentiments, the heart that will not permit sensitive human feelings and needs to be at best blithely ignored and, at worst, brutally trampled upon.

What I appeal for here is some show of the natural affection that sisters and brothers should have for each other and, together, some sensitive concern for the happiness of the parents and the total well-being of the family.

The first Jewish congregation in history was presided over by the patriarch Jacob who gave to his people the name he earned in a long, difficult but successful struggle—the title, Israel. Jacob was the founder of the family whose members, in turn, fathered the tribes of Israel. In his last hour, he convened the heads of these subsidiary families.

ויקרא יעקוב אל בניו ויאמר: האספו ואגידה לכם את אשר יקרא אתכם באחרית הימים.
Jacob called his sons and said: "Gather yourselves together that I may tell you what shall befall you in the days to come."

However, instead of predicting any future events, the Patriarch proceeded to give an analysis of the virtues and deficiencies of each of the grown-up children in his large and ever-growing family.

Our sages explain this seeming non-sequitur, by telling us that the whole of the prophecy is contained in the very first sentence, which is to be understood as follows: "If you do gather together, if you behave as a unit, as mutually respectful members of one family, concerned for each other and for your united destiny as an important social organism, you will, by this very getting together itself, take the first necessary step to insure that you will have a future."

The future is for and with families and congregations and societies and nations who sensibly set their mutual welfare above their petty, destructive, competitive instincts.

The function of love in the Divine Plan is that the satisfaction of this need and passion requires us to make those personal adjustments in our own character and conduct that will, in turn, make us suitable, appreciated, and loved mates, each for at least one other member of the human family. Such a loving pair finds its fulfillment in the fruit of love's sharing: a family.

The existence of other lives, growing out of and depending on our own, makes demands of us, which expand the scope of our love. Through such slow, gradual out-reachings of the tendrils of the seeds of love within the human heart, seeds implanted there by God, man grows to humanness, which is to say, toward reverent concern for all of life and toward the Creator of this life, toward God. This is religion. This, need I remind you, is the business of this House, and hence, the business before this meeting and, indeed, before every meeting of this congregation. 🌺

❧ Addendum

❧❀ Intelligence
The Solution to the Problem of International Peace

Whatever the forms that the causes for war may take, they all of them go to a single taproot of evil, selfishness. Nor is this selfishness some impalpable miasma that pervades States, and it would be well if we would expunge from our discourse and from our minds all concepts that further this loose way of thinking. It is peculiar how deeply ingrained, in the consciousness of most of us are vestiges of the idea that social forces are entities with personality, consciousness, and will of their own. "The effects of economic pressure," "the force of circumstance"—phrases like these slip from glib tongues as easily as if they were explicit, which they are not, or people who utter them were oblivious to their implication, which is mostly the case.

The conception of the existence of society apart from and over against the individuals who compose it, a thought embodied in Spencer's "social organism," is an idea that has been discarded by thinkers at least since Comte. Consideration of the facts of social life cannot but lead to the conclusion that social situations and circumstances, social forces and processes are merely intellectual ways of viewing the reality of individuals living in groups; they are aspects of the interaction of people on a mental plane and not dynamic powers. When it has become part of the primary philosophy to speak of whatever conditions, either of the urban community or of the society of the world, as having come about through the energy exerted by individual people and not through the instrumentality of blind and relentless forces, the thought process of all of us shall have been materially improved. People will then begin to analyze their milieu scientifically, to apply intelligence to economic and social problems rather than to make moral or, which is the same thing, fighting issues of them.

One of the alleged prolific sources of war, an economic condition long claimed to be unavoidable, which makes war not only inevitable but even desirable, is overpopulation. Moreover, it is argued, a surplus of men is to be wished even though the reduction of the excess is necessary, but war is an adequate and efficient eliminator. Those who make these affirmations are in general of two classes, militarists and jingoists who seem to urge war as an end, and certain theoretical biologists who take war with disease and other "accidents" of the course of events as a natural means. We treat of this latter group at once.

The contention is that no progress is ever made without waste and that, therefore, there will always be more people on the earth than it can amply provide for, so that only the best may continue and carry on or, at all events, the least good may be excluded. Does not such a view bespeak an exaggerated self-esteem on the part of any living person? Such an individual looks back on the endless stretch of history and sees himself as the thus-far most desirable product of a timeless weeding-out process; he confidently admits his superiority and that of his race over all the great peoples of antiquity, the resplendent Egyptians and Mesopotamians, the wisdom-loving Greeks, the prophetic Israel, the bellicose Romans; he assumes that our own civilization is the best in all of these that has endured the racking test of the ages and is the last word in the perfection toward which the world is marching. To multiply evidence of the fallacy of the proposal of war as an agent of the process of "the survival of the fittest" would be as absurd as the theory itself. Over-population is an existing state in some countries; it is a problem, but war is not its solution and it is not a real cause of war.

With the knowledge at our disposal today there need never be a population anywhere in excess of the means of sustaining it. Ways of controlling the rate of population increase are known and if this information were made common there would be no more over-population. But this would eliminate a most popular and much-employed excuse for war, so people who are in power, not the mystic State, but individuals in office and in power because of wealth see to it that any effective, intelligent means of reducing the population are not taken. Let us look at the matter clearly. It is evident that wars are not actually caused by too many people, quite the contrary, those for whom and by whom they are declared are numerically insignificant and the crowded conditions of the masses is a rationalization, a good rather than a true reason for war. This rationalization draws attention, and such is its intent, from the crude and simple fact that people with power or money, which is the same thing, are anxious for markets for the disposal of surplus merchandise, not merely territory for the colonization of surplus people. These magnates and statesmen care not a whit for the crowded masses, but are nothing loath to exploit them to over-production, encourage their increase, and use the fact of their numbers as an excuse for getting themselves killed off in battle to obtain more land, ostensibly to provide a haven for their overflow. Is it not about high time that this stupidity should cease? And stupidity it is, both from the point of view of war itself, where for example unthinking

obedience is classed a virtue and goes by the misnomer of
courage, and of that of the real underlying reason for war,
where if every group of those who had the means to start
war would do so there would be no one left to manufacture goods for export, no buyers in distant or near markets,
no wealth and no power. Each war, as it surpasses its predecessor in carnage and destruction, comes nearer to the
ultimate goal of universal and utter annihilation. Let us at
last come to our senses.

Immanuel Kant, profoundly affected by the principles of the French Revolution, under the exhilarating inspiration of Liberty, Equality, and Fraternity, indicted his
philosophic essay on "Perpetual Peace." In it he asserts,
contrary to the then popular notion, that it is not alone in
the graveyard that eternal peace can be found. True, a condition of peace among nations existing side by side is not a
state of nature. The state of nature is rather a state of strife.
But the establishment of a State of peace is feasible when
there is a *brotherhood of nations*. What could more reasonably
be expected that that as men in a condition of nature had
concurred in a compact to found a state to the end that
peace among themselves might be secured, so states should
join together to form a confederation of the world for the
purpose of maintaining universal peace? Such a universal
federation would be permanent, however, only on condition that the civil constitution of every state were republican, or, in other words, in case the legislative and executive
processes were separate.

Psychologically, one of the best cures for *selfishness*,
whether individual or national, is the formation of friend-
ships whereby the interests of the individuals or nations
concerned become identified. Insurance of peace is, for
one thing, the problem of replacing narrow selfishness
with open-minded generosity. The road to success in the

matter of universal peace lies through good understanding among the peoples of the earth. If once that understanding is made permanent and statesmen learn that they must not play tricks with it but must use it carefully for the sake of themselves and for the sake of the whole world, we shall have taken an enormous step in the right direction. But though our union be exclusive in sentiment it must never be exclusive in action. When it was proposed to make peace with Russia under the Bolshevists, there were some most excellent people who cried out in horror: "We can never clasp the gory hand of Lenin?" Why not be sensible? We have got to effect some relations with some representative of Russia, and it is doubtful whether there is much to chose from between the Red terror and the White.

But the interposition of personal ethics in such a matter is entirely out of place. We did not create the situation; our duty is to do the best thing for humanity in all the circumstances we find actually to exist. If any individual fancies the weal of the human race to be staked on the continued refusal of one group of officials to recognize another, which indeed has countenanced and condoned unspeakable and flagitious atrocities; if any one believes it to be at all worthwhile to leave innocent people to the physical anguish and moral catastrophe of starvation, that creature who holds this startling opinion is acting in his own right in his persistence in a policy that precludes the very existence of Russia. But it is senseless and perniciously wrong to suppose there is in such matters some absolute moral claim. Let us make no mistake; we are bound, for the sake of peace, to welcome to the peace banquet of the world the representatives of all of its people, for only so can honest international relations be a cause worth *living* for.

We must carefully eradicate from our minds the existing competitive standard of greatness and, in general, if we are to think of peace we must learn to regard other nations as comrades whom we would help toward a common welfare of humanity in which all share, rather than as rivals whose success involves disappointment to ourselves. This is the fundamental idea which finds expression in the League of Nations. But if the League is confined to its primary function of checking the outbreak of war, it will fail even in that. It will succeed only to the extent it is progressively accepted as the representative of a common human welfare which includes that of all nations. It will be much easier for people who control states to eschew self-seeking and vindictiveness if they bear in mind constantly the truth that all law is but an expression of the Divine Creator Who has made us so that if one member of us suffer all must suffer with it, and if one rejoice all rejoice.

The sum of it all is peace, and if peace is to be secured there must be an end of self-seeking and rivalry, personal, sectional and national; not only must there be no seeking for more than is right, but there must be no *insistent claim* even for just rights. There must be the pursuit, first and foremost, of the highest *general welfare* without regard to claims arising from the violation of that justice in the past. If man has been injured, he has a just claim for redress, so for the group and the nation. But if the claim is *pressed* it may lead only to a sense of injury on the other side. It would be well if more often in public affairs men would see the inanity of wrangling and cry, "Enough!"

We will find peace only when those who have both the right and the power to punish, choose instead to promote the common interest, for the, moral foundation of peace is a perfectly ordered world of justice. But our world as it exists today is disordered and when evil has come in it can only be expelled by suffering voluntarily endured by the innocent; in our world the moral foundation of peace is mutual understanding and a consequent spirit of *self-sacrifice.*

As an aid to the development of this spirit of self-sacrifice there might be elaborated an international educational institution—that at Geneva is a good beginning—whereby efficient education in international sympathy shall become a usual, if not an indispensable, prerequisite to candidacy for national leadership in all countries. These leaders would instill their people with the moral duty incumbent on every citizen of every country to acquaint himself with the main facts governing the policy of his own and other countries and to understand them. They would teach that it is the duty of citizens of a country belonging to any one section of society to know the interests, aspirations, and attitudes of members of other groups and to understand the causes which lead these others to view life as they do. Mutual knowledge, intelligent understanding is the only remedy for ignorance, the breeder of hate and strife, and plainly it is upon those who have the greatest opportunity of education that the responsibility in this matter rests most heavily. These universally taught leaders would stimulate the intellectual and scientific curiosity of their people. They would fire the people's imagination to appreciate all knowledge in terms of human joy and sorrow, for imagination added to knowledge is a sure source of sympathy.

The establishment of an international school for the education of national leaders would be beset with great difficulties, but surmounting them would be a facile task after the grim horrors of war thereby to be forever ended. For such international education must probably cause the last most horrifying universal disaster to be also the last example of the most calamitous of all forms of human selfishness and stupidity.

As the course of history proceeds the making of war and peace comes to depend on and reflect the moral condition of mankind in ever increasing degree. When governments were relatively independent of the people in whose name they acted, and when armies were the opportunities for kings to display or augment their glory, the connection between foreign policy and the moral quality of civilization generally was not intimate. No doubt there was some connection, for no war could be waged without some measure of popular support. But it is clear that in such wars as those which Edward III and Henry V waged in France, the personal ambitions of a very few individuals were almost alone in deciding the issue, while the country at large accepted its policy, sometimes with enthusiasm born of the chauvinistic twaddle of state mongers and demagogues, mostly with resignation, and often in despair. The development of nationalism and especially democracy has made a vast difference.

Taking the world as it is, there can be no successful basis for a firm peace between nations unless those nations are in the last resort self-governing and the will of majority prevails and not the will of some autocrat or oligarchy. According to the sage of Königsberg, Kant, under a republican constitution the consent of citizens as members of the state should be required to determine at any time whether or not there should be war. For while rulers fly to arms with an easy conscience and a heart as light as their head, the people, on whom falls the burden of war—the fighting as well the other cost, and the restoration after the storm—the people would come in time to detest the very name of war and refuse their consent to waging it.

But if the consent and moral support of the people is necessary for the declaration of war it is no less so for the making of peace. No durable or enforceable contracts can be made with any nation which has not got a democratic basis. The reason is obvious; some pretender will always claim to speak for the people, though he has no such right. He will say he cannot maintain this or that former contract of his government, because that contract was not recognized by the people. To make stable contracts there must be plenipotentiaries and no man can be the true diplomatic agent of any nation unless he is appointed by a government that rests on the popular will. This is neither subtlety nor political metaphysics. It is plain common sense. A stable universal peace must rest upon international contracts; these cannot be entered into by minors, slaves, or persons in any form of tutelage. To produce a firm set of contracts, there must be a firm set of free contractors. True, as contrasted with sham, democracy is essential to the peace of the world. This is a fact which ought to be recognized fully. If it is, the maintenance of peace and of a democratic system of government will go hand in hand. To this end the nations should do everything in their power, rulers and people.

But what shall we do about those whom Mr. Santayana calls "panegyrists of war?" The exponents of the barbaric hedonism of the pleasure and glory of war, who insist that *periodical bleedings* are requisite to the health of a nation.

These people can multiply their encomiums to the great god Mars only because they refuse to allow the facts of experience to stare them out of countenance, nevertheless it is very easy for them to make their appeal to the populace. And William James calls to our attention the fact that although none of us would vote for a new war for independence, negro emancipation, or world democracy, only a few odd ones among us would vote—were the thing possible—to have any of the past wars for "ideals" blotted out from our annals. Military feelings, he thinks, are too well-grounded to be simply uprooted. This is so because since childhood we have been nurtured with mawkish sentiments in favor of war, so that when we grow up we have, as John Erskine says, a predilection for making moral issues of economic and social problems and we think it cowardly to confess that these are merely problems for intelligence. We are so reared that we delight in flamboyant pseudo-patriotic propaganda with large doses of mouth-filling phrases, "argumenta ad populum" to invoke our traditional deities, and a great waving of flags—all of this when the question is one that needs for its solution only a bit of reflection or perhaps a good deal of cooling-off to die of itself.

We are taught to be loud in our praise of those of our leaders who are aggressive and persistent, who, when they cannot scale a wall, threaten to butt it in, if they have to do it with their heads. If our leaders used more brain and less skull there would be fewer concussions of many sorts.

It is these leaders who in turn tell us that war is the romance of history, that the army is the perfect school for the manly virtues. But the world over people are growing wiser; no more in England, for example, do her choicest young men compose the army, no longer are soldiers considered the very acme of physical and gentlemanly perfection. Once we dimmed into forgottenness the frightful blunder of the Light Brigade and glorified the manly courage of the obedient but unintelligent men who helped make so much target practice. It is time that we discontinued interpreting such stupidity in the glowing terms of the tragic courage that suffers its results. When will come the age of reflection? That we cannot tell, but the rapidity of its approach will be in proportion to the extensiveness of the movement to educate people the world over. It will come through the development of the intelligence and the teaching that it is the moral obligation of the more intelligent to help others see their place in the world and aid them in adjusting to their position in life.

In itself, the awful ride of the Light Brigade, like the loss of Varus' legions, is but a small thing when compared to the immeasurable havoc wrought by war since time out of mind. Shall we continue to rely for succor on those virtues supposedly imbued nowhere so well as in war?—on courage and steadfastness. Courage and steadfastness are doubtless good in themselves and good for men, but everything in its time and place. If one wishes to flee prison, what is needed is the key. Lacking that, let one have courage and steadfastness by all means. This world of ours is incarcerated and bound by ignorance and must out. The key is intelligence.

If military power could prevail; if by its very nature it were not so variable and shifting, it is possible, as Arthur Balfour suggests, that after "the long struggle with Mohammedanism, there might still be an Empire in the East, largely Asiatic in population, Christian in religion, Greek in culture, Roman by political descent" and "Had this been the course of events large portions of mankind would doubtless have been much better governed than they are." But such is not the case, and we need a moral substitute for war to de the things that war could not do. And surely, in all the multifarious panorama of the world's work today, there should be those things which supply whatever elements of good there are in war without its devastating effects. Mr. Balfour posits the alliance of science and industry as the social force which will substitute for war. To be sure, there are those who would question the moral of this force as much as we question that of war. There are even some who identify science and industry with war. But these cannot be corrected in a short time nor by any one essay. The alliance of science and industry is none the less "a force fitted to arouse and sustain the energies of nations and may be ranked with those other forces which most deeply stirred the emotions of great communities, have urged them on to the greatest exertions, have released them from the numbing fetters of merely personal preoccupation—with religion, patriotism, and politics. Industrial expansion under scientific inspiration is not, at best, but a new source of well-being; at worst , the prolific parent of physical ugliness in many forms, machine made wares, smoky cities, polluted rivers, and desecrated landscapes—appropriately associated with materialism and greed."

Such a judgment merely confounds essence with accidental manifestations. What are we to say of the other forces that are so provocative of war? What are we to say of the narrow bigotries and hateful persecutions in the name of religion? of the thoughtlessness and avarice and tyranny of politics? of the selfish and often criminal brutality perpetrated in the name of patriotism? It is a lamentable, but no less veritable fact that all great social forces are not only subject to corruption, but are being corrupted continually, and that, because they are not superhuman powers but only ways of looking at the activity of people. But if, because of this, men were to seek their self-expression in the privacy of their own chambers and ignore the world, there would be no peace but degeneration. For Plato well-knew that the state is the best medium for the fulfillment of man's capacities, and that truth has not yet been gainsaid.

To quote Mr. Balfour again, "It may seem fanciful to find in a single aspect of this force an influence which resembles religion or patriotism in its appeal to the higher side of ordinary characters—especially since we are accustomed to regard the appropriation by industry of scientific discoveries merely as a means of multiplying material conveniences of life. But if it be remembered that this process brings vast sections of every individual community into admiring relation with the highest intellectual achievement and the most disinterested search for truth; that those who live by ministering to the wants of average humanity lean for support on those who search among the deepest mysteries of nature; that their dependence is rewarded with growing success; that success gives in its turn an incentive to individual effort in no wise to be measured by personal expectation of gain; that the energies thus aroused may affect the whole character of the community spreading the beneficent contagion of hope and high endeavor through channels scarcely known, to workers in fields the most remote; if all this be borne in mind it may perhaps seem worthy of the place I have assigned it"—as a moral substitute for war.

William James, firmly convinced that the benefits of the martial virtues are absolute and permanent goods, proposes the institution of a new kind of service—"the army against nature." In it, he believes, "The military ideals of hardihood and discipline would be wrought into the fiber of the people; no one would remain blind as the luxurious classes now are blind, to the permanently sour and hard foundations of his higher life. To coal and iron mines, to fishing fleets in December, to dish washing, clothes washing, and window washing, to road building and tunnel making, to foundries and stoke holes, and to the frames of skyscrapers would our gilded youth be drafted off, according to their choice, to get the childishness knocked out of them and come back into society with healthier sympathies and soberer ideas.

"They would have done their own part in the immemorial human warfare against nature; they would tread the earth more proudly... they would be better fathers and teachers of the following generation.

"Such a conscription, with the state of public opinion that would require it and the many moral fruits it would bear, would preserve in the midst of a pacific civilization the manly virtues which the military party is so afraid of seeing disappear in peace. We shall get toughness without callousness, authority with as little criminal cruelty as possible, and painful work done cheerily because the duty is temporary, and threatens not, as now, to degrade the whole remainder of one's life... So far, war has been the only force that can discipline a whole community... But the ordinary prides and shames of social man, once developed to a certain intensity, are capable of organizing such a moral equivalent of war as I have sketched, or some other, just as effective for preserving manliness of type. It is but a question of time, of skillful propagandizing, and of opinion-making men seizing historic opportunities."

After a long peace in a country capable of victory because un-bled by war, we may see a people's vital force bursting its bounds; it begins to create and conceive from the tremendous energy it has stored up in its long and unimpeded development. And a people, once having become industrious, will have formed busy habits which it will not soon or without out real cause relinquish. For there is a true and keen delight in delving into the possibilities of real things, molding, and reshaping, and fashioning new machines, and new tools, and new things of use. There is a creative impulse in man, a zest in the new, in improvement, in surpassing other men. There is something intriguing in forcing the earth to unburden itself of its hidden treasures, and watching these succumb to man's wheedling and

assume undreamed forms. The greatest scientific achievements: the longest air flight, the tallest structure, the fastest
automobile, the latest thing in cinematography—all these
deserve respect. It is the wish for new experience which
makes men like war for itself and the work of the world has
all of the elements of pursuit, and flight, capture, escape,
and death that are the very soul of this wish, but men must
be taught and we must be patient; there is much to learn.
🐾

This essay, dated June, 1928, was the first winner of the Goldman Peace Prize offered at the University of Cincinnati. Robert
Goldman, who offered the prize, was then Chair of the Board of
the Union of American Hebrew Congregations (now, the Union for Reform Judaism).

❧ Benediction